# PEOPLE POWER

UNIVERSITY PRESS OF FLORIDA

Florida A&M University, Tallahassee
Florida Atlantic University, Boca Raton
Florida Gulf Coast University, Ft. Myers
Florida International University, Miami
Florida State University, Tallahassee
New College of Florida, Sarasota
University of Central Florida, Orlando
University of Florida, Gainesville
University of North Florida, Jacksonville
University of South Florida, Tampa
University of West Florida, Pensacola

★ ★ ★ ★ ★ ★ ★ ★ ★ ★ ★ ★ ★ ★ ★ ★

# PEOPLE POWER

**History, Organizing, and Larry Goodwyn's
Democratic Vision in the Twenty-First Century**

★ ★ ★ ★ ★ ★ ★ ★ ★ ★ ★ ★ ★ ★ ★ ★

EDITED BY

WESLEY C. HOGAN AND PAUL ORTIZ

University Press of Florida
Gainesville · Tallahassee · Tampa · Boca Raton
Pensacola · Orlando · Miami · Jacksonville · Ft. Myers · Sarasota

26  25  24  23  22  21    6  5  4  3  2  1

Library of Congress Cataloging-in-Publication Data
Names: Hogan, Wesley C., editor. | Ortiz, Paul, 1964- editor.
Title: People power : history, organizing, and Larry Goodwyn's democratic vision in the twenty-first century / edited by Wesley C. Hogan and Paul Ortiz.
Description: 1st. | Gainesville : University Press of Florida, 2021. | Includes bibliographical references and index. | Summary: "Featuring contributions from leading scholar-activists, this book demonstrates how the lessons of history can inform the building of new social justice movements today"—Provided by publisher.
Identifiers: LCCN 2021007304 (print) | LCCN 2021007305 (ebook) | ISBN 9780813066912 (hardback) | ISBN 9780813068473 (paperback) | ISBN 9780813057903 (pdf)
Subjects: LCSH: Goodwyn, Lawrence. | Social justice—United States—History. | Social movements—United States—History. | Democracy—United States—History.
Classification: LCC HM671 .P453 2021 (print) | LCC HM671 (ebook) | DDC 303.3/720973—dc23
LC record available at https://lccn.loc.gov/2021007304
LC ebook record available at https://lccn.loc.gov/2021007305

The University Press of Florida is the scholarly publishing agency for the State University System of Florida, comprising Florida A&M University, Florida Atlantic University, Florida Gulf Coast University, Florida International University, Florida State University, New College of Florida, University of Central Florida, University of Florida, University of North Florida, University of South Florida, and University of West Florida.

University Press of Florida
2046 NE Waldo Road
Suite 2100
Gainesville, FL 32609
http://upress.ufl.edu

The law locks up the man or woman
Who steals the goose off the common
But leaves the greater villain loose
Who steals the common from the goose.

The law demands that we atone
When we take things we do not own
But leaves the lords and ladies fine
Who takes things that are yours and mine.

The poor and wretched don't escape
If they conspire the law to break;
This must be so but they endure
Those who conspire to make the law.

The law locks up the man or woman
Who steals the goose from off the common
And geese will still a common lack
Till they go and steal it back.

— *Anonymous (seventeenth-century folk poem)*

\*   \*   \*

This book is dedicated to those who organize to steal the common back.

# CONTENTS

# ACKNOWLEDGMENTS

Goodwyn lived deeply in his own mind. It was a source of strength only sustainable due to a remarkable family that kept him grounded. If we offer an account of his contributions in this volume, it would be half-baked without acknowledging the absolute centrality of his spouse, Nell Goodwyn, and his children, Wade and Lauren Goodwyn. They weren't simply the home and hearth he returned to each day to refuel. He married well, knew it, and stated it repeatedly. Nell was his best editor, his steadfast confidante, and his daily anchor. Wade and Lauren exposed him to fresh ideas, new ways of thinking, and challenged his more hierarchical habits. In ways that emerge throughout the pages of this collection, one cannot help but see the significance of these three individuals to Larry's insights, his rootedness, his tender side, and his self-discipline. We are particularly grateful that Wade Goodwyn's piece anchors part 2, and we are both deeply indebted to Nell, Lauren, and Wade for their support of this project.

We're indebted also to two early readers who provided invaluable feedback, Ed Balleisen and Ken Wissoker, and to our steadfast contributors, who stayed with us through multiple edits and kept our spirits high. Val Gillespie supported the creation of an archive of Goodwyn's papers at Duke.

Many thanks to Xaris Martínez, who kept us on track, set up a hundred meetings, reminded us of due dates, and helped us to stay organized. Xaris, thank you so much for making sure that everyone's documents were treated with respect and full consent, and that each contributor remained up to date through a very long process.

We are also especially grateful to Sian Hunter and the University Press of Florida for believing in the project. One of the highlights of writing this book has been getting to know Sian and learning from her superb editorial interventions. We also know this book is much better for the superb work of UPF's Michele Fiyak-Burkley, Mary Puckett, Rachel Doll, and Ann Marlowe.

Wesley Hogan thanks Hasan Kwame Jeffries, Jim Hightower, Jay Harris, and Deanna Zandt, who keep Larry's spirit alive through the *Teaching Hard*

*History* and *Jim Hightower's Radio Lowdown* podcasts. Important conversations with Thelma Kithcart and Linda Greider revived her spirits in the seven years it took to bring this project to print. The work of Donnel Baird building BlocPower, of Malinda Maynor Lowery and Danita Mason-Hogans as community-university bridge leaders in Chapel Hill, of the younger historians and artists Sharrelle Barber, Kenneth Campbell, Destiny Owens, Amber Delgado, and Ajamu Dillahunt-Holloway, and of Nsé Ufot leading the New Georgia Project have been particular inspirations. This collection would not have the verve and clarity it does without the editorial gifts of Dirk Philipsen. He first met Larry in Berlin in 1982 and came to the United States to study with him. Dirk's clear eye on the complexity and depth of Goodwyn's gifts and challenges in equal measure allowed us to share key insights on movements, organizing, teaching, and economic justice that the book would otherwise neglect. Now married fifteen years, Dirk and Wesley met because of their connection to Goodwyn, and Wesley can only say, *thank the Lord Almighty above for that.*

Finally, though Wesley and Paul have known each other since 1993 in several contexts, Wesley is grateful this book allowed us the time to work together on something that meant a lot to both of us. What joy to bring this book to life with Paul, who always has my back and keeps the spirit flowing with energy and brilliance. In sum, a damn fine man to ride the river with.

Our graduate school comrade Mary Wingerd deserves a special shout-out, as it was her idea to convene many of the participants in this volume with Larry during the 1990s for vibrant discussions about the past, present, and future of the labor movement.

Paul Ortiz is humbled by the patience, love, and editing expertise of Sheila Payne, his wife and social movement comrade of twenty-five years. Sheila knew Larry quite well, argued with him vociferously, and cared enough about this book to read many of the essays in their early stages.

Paul thanks Bremerton High School teacher Don Bidwell and Olympic College history professor Philip Schaeffer, who intellectually prepared a first-generation university student to succeed in higher education, while Evergreen State College faculty members Stephanie Coontz, Beryl Crow, and Tom Grissom insisted that Ortiz go to Duke to study history with Larry Goodwyn and Bill Chafe.

*People Power* has been a kind of extended community organizing reunion for many of us, a labor of love that took a few more years than originally planned. Paul is grateful for Wesley's comradeship and determination to see this project through to publication.

# In the Activists' Kitchen

## An Introduction

WESLEY C. HOGAN AND PAUL ORTIZ

As we put the finishing touches on this book, millions of people worldwide took to the streets inspired by the Black Lives Matter democracy movement. The 2020 protests were initially sparked by the police murders of Breonna Taylor and George Floyd. Organizers used picket signs, storytelling, social media, graffiti, oral history, and audio podcasts in order to force the nation to face up to the pervasive nature of racist violence in American society, past and present. While urging us all to remember the names and lives of African Americans killed by state violence, the protests have helped to rekindle movements against state violence in countries in Latin America, the Caribbean and Africa. This popular insurgency has been a long time in the making. Organizers in the Movement for Black Lives had been working for years to build awareness of systemic racism while participating in a variety of coalitions including immigration reform, prison abolition, gender and LGBTQ+ equity, and an end to US imperialism.

This organizing work has been especially strong in the South. Black, Latinx, and Arab youth built the Florida-based Dream Defenders in the immediate wake of the killing of Trayvon Martin in 2012. Subsequently the group joined efforts across the state in promoting the "Fight for $15 and a Union" campaign as well as building solidarity with Palestinians and garnering signatures for a petition to restore voting rights to formerly convicted felons in Florida.

At the moment of its inception in July 2013, police and conservative radio hosts attacked the term "Black Lives Matter" (BLM), for a variety of reasons. Critics demanded that activists instead use the phrase "All Lives Matter." They argued that the social problems highlighted by BLM organizers were not rooted in structural flaws of the United States. These critics believed in the doctrine of American exceptionalism, that the US was the greatest country in history. Just a few short years later, however, many of the skeptics had changed their minds, and pollsters reported a massive increase in support for the Black Lives Matter movement.[1] Suddenly journalists were describing the once-vilified insurgency as "the largest movement in U.S. history."[2] Like the upswelling of the Mississippi Delta after a record flood, the Black Lives Matter democracy movement in 2020 opened new spaces for reckonings with US history and realities as well as critiques of institutions that had once seemed impervious to change. From police budgets to Indigenous treaties to capitalism and Confederate monuments, nothing was any longer a sacred idol.

Lawrence Goodwyn (1928–2013) would have loved this moment. Goodwyn was an activist, a professor, and a historian who wrote and lectured on social movements built by Texas farmers, Polish trade unionists, civil rights activists, Latino/a farmworkers, and others who challenged the status quo. As a radical journalist and a political organizer in Texas, Mississippi, Florida, and other states, Goodwyn was a direct participant in the historic changes ushered in by movement organizers in the 1950s and 1960s.

After earning his PhD at the University of Texas, Goodwyn moved with his wife Nell to Durham, North Carolina, in 1971. He taught at Duke for more than three decades while Nell taught high school English. He offered classes that challenged students to question the premises of the world they lived in, including a course on agrarian insurgencies based upon his 1976 book *Democratic Promise: The Populist Moment in America*. An abridged version of the text became a staple of history and political science seminars as well as labor and community organizing workshops for decades to come. The opening sentence of the book reflected Goodwyn's goal of rescuing rural populism from middle-class scorn while ringing an alarm bell on the decline of democracy in America: "This book is about the flowering of the largest democratic mass movement in American history. It is also necessarily a book about democracy itself. Finally, it is about why Americans have far less democracy than they like to think and what would have to happen to alter that situation."

*People Power* is written by former colleagues of Goodwyn who worked with him or who felt their own lives impacted by his ideas. It is not an homage; rather, it is created by individuals who have found Goodwyn's life and works to be vital in reigniting discussions on democracy, equity, and reigniting our civic square. While the essayists in this book come from diverse backgrounds, they have in common a belief in the efficacy of people power highlighted in Jim Hightower's assessment of Larry's theory of history: Goodwyn "revealed that real progress comes from the mavericks and mutts who dare to challenge 'the great men.'"[3]

We wrote this book for people who believe that we are living in a time when large corporations and monied interests have seized control of the most important decisions that govern our lives. *People Power* is dedicated to people who want to democratize the nation by merging the lessons of the past with the creative energies of today's emerging justice movements. As contributor Adam Lioz notes, "To say that our country is at a crossroads, our democracy on the brink, is a cliché at this point—which doesn't make it any less true."

The symptoms of decay are everywhere. Donald Trump used racism and racial scapegoating to win the 2016 election. Federal and state authorities botched the nation's response to the global pandemic, costing 600,000+ American lives. The election of Joe Biden and Kamala Harris in 2020 represents a moment of opportunity, but it does not change the fact that billionaires have seized control of education reform, health care reform, energy policy, artificial intelligence policy, and, above all, who has access to money. The republic is embroiled in endless wars that the majority of the population oppose. Militarism has generated global refugee crises, drained the national treasury, cost thousands of lives, and added mightily to the corruption marking contemporary politics. Toxic masculinity has contributed to outbreaks of deadly school shootings that admit of no solutions other than "thoughts and prayers" while traumatizing generation after generation of children.[4]

A decade after the Great Recession and the taxpayer-funded bailouts that saved the auto industry and investment firms in 2009, people outside of Wall Street have yet to experience anything approximating a "recovery." Meanwhile, income inequality has soared to heights never before seen.[5] Working-class neighborhoods from the South Bronx in New York to rural counties across the nation to Los Angeles's Boyle Heights are living in a state of siege as affluent politicians, untouched, promote over-policing, anti-immigrant hysteria, and gentrification schemes that undermine communities at an alarming rate. Economists, hardly sobered by their admitted failures in the global economic system's collapse in 2008 or 2020, continue to sit in powerful political posts. White nationalism, anti-Semitism and

Islamophobia are on the rise. An *ABC News/Washington Post* poll revealed that nearly 10 percent of Americans "call it acceptable to hold Neo-Nazi or white supremacist views, equivalent to about 22 million Americans."[6]

*People Power* calls an emergency town hall meeting, bringing people together to find ways to confront these dismal realities. The contributors to this volume bring a wealth of experience to the discussion. They have studied slave revolts, popular insurgencies in Latin America, and rural rebellions in the United States. The participants in *People Power* have been on the ground as organizers in a broad array of struggles including the Chicano movement, women's liberation, union organizing, consciousness raising, Mississippi Freedom Summer, the Central American solidarity movement of the 1980s, and the 2008 and 2012 Obama presidential campaigns. This book is designed to generate deep discussions on the multiple crises of our time. We hope these dialogues will be held in community centers, churches, synagogues, mosques, union halls, bars, Zoom calls, workshops, retreats, and other spaces on the best ways to get free together. We hope to promote the sense of democratic possibilities generated by people's movements for justice.

One such moment of possibility is recovered in Connie Lester's essay on the visions of Black and white farmers in the 1880s South to create a small-*d* democratic money supply and an economy free of the legal theft of mega banks. How do we generate momentum today to break through the power of Wall Street to twist government to its own ends?

The writers here approach these challenges from divergent perspectives. However, we have one thing in common. We are journalists, historians, organizers, staff, or students who worked with Professor Lawrence Goodwyn, or "Larry," as he insisted his students at Duke University call him to the very end. Larry could be abrasive, he chain-smoked, very often he could be profane. Goodwyn's self-professed aim: to rescue US history from "the enormous condescension of academics and damn fools," as he often told us in university seminars, in taverns, on road trips through rural America, and during Industrial Areas Foundation meetings, among other venues.

Goodwyn served as a lightning rod who gathered together dissident politicians, renegade journalists, graduate students, Polish Solidarity members, Scottish socialists, antiapartheid activists, civil rights movement veterans, and many others. Some knew him as an investigative journalist who had worked with the legendary muckraking *Texas Observer*. Others knew him as a political operative in Texas maverick senator Ralph Yarborough's campaigns. Goodwyn was the author of *Breaking the Barrier: The Rise of*

*Solidarity in Poland* (1991), *Texas Oil, American Dreams* (1996), and *The Populist Moment: A Short History of the Agrarian Revolt in America* (1978), among other books, essays, and op-eds during a distinguished career as a historian at Duke University. *Texas Observer* editor Molly Ivins characterized *The Populist Moment* as uncovering a long-forgotten rural insurgency which personified "the self-empowering fulfillment of real democracy that it was at its best."[7] That is also the goal of this book.

Larry identified himself in a 1965 essay as a "contributing editor" of the *Texas Observer* as well as a person who "takes part in Texas politics." In the 1960s he took part in a coalition of organizers who built a movement of African American, Latina/o, and progressive white laborites depicted in Max Krochmal's book *Blue Texas: The Making of a Multiracial Democratic Coalition in the Civil Rights Era*. And, as Gunther Peck and Faulkner Fox note herein, Larry played an active role in the campaign to turn North Carolina "blue" and elect Barack Obama president.

Today, many ask if democracy will survive the twenty-first century. History may provide helpful ideas, but only if used with skill and care. Journalists such as Andrew Sullivan and scholars like Jason Brennan have argued that the Trump Era signals that we have "too much" democracy, too much popular input.[8] Indeed, the week after Trump's 2016 victory, the *Washington Post* even recommended Goodwyn's *Populist Moment* as a key read to understand the revolt of white working-class citizens.

Goodwyn would have argued to the contrary that the real problem is not that we have too much democracy in the form of Trump voters, but that their votes are an alarm bell, alerting us to how remote we are from living in a world where ordinary people have a meaningful say in the circumstances of their own lives. This is why Larry taught about the overlapping themes of racism, white supremacy, and the power of monied elites to distort democracy—from the beginning of the republic through the present day.

Goodwyn urged everyone around him to read novels as a way to understand the flaws of the republic that historians had papered over with odes to American exceptionalism. He firmly believed that novelists were better storytellers than historians and that storytelling was an essential tool in community organizing and in the pursuit of truth. Larry enthusiastically introduced students to the works of Alice Walker, Mark Twain, William Faulkner, and other dissident writers who explored American hubris with greater candor than most scholars ever achieved. Goodwyn pressed us to ask the question, why had historians largely refused to learn from the American literary tradition that our history was a narrative of tribulation and struggle, not a chronicle of stable advancement as presented in textbooks? This was not merely an academic exercise. Governments may promote myths of inevitable progress in order to encourage acquiescence in the citizenry. In contrast, the dilemmas of characters peopling the pages of James Baldwin's *Another Country* or Toni Morrison's *Beloved* demand intense engagement, a reckoning with profound injustice, and a stand against cruelty, inhumanity, and indifference.

Larry's broadsides against the status quo, which many of his academic colleagues found to be rude and mean-spirited, were rooted in an understanding of the failures of "Western civilization" to solve its own contradictions. While some leftist scholars drew on Marx to solve these problems, Larry turned toward writers like Toni Morrison to pick through the wreckage of capitalism and imperialism—like the narrator of Morrison's *Tar Baby*, who ruminates on a tradition that creates "the people who in a mere three hundred years had killed a world millions of years old. From Micronesia to Liverpool, from Kentucky to Dresden, they killed everything they touched including their own coastlines, their own hills and forests. And even when some of them built something nice and human, they grew vicious protecting it from their own predatory children, let alone an outsider."[9]

As a movement scholar, Goodwyn never tired of reminding students and younger organizers that "all learning is experiential." In this vein, Goodwyn drew on Herman Melville because the whaler-turned-novelist used his own experiences to grapple with the profoundest philosophical problems of his time. In the final years of the antebellum era, Melville wrote from his knowledge as a common seaman to explain why the ship of the republic was sailing to its doom: hierarchy, deference, and totalitarianism in the form of the captain were metaphors for the death of the democratic experiment. In *White-Jacket; or, The World in a Man-of-War*, the novel immediately preceding *Moby-Dick*, the book's narrator cries:

Who put this great gulf between the American Captain and the American sailor? Or is the Captain a creature of like passions with ourselves? Or is he an infallible archangel, incapable of the shadow of error? Or has a sailor no mark of humanity, no attribute of manhood, that, bound hand and foot, he is cast into an American frigate shorn of all rights and defences, while the notorious lawlessness of the Commander has passed into a proverb, familiar to [sailors]: *the law was not made for the Captain!*[10]

In a review of David Herbert Donald's *Liberty and Union: The Crisis of Popular Government*, Goodwyn expanded on his belief that the nation's historians were teaching democracy as a spectator sport in contrast to literary traditions that urged dissent:

> Our novelists, taking as their premise the condition of man—tormented, unfulfilled, endlessly striving—have produced a literature of American endurance under tragedy. In contrast, our historians, as guardians of the national covenant, have determined to find an explanation for our progress. Their song is one of celebration. The American tribe portrayed by our historians is triumphant, without tragic dimension. Those humans called Americans have somehow been spared the vicissitudes elsewhere afflicting the species. Two literatures, two Americas. A puzzle indeed.[11]

Larry frequently told students and organizers that the history profession was beyond reform because, as he explained in his review of *Liberty and Union*, the nation's historians refused to grasp that the arc of history did not necessarily bend toward "progress." This was not an excuse for sardonic detachment; indeed, it was a call for continuous rebellion. As William Greider fondly recalls, Goodwyn "gave me the language and the nerve to write seriously about the idea of democracy, to reject the dominant culture's cynicism and self-congratulations, to tune out the mass-market propaganda that passes for political speech. What a wonderful gift."

Many groups have aspired to democracy in the United States, yet we've never lived it. The tyrannies of settler colonialism, slavery, and, as Faulkner Fox, Marsha Darling, and Elise Goldwasser remind us in this volume, patriarchy, have poisoned our social relations and deepened our distrust of institutions. Tim Tyson echoes this theme, observing: "Goodwyn believed that people commonly live in a quiet posture of resentful resignation toward their governments and that many forces, internal as well as external, keep them from protesting."

The Supreme Court's *Citizens United* ruling in 2010 and its subsequent evisceration of the Voting Rights Act in 2013 have expanded the capacity of Wall Street to undercut democracy while the elderly, African Americans, Indigenous people, youth, and immigrants face an increasing regime of voter suppression tactics implemented by Republican-dominated state legislatures. During the 2016 presidential election, nearly 100 million eligible voters did not vote. The 2020 election presented an even greater catastrophe for the principle of "one person, one vote," as states continued to create barriers to voting. We need fresh perspectives on what Goodwyn referred to as the "mass resignation" of the American people in the face of corporate power and soul-crushing inequalities. What motivates ordinary people to move from their kitchen table, where they discuss real-life issues, and to get involved in politics? The authors *of People Power* explore the ways that history and the chronicles of past social movements can inform civic engagement today.

Goodwyn worked with an eclectic array of organizers, historians, and social scientists willing to confront stark truths about hierarchy and liberation. Of these, none was more important to him than C.L.R. James, the Caribbean revolutionary. As Benj DeMott remembers, Larry met James during a conference at Duke. In subsequent years, he shared this breathtaking experience with many of his students. James's *Black Jacobins: Toussaint L'Ouverture and the San Domingo Revolution* (1938) anticipated the central themes in Goodwyn's *Populist Moment*, especially the relationships between self-activity, self-confidence, and solidarity as necessary building blocks to social movements. Neither the slaves of eighteenth-century Haiti nor the embattled farmers of nineteenth-century rural Georgia could find the answers to the problems facing them in their received cultures. Instead, as James argued, "People find out these answers only by activity, they make experiences and from these they learn. . . . You have got to know what you are, and what you can do. And this nobody can teach you except yourselves, by your own activities and the lessons that you draw from them."[12]

The contributors to *People Power* provide us with numerous examples of people learning these lessons, getting together, challenging the status quo, being knocked down and getting up again to fight another day. It is significant that a good deal of this work happened at Duke University, a microcosm of ruling-class America—not an institution associated with social change. Wendy Jacobs recalls helping to build a vibrant culture of student activism and the fostering of coalitions at Duke in the 1970s, while Thelma Kithcart explains how the Duke Oral History Program led by Goodwyn and Bill Chafe helped build bridges between staff, faculty, and African American graduate students. Organizing means breaking down the divisions, borders, and walls that nationalist politicians erect in order to divide us. In an era of rising ethno-nationalism, we must find new ways to talk to each other.

This is difficult work. Lane Windham reminds us that in any study of the past designed to inform the present, what matters is "learning that social progress is never inevitable; it grows from collective efforts, and those collective efforts rarely succeed without mindful and careful organizing." This means casting off what Goodwyn identified as the "sophisticated deference" of the present whereby ordinary people defer to authorities and waste precious years—perhaps decades—hoping great leaders will save them.

The problem of deference is especially acute in a society such as ours which is supposedly based on meritocracy *and* democracy. During election seasons this is painfully obvious as one side or the other waits on the perfect candidate, "the one who speaks directly to me." Our collection of essays offers readers and organizers a way out. Each author here explores elements of critical questions: What's my role in this democracy? What's your role in this? And what do we need to work together? Furthermore, what in the hell is "democracy" in the first place? What are its limits?

*　*　*

When the coeditors of this volume arrived at Duke University in 1993 as first-year graduate students unknown to one another, the stultifying hierarchy of the history profession and academia writ large was alienating. There seemed to be as much distance between professors and graduate students as between high priests and confessants. In the hallways of a history department in a building named after a Confederate general, sophisticated deference structured relationships between tenured professors, staff, and terrified graduate students. As professors ourselves now, we see how deference between students and teachers leads to intellectual timidity and timid prose. Those in turn reproduce the discourse of American exceptionalism that prevents the United States from facing its most ingrained problems. For us, Larry was the first professor to flatten that hierarchy, to clarify that prose. And in true Goodwyn fashion, he did it through direct action. He walked up to both of us one day and stuck out his hand to shake. "C'mon, comrades, I'm just an old cowboy from Texas," he rumbled as we stood there, mouths agape, staring at his outstretched palm.

Goodwyn provided a working model of a life of the mind, using his commanding powers of concentration to try for a permanently useful fix on the inheritance of history, on the writing that'd come before him, and all the people he'd met that represented the different stages of that literature and the varied ideologies within it. This working life of the mind was as close to a religious discipline as he got, though certainly one can see religious themes in his understanding of humans as deeply flawed and constantly reaching for redemption.

He told people at the university that they would confront challenges: "Once you have your degree, so what? You have to be able to go back to the community you grew up in, where most people may not have high school or college degrees. How can you be a fellow citizen there?" he'd ask. How do you accompany others fighting for justice? How can you be useful to a social movement where you are an outsider? Once you learn something from experience, how can you pass this on to newer recruits in the movement, to keep people on the same page? Speaking of which, how do you most effectively recruit new members? How do you work out strategic differences in an egalitarian way?

*People Power* addresses these perennial questions. Political education is contentious, and challenging. Movements often splinter in the face of internal disagreements. As Goodwyn insisted, the legacies of white supremacy and settler colonialism must be placed in the foreground of this discussion. Democracy, as Nēpia Mahuika and Mentan Tatah among others have noted, must be decolonized.[13] Yet studying earlier movements can provide solace and insights for everyday people working to make their government accountable and just.

*People Power* ruminates on the fate of democracy in the contemporary world, relayed as a series of pivot-point connections and challenges and continued frank discussions about the disaster of American economic policy. And a reckoning with the power of white supremacy to destroy all hopes for "liberty and justice for all." These were the great questions that Goodwyn, a self-described white southerner, grappled with his entire life. In turn, these became the organizing problems and research questions that he demanded his students and "comrades" wrestle with as well: what were the origins of modern social movements and what could we learn from them in order to rebuild the "democratic promise" of the republic?

The insurgents that Larry painstakingly and eloquently chronicled— Populist farmers in Gilded Age America, interracial movement organizers in East Texas in the 1890s and 1960s, Polish workers in the 1980s—all lost in the end. They were defeated by corporate capital, white supremacy, and/or the greed of politicians; however, "the people" also made terrible errors of judgment, and the vaunted *vox populi* was not infallible. Larry did his students and future organizers a fundamental public service by insisting that "you can't honor the people by romanticizing them." Assessing failure right alongside success builds stronger democratic cultures moving forward.

Goodwyn had a term for those with whom he had sustained intellectual friendships. He'd say that person "would do to ride the river with."

Goodwyn's work centered around the relationships he built as a journalist, political organizer, family man, scholar, and teacher. As many attest, he served as a decisive intellectual presence for historians, journalists, historians-in-training, and undergraduates who went on to become what civil rights activist John Lewis would call "good troublemakers" no matter their chosen pursuit or profession.

In part 1, the life-altering contours of these political relationships emerge. Since Goodwyn understood that relationships of trust form the building blocks of social movements, he treated them as sacred. His work within political and social movements, as well as the roles he played to encourage other political organizers, can be seen here.

Repeatedly, Goodwyn noted to any who would listen that the "point of the whole thing is working with young people." Part 2 focuses on those students and his pedagogical approaches, including the pathbreaking Duke Oral History Program created by Goodwyn and fellow historian Bill Chafe between 1972 and 1981. Oral history and storytelling were important to Larry, and he used them as techniques to bridge the rarefied halls of academia with the rough-and-tumble worlds of working-class life and culture. Teaching oral history was a way of putting his students in contact with local people and organizers who were frequently left out of mainstream historical narratives. "If one really wishes to know how justice is administered in a country," James Baldwin remarked, "one does not question the policemen, the lawyers, the judges, or the protected members of the middle class. One goes to the unprotected—those, precisely, who need the law's protection most!—and listens to their testimony. Ask any Mexican, any Puerto Rican, any black man, any poor person," he urged, "ask the wretched how they fare in the halls of justice, and then you will know, not whether or not the country is just, but whether or not it has any love for justice, or any concept of it. It is certain, in any case, that ignorance, allied with power, is the most ferocious enemy justice can have."[14] This is a vital truth to share in our moment in history. How Goodwyn taught this truth to younger people, and what they did as a result, is the focus in this section.

One of Goodwyn's signal contributions to US history was his recovery of the farmers' organizations that made up the base of the Populist movement of the nineteenth century. In *Democratic Promise: The Populist Moment in America*, Goodwyn showed that the farmers of this period, working through cooperatives and the Farmers' Alliances, created the "Sub-Treasury Plan," a low-interest sustainable credit system. In this plan, farmers would store their crops in federal government silos as collateral, while

Larry Goodwyn talking with
a long-time friend at home,
Durham, 1990. Photo by Dirk
Philipsen.

the federal government loaned them money at cost. In order to establish whether the Sub-Treasury Plan was viable in its own historical context, Goodwyn gave a draft of the plan to Duke economist William P. Yohe, who established that the plan was sound and indeed would have been workable if not for the opposition of Gilded Age bankers, corporations, and mainstream politicians.[15]

This blueprint for what Larry called "democratic money" provides an egalitarian path forward in the face of twenty-first-century debates over global bankers' lack of accountability. Recently the International Monetary Fund apologized for the institution's role in draining wealth from the global South and redistributing it to the already affluent North. A modern Sub-Treasury Plan could be one way to put that apology into action.[16] Part 3 includes Connie Lester's reframing of Goodwyn's central historical recovery within this current debate, as well as two historians writing new chapters of the nation's legacy, informed by Goodwyn's signal insights. This intellectual body of work allows future journalists and historians a head start, enabling them to avoid the common pitfalls of the "guilds" of journalism and the history profession that Goodwyn himself tackled.

Like every human being who has ever lived, Goodwyn was a person full of paradox. Though a loving spirit pervades these essays, Goodwyn sometimes came up short by his own standards, and he had an ability to agitate, aggravate, and infuriate his students, friends, and fellow organizers. The angry and hurt qualities reflected in several pieces mirror that truth. And there are of course downsides to bridging scholarship, activism, and civic engagement—it risks the likelihood of partial perspectives. Several submissions warn against lifting up anyone as a heroic figure. No one of us has the ability to move the culture forward by ourselves. In these pages, we gather to share stories of our past that can move us forward, out of the proverbial kitchen and into the political sphere, together.

## Notes

1. Nate Cohn and Kevin Quealy, "How Public Opinion Has Moved on Black Lives Matter," *New York Times*, June 10, 2020.

2. Larry Buchanan, Quoctrung Bui, and Jugal K. Patel, "Black Lives Matter May Be the Largest Movement in U.S. History," *New York Times*, July 3, 2020.

3. Quoted in Ronnie Dugger, "Lawrence Goodwyn, A Man of Words and Ideals," *Texas Observer*, November 7, 2013, https://www.texasobserver.org/man-words-ideals/.

4. Phillip Reese, "When Masculinity Turns 'Toxic': A Gender Profile of Mass Shootings," *Los Angeles Times*, October 7, 2019, https://www.latimes.com/science/story/2019-10-07/mass-shootings-toxic-masculinity; Mark Follman, "Armed and Misogynist: How Toxic Masculinity Fuels Mass Shootings," *Mother Jones*, May/June 2019, https://www.motherjones.com/crime-justice/2019/06/domestic-violence-misogyny-incels-mass-shootings/.

5. Gina Heeb, "US Income Inequality Jumps to Highest Level Ever Recorded," *Business Insider*, September 27, 2019, https://markets.businessinsider.com/news/stocks/income-inequality-reached-highest-level-ever-recorded-in-2018-2019-9-1028559996.

6. Gary Langer, ABC News, August 21, 2017, https://abcnews.go.com/Politics/28-approve-trumps-response-charlottesville-poll/story?id=49334079.

7. Molly Ivins, "Molly Ivins February 6," Creators Syndicate, February 6, 1996, https://www.creators.com/read/molly-ivins/02/96/molly-ivins-february-6-1996-02-06-2f3916f2.

8. There has been a small cottage industry of books and articles in the last decade centered on "too much democracy is destroying democracy." The representative arguments are present in Jason Brennan, *Against Democracy* (Princeton, NJ: Princeton University Press, 2017); Andrew Sullivan, "Democracies End When They Are Too Democratic," *New York Magazine*, May 1, 2016, http://nymag.com/intelligencer/2016/04/america-tyranny-donald-trump.html.

9. Toni Morrison, *Tar Baby* (New York: Knopf, 1981), 269.

10. Herman Melville, *White-Jacket; or, The World in a Man-of-War* (1850; New York: Michael Wilson and Watersgreen House, 2014), 207.

11. Lawrence Goodwyn, review of *Liberty and Union*, by David Herbert Donald (Boston: Little, Brown, 1978), *New Republic*, November 18, 1978, 33.

12. C.L.R. James, *Party Politics in the West Indies: With an Introduction by R. M. Walters* (San Juan, Trinidad: Inprint Caribbean, 1984), 3–4.

13. Nēpia Mahuika, *Rethinking Oral History and Tradition: An Indigenous Perspective* (New York: Oxford University Press, 2019), 32–44; Audra Simpson, "Consent's Revenge," *Cultural Anthropology* 31.3 (2016): 326–33; Mentan Tatah, *Decolonizing Democracy from Western Cognitive Imperialism* (Cameroon: Langaa, 2015); Christine Keating, *Decolonizing Democracy: Transforming the Social Contract in India* (University Park: Pennsylvania State University Press, 2011).

14. James Baldwin, *No Name in the Street* (1972), reprinted in *Collected Essays* (New York: Library of America, 1998), 445.

15. William P. Yohe, "An Economic Appraisal of the Sub-Treasury Plan," Appendix B to *Democratic Promise: The Populist Moment in America*, by Lawrence Goodwyn (New York: Oxford University Press, 1976), 571–81.

16. International Monetary Fund, "Greece: Ex Post Evaluation of Exceptional Access Under the 2010 Stand-By Agreement," June 2013, available online through https://www.imf.org/external/pubs/ft/scr/2013/cr13156.pdf. See also David Graeber, *Debt: The First 5,000 Years* (Brooklyn, NY: Melville House, 2011).

# PART I

★ ★ ★ ★ ★ ★ ★ ★

## Making the Common Good
## the Common Will

### Social Movements and Political Organizing

★ ★ ★ ★ ★ ★ ★ ★

The debate is as old as the idea of democracy. For some of the people fighting for justice, electoral politics is a largely futile effort. It is fraught with corrupt compromises and selling out to established power. As the old saying goes, "If voting made any difference, it'd be illegal." Instead of focusing on the ballot, those activists march, sit in, organize unions, set up cooperatives, promote armed self-defense—using tools outside the official political script. On the other hand, many citizens rely on elections to defend and to expand the precious gains made by the Black Freedom Struggle, the women's movement, LGBT organizers, and other activists. Malcolm X captured the matter succinctly—"It's the ballot or the bullet."

Goodwyn waged a lifelong struggle to plant his feet squarely in both camps, to explore them not as contradictory but as complementary. He never gave up on electoral politics, and the 2007–8 Obama campaign reignited his sense of the country's democratic possibilities. The Faulkner Fox and Gunther Peck chapters in this section detail their own sharpening of the lessons Goodwyn had learned from his years working as a Democratic Party operative in 1950s Texas. He helped to organize a powerful multiracial coalition in that state in the 1960s where working-class Mexican Americans and African Americans formed effective political alliance with white liberals, as Max Krochmal's chapter recounts. The problem for post-civil-rights-era Democrats was already clear to Goodwyn in late 1965:

"the unconscious assertion of white power on the part of white liberals." Faulkner Fox had to figure out how to respectfully listen to Black organizers in Durham in 2009, just as Goodwyn had in Huntsville in 1965.

But electoral politics have limits. Goodwyn's work is an ongoing argument that democratic movement in the direction of justice only happens if triggered from outside, and from the bottom up. Without organized people at the base cracking open received habits, without people arguing and kicking and screaming and experimenting, deeply ingrained power structures of governing don't change. Larry celebrated alongside his students when they uncovered long-forgotten strikes, voter registration drives, or insurgences created by "ordinary people" through rigorous archival research or by interviewing movement veterans. Historical research, shared experiences, and patient listening were—and are—keys to recovering the democratic promise. The struggle for democracy, Goodwyn understood, is, at its core, not about civility or morality, or even about being "right," but about power. People power.

Organizers like Ernie Cortés, Donnel Baird, Jim Hightower, and Adam Lioz share in this section how they drew inspiration and information from Goodwyn. He was particularly good at helping them understand the many dead-end paths of previous justice advocates. As Hightower vividly testifies, Goodwyn urged people to listen to those at the base of the society—workers, people of color, the marginalized—and to use the history of their struggles to inform our political engagement. Spending thousands of hours in conversation, Goodwyn encouraged people like Baird and Lioz over the decades to keep up their essential work as organizers, building the country's democratic potential one relationship at a time. Given that there is no movement if nobody moves, he also persistently encouraged his closest writer friends to leave their desks and libraries and meet people where they lived, in their homes, in the barrios and workplaces, as Peter Wood and Benj DeMott share.

The chapters in this section portray a thinker and fighter who represented and encountered his share of contradictions, or what he memorably called "the barnacles of the received culture." By turns lovely and abrupt, patient and fed up, encouraging and dismissive, Goodwyn realized his close association with a long list of brilliant freedom fighters who, in the words of Bertolt Brecht, "wished to lay the foundations of kindness, [but] could not ourselves be kind." Contradictions and health problems did not stop him, however. Throughout his adult life, whether in Texas or North Carolina or Poland, he persistently tried to find and learn from activists about new ways for people to achieve a say in their own lives. To the very end, he did not give up on democracy. One of his last political acts is chronicled here, persuading a disillusioned Vietnam veteran to register to vote just by being patient enough to listen to the veteran's story.

# 1

## Goodwyn and
## the Democratic Coalition of Texas

MAX KROCHMAL

In 1962 Larry Goodwyn bulldozed the Lone Star political scene like a Texas tornado, sudden, deafening, and leveling everything in his path. He was not unknown to the state's Democratic Party activists: he'd been a volunteer and sometime staffer in the barnstorming campaigns of Ralph W. Yarborough in the 1950s. Larry had grown up in the "liberal movement"—the largely white fight to make the Texas body loyal to the party of Franklin D. Roosevelt. Years of work as a journalist around the legislature and as a foot soldier in the party's perennial convention battles earned him a reputation as a straight shooter and committed activist. But in 1962 Goodwyn landed a high-profile gig as the head PR man for Don Yarborough (no relation), the first gubernatorial candidate to embrace the burgeoning civil rights movement.

Larry's new post propelled him to the center of several tumultuous transformations, all of which swirled around Don's campaign. He looked on as conservative white Dixiecrats began their defection to the Republican Party, as African American and Mexican American activists demanded faster change with increasingly militant tactics, as organized labor struggled to expand its base, and as white liberals charted a new course in the age of civil rights.

Over the next three years, Goodwyn would navigate this minefield to emerge as a leading voice in Texas politics, and indeed in the civic life of the entire South. Always learning from experience, he would develop new alliances among white liberals, Black and Brown civil rights activists, and the white-led labor movement. He would inhabit the eye of the storm as these groups came together to form a multiracial coalition, living through the exhilarating promise and ultimate tragedy of trying to come together across the color line. Larry's activism would eventually lead him to become a pathbreaking historian of social movements. But before he became Goodwyn the scholar, his work as an organizer and journalist in Texas in the 1960s taught him lessons that still resonate for community organizers in 2020 and beyond.[1]

## "New Shapes in Texas Politics"

In 1961 president H. S. Hank Brown of the Texas AFL-CIO convened the first meetings of the simply named Democratic Coalition, a smattering of African American activists with ties to the NAACP, Mexican American leaders of the Political Association of Spanish-Speaking Organizations (PASO), labor leaders, and "independent" white liberals from the Democrats of Texas (DOT), a left-wing party caucus that had collapsed the year before. After much acrimonious debate, the diverse group agreed to work together on a poll tax drive, the annual winter ritual of registering their constituents, people who today would be called "unlikely voters." As Don Yarborough's campaign picked up steam, with Larry Goodwyn as his spokesman, the Coalition hired two temporary staffers, one African American and one Mexican American, who canvassed the state's barrios, ghettos, and rural crossroads. They trained local activists who, in turn, registered thousands of Black and Brown Texans who had never before connected to the "liberal movement." Change was in the air.

Yet the Coalition's members could not agree on a gubernatorial candidate. Despite Don's and Larry's pleas, many African American leaders instead supported John Connally, an ally of Lyndon B. Johnson, former secretary of the navy in the Kennedy administration and the first establishment politician to actively court the Black vote. Mexican Americans in PASO split when a pragmatist faction secured the group's endorsement for the incumbent, Governor Price Daniel, a previously rabid segregationist. White liberals and labor leaders backed the liberal integrationist Yarborough, as did PASO's dissidents and some African American groups. Don beat the odds and advanced to the Democratic primary runoff (a hallmark of the one-party Solid South), and Goodwyn rushed to bring as many Black and Brown voters as possible into the candidate's fold. The Coalition, which had fractured after the joint registration drive, was reborn on the ground in the final month of the campaign. In the end the insurgent failed, but by only 26,000 votes out of more than 1.1 million cast, 51 to 49 percent.[2]

While many liberals despaired, Larry crunched the numbers. The heartbreaking campaign had given him reason for hope. African Americans, Mexican Americans, urbanites, and Republicans had all voted in record numbers, creating a viable two-party state, and inexorably shifted the political terrain. Many whites had abandoned the "Party of the Fathers" for the GOP, which meant that the conservative Democrats were losing their base. The Coalition's establishment opponents won only because they made special appeals to African American and Mexican American voters, but those groups could also be organized for the cause. The state appeared likely to follow the example of San Antonio over the previous six years: there Black, Brown, and white liberals, labor leaders, and small farmers organized the Bexar County Democratic Coalition and proved that they could wield a majority if they stuck together.

"For liberals as for the G.O.P.," Goodwyn wrote in the *Texas Observer*, "1963 can be a year of consolidation or—if they are diverted—a year in which that consolidation is postponed." Conservatives would attempt to maintain their "coalition of big business interests with minority voters," he wrote, so liberal candidates "must be more liberal, more explicitly integrationist," and more committed to the statewide Democratic Coalition. These were the "New Shapes in Texas Politics," he added. White activists must take unequivocal stands and catch up to the Black freedom struggle. Yet "this is easier said than done," Goodwyn noted, "because the pace of change, in racial attitudes and in racial expectations, is far swifter than most liberal politicians realize."[3]

Never content to write in a vacuum, Larry hit the road to sell his theory. He prepared thirteen hand-drawn graphs that demonstrated the trends of the changing electorate, analyzing the previous decade of contests to demonstrate the defection of conservatives to the GOP and the rise of the Black and Brown votes since 1960. He took his case to labor leader Hank Brown and to white liberals around the state. He did not believe that there was any natural affinity for white liberals among Black and Brown activists, nor much love in either group for the other. But the numbers meant that liberal Democrats needed to woo nonwhite voters first and foremost, and that meant fighting for civil rights. "If we're gonna get those votes, we're gonna earn them," Larry told his white audiences. "These are our folks." But, he added, "They ain't votin' for us because we ain't doin' right by them."[4]

Goodwyn also shared his analysis with his friend Arthur DeWitty, an African American journalist and leader of the NAACP in Austin. DeWitty was convinced and agreed to join the roadshow. They shared Larry's graphs and call to action with Black political activists in Dallas, Houston, San Antonio, and rural East Texas as well as with Mexican American audiences in San Antonio and across South Texas. Brown joined them in pitching it to labor's Committee on Political Education, urging local leaders to recognize that "civil rights" fell within their own self-interest. Finally, Larry took his case to East Coast foundations: the Rockefellers in New York, several groups in Washington, DC, and the Voter Education Project in Atlanta.

As they traveled, Goodwyn and DeWitty hatched plans for a biracial "Team Program" centered on voter registration and mobilization, an ambitious field campaign in which pairs of Black and white organizers would develop Black political organizations throughout the state and then connect them with the extant white liberal groups in their counties. Yet the proposal to create the Team Program, like Don Yarborough's campaign, turned out to be an exercise in social learning. Despite DeWitty's intimate involvement, Goodwyn's first drafts were steeped in latent white supremacist assumptions and straitjacketed by a binary analysis of the state's racial problems.

The Coalition's activists of color pushed back hard against the initial proposal, making their voices heard in countless meetings as well as, critically, on the streets. Mexican Americans in the South Texas agricultural hamlet of Crystal City had just come together with Coalition leaders from nearby San Antonio to overthrow the Anglo planter oligarchy that had dominated rural South Texas for the previous century (Larry hand-delivered donations from Coalition partners and was the first Anglo reporter on the scene). African Americans across the state were on the march to desegregate the holdout businesses, to demand jobs at ghetto grocery stores, and to win ordinances that would guarantee their civil rights. White liberals like Goodwyn were forced to come to grips with the growing power of their Black and Brown counterparts—and to treat them as full rather than junior partners.[5]

## "A Four-Group Coalition"

In late April 1963 the leaders of the Democratic Coalition gathered to restructure their organization. Since its inception in 1961, the body had convened haphazard meetings of activists of all races, but in the end each partner was free to go its own way. Now Black and Brown activists convinced their white counterparts, including Larry, that the multiracial alliance must be more deliberately democratic. To move forward, it must guarantee equal representation and leadership roles for its Black and Brown participants.

The traditional lack of structure was no longer viable. Although they refrained from creating a constitution and by-laws, Coalition leaders recognized the need to appoint cochairs and develop a formal power-sharing arrangement. The old informal agenda committee of about ten members gave way to an official "policy committee" of sixteen leaders, intentionally organized to include four members from each "leg" of the Coalition: Mexican Americans, African Americans, organized labor, and "independent" white liberals. The new policy committee translated the years of experimentation in coalition building into a more intimate partnership in which each group had an equal voice.[6] Although many of the activists were holdovers from earlier collaborative efforts, this newest incarnation of the Coalition constituted a significant departure from the past. It formally recognized—for the first time—the independence and agency of its nonwhite participants. The new structure allowed for dialogue to take place in the open and on equal terms. And it allowed them to raise money and hire a sole full-time staffer, one Larry Goodwyn.[7]

The Coalition's first statement of principles set out an expansive vision of civil rights, declaring the issue the group's highest priority. Although it may seem obvious today, such a pronouncement carried great symbolic weight. As the liberal *Texas Observer*'s Ronnie Dugger noted, "For many years Texas liberals treaded softly . . . on civil rights, evolving integrated practices in their meetings, but generally emphasizing advanced policy positions in other areas." In contrast, the Coalition's new leadership structure prioritized racial equality, marking a radical departure for Texas liberalism, one that made it possible to envision a truly multiracial movement.[8]

The Coalition also revised its plan of action. Following months of social learning, Goodwyn penned a revised Team Program proposal that reflected both the growing power of the Black and Brown legs of the Coalition and the white liberals' growing acceptance of nonwhite leadership. Instead of hiring a predominately white staff to attract African Americans and Mexican Americans into established white groups, as early drafts had dictated, most of the staff would now be Black and Brown organizers. The sole white coordinator remaining in the new plan would be asked "to prod existing local [white] liberal organizations into incorporating the Negro and Latin-American organizations in the local Democratic Coalition, *with the minority group leaders in policy-making positions in the Coalition's leadership.*" The local alliances needed to follow the example of the reformed statewide body, which soon elected four cochairs, one from each leg of the Coalition, and a steering committee of one hundred, twenty-five per group.

In this reimagining of the Team Program, the fundamental problem to be solved was the historic failure among white liberal groups to substantively include African Americans and Mexican Americans as leaders and equal partners. Goodwyn gave his white comrades the benefit of the doubt even as he called them to action: "Most white liberals in Texas now realize—for reasons of internal Texas politics—the need for a rapid revamping of the old power relationships among reform-minded persons in all races," Goodwyn began. Yet white liberals needed to move beyond acceptance toward active inclusion. "Habit, left to itself, dies hard," he wrote. "At this stage of the development of Texas liberalism, segregation, as an idea, is dead, but the *political habits* of segregation tend to pop up from time to time in such matters as the internal structure of the local liberal political organization." Newly egalitarian leadership structures represented the key to moving forward together. Larry then offered a series of warnings: "Unless white liberal Texans, at the local level, abandon the old practice of meeting alone, adopting their own program, and then going out to 'sell' the finished product to their political allies among minority groups—unless this folk custom ends, any success attained by a mass voter registration drive will be illusory and the political 'coalition' that is projected will be a soap bubble." The Team Program was about more than votes, Goodwyn concluded. Rather, it "is an attempt to forge a political weapon against segregation—to complement legal and mass action weapons," he wrote. It was a campaign for freedom, and only a robust, democratic multiracial partnership could make it work. Otherwise, Larry concluded, "the political assault on segregation will be blunted."[9]

The Coalition's multipronged war on Jim Crow and Juan Crow would soon capture the attention of the state and, indeed, the nation. Its radical experiment in multiracial democracy would take many twists and turns in the coming years, and Larry Goodwyn would have a hand in many of them. One upsurge occurred on August 28, 1963, the same day as the March on Washington, when some one-thousand demonstrators paraded from all-Black East Austin to the state capitol demanding "Freedom Now." The Democratic Coalition was visible throughout the protest: veteran Black and Brown activists pledged fealty to the multiracial alliance, praising the unprecedented unity among the four groups in their speeches. Larry and white labor leaders joined them in blasting Governor Connally and his conservative Black and Brown allies, promising still more demonstrations.

Even the most stolid white liberals, who had long practiced respectability politics, openly embraced direct action.

On the ground, the Coalition built upon the revised Team Program to conduct the state's largest grassroots registration and voter turnout effort to date, an initiative that permanently enlarged the Texas electorate and brought the seeds of democracy to the state's major cities. Although the assassination of JFK slowed their assault on the Texas establishment, the newly organized Black and Brown precincts carried LBJ and Ralph Yarborough to easy reelection in 1964. The Coalition had broken open the doors of the Democratic Party to Black and Brown activists, remapping state and national politics. Local coalitions flourished in the big cities by modeling their structure on the statewide bodies, drawing on the interpersonal relationships forged over the previous years, and mobilizing activists of all colors—by taking the lessons that Larry helped them learn to heart.

Yet at the same time, the limits of their power became ever clearer. The governor's mansion was no longer in sight: after Connally took a stray bullet that day in Dallas, his polling skyrocketed. The longtime gradualist governor also doubled down on dispensing patronage to his Black and Brown supporters, weakening the hands of the more militant Coalition activists who demanded independent political power. White reaction and white flight took their toll on the movement as well. For his part, Larry Goodwyn left his position as the Coalition's director in the spring of 1964 and, after working a stint on a congressional campaign, announced plans to write a book on the movement while attending graduate school at the University of Texas. The Coalition ceased holding meetings, and many Black and Brown activists flirted with new biracial partnerships free from white interventions. White "independent" liberals chafed at such moves and feuded with organized labor over its pragmatic embrace of President Johnson.[10]

There were ample signs of growing splits, but democracy still seemed attainable, and not too far beyond the horizon. Senator Yarborough remained upbeat, praising the Coalition and, by extension, Goodwyn. Yarborough wrote that he had heard "rumblings of rivalry, of defeatism, of Quislingism for a few bones—bones with less meat on them than cabrito barbecue." The senator added that the work put into "building this effective political instrument" might be for naught if its leaders didn't strengthen the Coalition. "It is imperative that the leaders and the various organizations dedicated to the welfare of the people stay in close and continuous communication," Yarborough wrote. "The immediate future for the progressive forces of democracy in Texas is bright" if they could all stay together,

Yarborough added, and not allow the "corporate power structure" to divide them. "Those who exploit the people . . . realize the dangers of their impending political defeat better than do many of our friends," he concluded. "That's why they are working so hard to bury the Democratic Coalition."[11]

### "'Hey-You' in Huntsville"

Yet the alliance faded by the summer of 1965, leaving Larry Goodwyn and other longtime activists to search for new ways to carry the struggle forward. They found it in an unlikely place: the East Texas city of Huntsville, home to the state's largest prison, an Old South plantation economy, and an all-white political system devoid of any liberal pretense—indeed, it remained rigidly segregated a year after the Civil Rights Act had taken effect. The battle to integrate Huntsville would put Larry at the center of the civil rights storm yet again, giving him new experiential knowledge that still reverberates today.

With support from the fledgling Coalition, a pair of students, one Black, one white, arrived in the city on July 15, 1965. They had attended organizing workshops led by the Texas AFL-CIO in Austin and by SNCC in Mississippi, and they now hoped to bring the fight home to Deep East Texas. Within hours of their arrival, police arrested the white student for traveling in an integrated car, igniting the tinderbox. A local Black youth who had attended the Austin training began mobilizing local high school and college students, while his father, a union leader, worked on the adults. Within seventy-two hours they had recruited forty friends, founded a new organization, opened an office, and prepared for demonstrations. On July 18 they staged stand-ins at the town's movie theaters, and that same afternoon they staged sit-ins at two of the segregated restaurants lining the county courthouse square. Most of the businesses caved quickly, but the Raven Café refused to integrate. The protestors returned to their office but escalated their actions each day thereafter, adding mass marches to their tactical repertoire. Law enforcement arrested a half-dozen students and beat up an out-of-town reporter, but Governor Connally refused to intervene. When organizers called a mass meeting at a local church, the town's Black Ministerial Alliance refused them entry.

The new group, Huntsville Action for Youth (HA-YOU, pronounced "hey-you"), turned instead to allies across the color line and beyond their local community. The remnants of the state Democratic Coalition heeded their call. First came a stock of Freedom Badges left over from the 1964 get-out-the-vote campaigns, which local youth pinned to their chests as they began a house-by-house, block-by-block canvass of the county. Next came the arrival of organizers from the Southern Christian Leadership Conference (SCLC), including veteran Texas activist B. T. Bonner, a close friend of Goodwyn's who had led the March on Austin in 1963.

Larry arrived on the scene on July 25, ten days after it all began, carrying his pen and reporter's notepad while also wearing his activist hat. The night before, an SCLC staffer and allied white minister had hit the phones, contacting Goodwyn and other liberals across Texas who promised to support the struggle. By morning, Larry and two dozen other veteran white activists made their way to Huntsville to join the fight.[12]

That afternoon, HA-YOU staged a picnic fund-raiser at a nearby state park, with some three hundred people in attendance, all "dressed in their Sunday finery," as Larry would later put it. Reverend Alfred Sampson of SCLC denounced the Negro Chamber of Commerce, the leaders of which had called for a "cooling-off period" and then secretly negotiated for partial integration with the white restaurateurs. Sampson got to the crux of the matter: "Who speaks for the Negro?" he asked. "The same man who asks the question answers it. No longer, white man, can you pick X-amount of Negroes and put them on committees and continue the substance of segregation by slightly altering the forms. That day is over."

The out-of-town white liberals got his message. As Goodwyn wrote, "We [whites] believed that HA-YOU . . . represented the spirit of the overwhelming majority of the entire Negro community—from the checker players on the courthouse lawn to the maids and porters who brought food to the houses" of the movement's adult supporters. Meanwhile the Negro Chamber, "a roster of whose directors would make clear their economic dependence on the ruling powers in Huntsville, had not known what was going on and disclaimed responsibility." Larry and his companions decided that their role was to confer legitimacy on the city's new Black leadership: the students of HA-YOU.

That evening, twenty-six white sympathizers from six different Texas cities entered the Raven Café en masse, filling up every booth and counter stool and forming a line to the door. As customers left, the Coalition activists took their seats, ordered a cup of coffee, and lingered. Larry Goodwyn was among their ranks. "Our tactic was to create a circumstance that would force the town to ask, 'Who is HA-YOU?'" Goodwyn wrote. Several performances of the same scripted exchange took place. A server, then a manager, then a police officer would ask a demonstrator what was going on, and the demonstrator would reply that they were all here to integrate the café. The questioner would state that it was already integrated, that two Black men from the Negro Chamber had eaten there that very morning. The protestor would respond that the café owner simply needed to call HA-YOU to tell them that the restaurant was open to all. And then the reply: "What is HA-YOU?" The protestor would explain that HA-YOU was the voice of the city's civil rights movement and that it alone could sanction a settlement. After each exchange, the protestor provided HA-YOU's phone number and waited, repeating the dialogue until they were all rounded up, put in paddy wagons, and taken to the county jail. The reaction surprised HA-YOU leaders, who expected some fallout but did not think that the Dixiecrats of Deep East Texas would arrest an all-white group. One Black student from the University of Texas who had joined the movement told Larry that the fact that white people were in jail for their freedom had an "electrifying effect in the Negro community."

In response, movement activists marched again on the county court-house, now filled with their jailed allies. HA-YOU led three hundred demonstrators in a narrow column that stretched several city blocks by the time it arrived downtown. Goodwyn and the other white liberals remained in jail overnight. The following morning, a Black lawyer from nearby Beaumont negotiated their release, but the local judge required that each defendant post a $200 bond secured by local property. He would not accept cash, which the white liberals could easily obtain. Two African American farmers from surrounding Walker County put up the $5,600 bond, risking their own futures on the movement, and the prisoners were released. "This has turned everything upside down," the Black UT student concluded. "Whites went to jail while Negroes stayed out, and the whites were defended by a Negro lawyer and were bailed out by rural Negroes in the heart of East Texas." It was the kind of irony that would have elicited one of Larry's wry grins.

Thus the Huntsville movement grew directly out of the Democratic Coalition's statewide networks, revitalizing the relationships among its members and providing participants with an experiential education in interracial solidarity. Larry's account of the protests in the *Texas Observer* showed by example how white sympathizers could be useful to the movement while minimizing the paternalism exhibited by their counterparts in other locales.

Nonetheless, Goodwyn's powerful narrative of his own process of social learning failed to change the old "political habits of segregation" that he had long warned against, the intractable "folk customs" that revived as the statewide Coalition faltered. Indeed, a few months earlier, Larry's editor Ronnie Dugger had proposed his own agenda for Texas liberals: discard the Democratic Coalition and form a new organization, "this time as undifferentiated liberal Democrats—not as labor, not as Negroes, not as Mexicans, not as 'independents,' but as whoever they are, in whatever personal reality they live: as persons."[13] He later added that the Coalition "is not a democratic organization. Its very zeal for civil rights has trapped it into the structural segregation" of the four separate legs, a model that, he maintained, stifled its ability to achieve a unity of purpose.[14] For Dugger, the Coalition failed because it fostered divisive identity politics, because it was too close to the civil rights movement, and because organized labor was too powerful within it. Now was the time for all liberals to come together as one, checking their organizational affiliations at the door.[15]

Yet Dugger's solution overlooked history: the Democratic Coalition had grown out of years, even decades, of relationship building, experimentation, trial, error, success, failure, and, above all, social learning. In contrast, Goodwyn's analysis reflected the fact that he had gained firsthand insight that later engendered one of his trademark phrases, that "all knowledge is experiential." He and DeWitty had revised the Team Program after months of contestation, following countless acrimonious meetings while holding together the fragile alliances forged on the streets of San Antonio, Houston, and other Texas cities. The Coalition's huge step forward in 1963–64 reflected this social learning, shaking the foundations of Lone Star politics and forever reconfiguring the state's civic life. The Huntsville movement had taught Larry and other white liberals how to better support and uplift indigenous Black leadership. At the same time, the cleavages of race and class remained as important as ever within the Democratic Coalition, and not just for Black and Brown activists. Facing new challenges to their leadership, many white liberals retreated to the safer realm of party politics, or to new frontiers such as fighting the war in Vietnam. Meanwhile, the struggle for civil rights remained incomplete. Durable institutionalized racism could not simply be wished away.

## "The Caste System and the Righteousness Barrier"

Still, a faction of white activists plowed forward with plans to create a new organization, the Texas Liberal Democrats (TLD). Dugger, Goodwyn, and hundreds more attended its founding gathering in November 1965—old and young, not lily white, but paler than the Democratic Coalition's meetings had ever been. Perhaps predictably, the convention exploded as soon as it began. In a postmortem analysis in the *Observer*, Goodwyn attempted to explain what had gone wrong, in poetic, lyrical, and devastating form—vintage Larry. In addition to examining the Coalition's shortcomings and the imminent collapse of the multiracial alliance in Texas, the piece explored the blinders that many white liberals maintained. At its root, he argued, the problem at the TLD meeting was that white activists carried what would later be named "an invisible knapsack" of power, privilege, and—in perhaps the first use of another of his many trademark phrases—"unconscious white supremacy."[16]

The "liberal dilemma" at the convention centered on race, Goodwyn maintained. Virtually all of the conference's Black participants left the meeting upset, as did the legions of younger precinct activists who had joined the Coalition's campaigns throughout the 1960s. Most were "bitterly disappointed," he wrote, and some were "depressed." Their despair stemmed from a particular form of racial conflict, the tension between what Goodwyn called "the Politics of the Present" and "the Politics of the Future." Participants in the former sought to win the next election, while adherents to the latter wanted to win elections in order to destroy the caste system. The object was not simply to win but "to give people the opportunity to create fundamental changes in the quality of their lives." The division between these two political tendencies "conditioned" the debates throughout the meeting, Goodwyn noted, creating two distinct factions of attendees, split along racial lines, both trapped "by the brooding pressures of the Southern past" and "that most deadly of all political diseases—suspicion."

At a deeper level, Larry wrote, the problem facing the liberal movement was that Black and white activists did not know how to talk to one another and shied from candid conversations in interracial crowds. The liberal crisis "is the crisis of caste, and the fears that flow from that crisis," he added. It is worldwide as well as domestic, as "non-white people who want to breathe, really breathe, for the first time" assert their place on the world stage. There could be no reconciliation between the two political tendencies, and the two races, based on the old ways: "Any discussion of relationships among Texas liberals, white and black, must start with the simple statement that we have got to find ways to begin speaking our true feelings to one another." All Southerners, Black and white, conservative and liberal, have been conditioned to lie, and all were shaped by racism, he noted. "We have been children of a caste system for as long as we have lived, and segregation has created half-men in both races. We think in racist ways, even when we are trying not to." Indeed, he wrote, "It is not so much that we consciously lie to one another. We merely utter polite banalities in order to avoid speaking difficult truths." They were all guilty of lying by omission. Goodwyn contended that the breakdown of social relations and the lack of candor among Black and white activists would have profound consequences. He concluded, presciently, "Sooner than most of us think, there may be no possibility of our being able to communicate in ways that have relevancy."

Absent such relationships, white activists refused to understand that African Americans could be the leaders of the new "liberal movement"— a struggle that many whites believed they had waged for decades, largely on their own. This "barrier of righteousness" produced paternalism that led white liberals to offer direction to their Black counterparts rather than learning from the African American freedom struggle. Goodwyn cited two examples from the TLD conference. First, a self-styled white "radical student" proposed a march in Huntsville, but he did so "without once considering the views of the Negroes of Huntsville who have been enduring the most brutal repression for the past four months." For that student, as well as for many of the others at the conference who debated the issue, "Negroes seem to exist as an abstraction, but not as people." After this "confrontational" resolution was presented, another conference participant, "whose author had likewise not bothered to consider how it meshed with the plans of the people in Huntsville," offered a "liberal" alternative. The conference finally passed a third, "moderate" resolution, which asked for the students' release from juvenile prison but "the chief merit of which seemed to be its high degree of invisibility." It was no surprise, Larry noted, that two of the state Coalition's veteran Black activists lodged fierce objections to the proceedings. The discussion took on an "otherworldly cast," with the issue's main protagonists rendered objects without agency.

Larry's second example drove his point home. At the conference, "a very prominent white person from a medium-sized Texas city" approached Goodwyn and complained that African Americans in his town were "behaving in a racist way," refusing to join the local liberal organization and spurning the help of whites like him. They did so, he said, even though whites in the Coalition had "given" the African Americans the idea and the tools to organize in the first place. Regardless of the facts, the narrator's claim implied "that Negroes are incapable of making fundamental policy changes without whites' guidance." Moreover, Goodwyn wrote, his interlocutor erred in asserting that there exists "a thing called 'the Negroes.'" Just as whites disagreed, African Americans were not monolithic, and their political world was not instrumentally controlled by whites. Internal clashes characterized each group, Goodwyn contended, as they always did "when more than two human beings get together for politics." Despite possessing tolerant attitudes, many white liberals still "unconsciously speak of 'the Negroes' without any feeling of inconsistency." Moreover, the fact that the man confessed his frustration to Goodwyn and not to the Black activists in his own town suggested that the candor needed for functional dialogue had already disappeared. "The evidence is abundant," Larry added, that white liberals "do not accept, *in their daily political or private actions*, the premise that thrust for change in America comes mainly from Negro people, not white people. . . . A great body of liberals, however, cannot bear to relinquish their image of themselves as the sole conscience of the forces of dissent in the South."

White liberals could become relevant again by refocusing on the "Politics of the Future," Goodwyn argued. They needed to address the caste system head-on by developing new strategies that looked beyond the next election, prioritizing the issues of those who were still struggling for freedom. In rural areas, Texans could follow the lead of activists in Mississippi, who were organizing around land ownership and fighting for influence on federal Agriculture Stabilization committees. "The same principle—making our politics germane to the daily lives of people in the neighborhoods where they live—would of course apply in the cities, too," he wrote. New organizations could be created that focused on problems of urban life: jobs, housing, parks, taxation, antipoverty programs, fair housing codes, and more. White liberals needed to be brave enough to forgo "our illusions about ourselves," Goodwyn concluded, and instead recommit to civil rights.

The statewide Democratic Coalition of the early 1960s would never be reborn, and not because activists shouted "Black Power," or because African Americans and Chicanos/as stormed out of interracial gatherings and organized their own liberation movements into the 1970s. Rather, the problem, already clear to Larry Goodwyn in late 1965, was the unconscious assertion of white power on the part of white liberals. In the years ahead, veteran activists of all colors would have no choice but to follow Larry's formula of approaching the problem in new ways, through new issues related to caste at the local level. That work remains far from finished in the 2020s, but the lessons that Goodwyn and his comrades learned along the way might yet help us transcend the "Politics of the Present."

# Notes

1. This chapter draws heavily on Max Krochmal, *Blue Texas: The Making of a Multiracial Democratic Coalition in the Civil Rights Era* (Chapel Hill: University of North Carolina Press, 2016). For a short version of that text with explicit ties to the present, see Max Krochmal, "The Texas Senate Race Is Not 'Historic,'" *Los Angeles Review of Books*, November 4, 2018, https://lareviewofbooks.org/article/the-texas-senate-race-is-not-historic/.

2. "How It Happened: A Narrow Victory," *Texas Observer* [hereinafter *TO*], June 8, 1962, 1. For background, see George Norris Green, *The Establishment in Texas Politics: The Primitive Years, 1938–1957* (Westport, CT: Greenwood Press, 1979).

3. Larry Goodwyn, "New Shapes in Texas Politics," *TO*, December 13, 1962, 3–4.

4. Quoted in Ronnie Dugger, "Texas Politics," *TO*, January 10, 1963, 14–16.

5. See Krochmal, *Blue Texas*, chap. 8; Larry Goodwyn, "Los Cinco Candidatos," *TO*, April 18, 1963.

6. Memo from Larry Goodwyn to Mr. Ed Ball and fourteen other recipients, May 29, 1963, and memo from Larry Goodwyn to Co-Chairmen, Democratic Coalition, November 15, 1963, both in Texas AFL-CIO Papers, Democratic Party Correspondence, Special Collections, University of Texas, Arlington, AR110-26-9-5; Ronnie Dugger, "A Four-Group Coalition," *TO*, August 9, 1963, 3–5.

7. "The Democratic Coalition is a voluntary association of individuals . . ." [Statement of Principles], mimeograph on onion skin paper, attached to Agenda, Democratic Coalition, Granada Hotel, June 1, 1963, Rev. Claude W. and ZerNona Black Papers, Trinity University, Box 32, Folder 11.

8. Dugger, "A Four-Group Coalition," 3.

9. Revised proposal for the Team Program, June 1, 1963, on Democratic Coalition letterhead with blue ink, no title, no author [Lawrence Goodwyn], Black Papers, Box 32, Folder 11 (original emphases).

10. Krochmal, *Blue Texas*, chaps. 9 and 10.

11. "Yarborough Writes on the Coalition," *TO*, April 16, 1965, 12. "Quislingism" refers to collaborating with the enemy, in this case LBJ and his ally Connally.

12. Larry Goodwyn, "'Hey-You' in Huntsville," *TO*, August 6, 1965. Also see Krochmal, *Blue Texas*, 383–89.

13. Ronnie Dugger, "Observations: The Texas Liberals," *TO*, April 2, 1965, 15.

14. Ronnie Dugger, "The Liberals of Texas," *TO*, July 9, 1965, 1.

15. Ronnie Dugger, "Liberals in Texas to Meet in Houston," *TO*, October 15, 1965, 1; "Observations," *TO*, October 15, 1965, 15–16.

16. Larry Goodwyn, "The Caste System and the Righteousness Barrier," *TO*, December 31, 1965, 10–15 (all subsequent quotations); Peggy McIntosh, "White Privilege: Unpacking the Invisible Knapsack" (1989), in *Understanding Prejudice and Discrimination*, ed. Scott Plous (New York: McGraw-Hill, 2003, 191–96.

# 2

## Without Dissent
## There Can Be No Democracy

ERNESTO CORTÉS JR.

I first met Larry when I was active with the University "Y" and organizing a conference on civil rights in late 1965 or early 1966. One of the local civil rights attorneys had heard about my work to identify housing options that were open to students of all ethnicities, and introduced me to both Larry Goodwyn and Ronnie Dugger, founding editor of the *Texas Observer*. This was after the Voting Rights Acts had passed, and the question we were grappling with was where the movement should go.

Since we were a bunch of University of Texas students, we were planning the conference at Scholz Beer Garden, and Larry was being his usual curmudgeonly self, asking questions like "Well, what have you really done?" and "Who do you think you are?"

Despite that, Larry came to the conference, and he spoke. He was impressed by the students' energy and intentions. We organized a voter registration drive in East Austin as a result of the conference, and Larry continued to be impressed by the impact we made.

We followed the voter registration effort with a get-out-the-vote drive, which was significant in that the precincts that had voted for the conservative candidate for state attorney general in the 1966 general election went for the progressive in the runoff. The more progressive candidate had run his campaign with a "get tough on crime" slogan the first time around—not necessarily the best brand in communities where residents already felt persecuted by law enforcement.

At any rate, Larry saw that our work made a real difference in those precincts and he and I began a series of intensive conversations about my interest in organizing. He had significant relationships with people in the

Southern Christian Leadership Conference and had read Saul Alinsky and was intrigued.

We would have long conversations until two or three o'clock in the morning about politics, history, and economics. As I began to get more involved in organizing, he was particularly helpful in providing a sounding board for me, at some cost to himself and his family. I remember his wife calling at two a.m. and asking us to send her husband home.

I had always had an interest in history, but as a graduate student in economics, that wasn't necessarily a subject of emphasis. Larry reignited my passion, recommending to me writers like C. Vann Woodward and V. O. Key. My conversations with Larry were also where I developed a deep interest in Native American history. He introduced me to what he thought was the first-rate literature on the subject of Native Americans—books like *The Patriot Chiefs*. He introduced me to Pontiac, Chief Joseph, and Ten Bears. He would read me their speeches, and we talked about their lives. He was writing a book for Time-Life on Native Americans and spent some time doing research in Oklahoma. He delved into things as obscure as cavalry dispatches, which cautioned against ever getting into pitched fights with Comanches because to do so was "suicide." The depth of his scholarship was extraordinary.

Larry introduced me to authors like Edmund Wilson, who wrote *To the Finland Station*, as a way for me to understand the different types of leftist intellectuals. He would spend hours in conversations explaining to me the difference between someone like him, a democratic socialist, and people he identified as more authoritarian leftist intellectuals. He said some believed that in order to secure jobs, housing, and food for people, it might be necessary to curtail some other people's civil liberties. In contrast, he positioned himself as a democratic socialist, who believed that civil rights and liberties can never be relinquished. He taught me that you don't remove or inhibit the opposition, even if they are a hindrance or impediment to your goals— that without deliberation, negotiation, and compromise there can be no democracy.

Larry was also one of the few people I knew who was taking oral histories at this time. He was always working on what would become his most famous book, about the populist movement, and particularly in Texas there were still survivors of these violent struggles to be interviewed in the 1960s. Of course he also traveled to courthouses, read diaries, and dug into any and all sorts of records, but oral histories became one of his specializations.

Larry opened doors to me in the organizing community. I met James Orange, the field secretary for the Southern Christian Leadership Conference (SCLC), in Chicago marching for housing. He took me under his wing because I knew Larry, introduced me to people, even got me a phone call with SCLC leader Andy Young, who was preparing to come to Texas. It was through him that I first became aware of how close Larry was to people like Martin Luther King Jr.

When I was organizing with the United Farm Workers, Larry kept telling me that I had to get to know a guy named Herschel Bernard—a man who would ultimately become one of my closest advisors and dearest friends for the next four decades. I'd put together a caravan of students to go from Austin to the Rio Grande Valley in the spring of 1966, stopping along the way in places like Beeville, San Antonio, Corpus Christi, to organize rallies for support. Herkie came to the stop in San Antonio. I had talked to him a couple of times on the phone and thought he would be a much older guy. He was quiet, pretty laid back, very self-possessed. He kept his hands in his pockets, which sort of symbolized to me his sense of reserve. He had an extraordinary economy of words.

This was the opposite of Larry, who had a real flair for the dramatic. Larry would shout hyperbole, not just about the people on the other side of the political spectrum, but about potential allies. His words were sometimes accompanied by objects sent flying across the room. People either loved Larry or they didn't. I remember being at a dinner of civil rights luminaries hosted by Al Gore when he was vice-president. I introduced myself to John Hope Franklin and told him I was a friend of Larry's. He beamed at me and shook my hand, praising Larry for his scholarship. Yet Larry received both praise and criticism for his erudite book on the Solidarity movement in Poland. Regardless of how he was viewed, Larry was passionate and courageous—about politics, about people, about connecting them to one another.

He believed Herkie was representative of the few progressive liberals in San Antonio who were Anglo, and that was why it was important to him that we develop a relationship. San Antonio was undergoing a real transition at the time, having moved from a commission form of city government, which was essentially patronage or machine politics, to a council-manager system, which would theoretically be more accountable and democratic. City politics was a labyrinth during this transition, and Larry helped me understand the players, the relationships, really the kind of power analysis that is central to any significant community organizing effort.

At around the same time, a split was emerging among liberals in Texas more broadly, among Larry's own people. A number of prominent progressives got co-opted by the Johnson administration in the early days of the Vietnam War. Larry never did, but this split made the politics of Texas liberals tumultuous during this period. It represented another maze for me to navigate, and once again Larry was there to point me toward interesting people in the mix.

It was typical of Larry that one day he announced, "We'll drive to Houston!" The last-minute trip was occasioned by the need for me to meet a guy, in this case Bob Hall, one of the key progressive lawyers in Texas and someone who became a dear friend. A liberal graduating from law school in the state went to one of two firms—either the one Larry was about to introduce me to in Houston, or a group of like-minded folks in Dallas. Naturally he wound up connecting me to the folks in Dallas as well, where I met David Richards, another lifelong friend.

These kinds of connections and relationships were the keys to my development. Thinking back, the list of progressives who came out of San Antonio, my hometown, during this period is remarkable. The city was a crucible for the development of Texas politics, particularly the progressive wing. Larry Goodwyn, Herschel Bernard, Ronnie Dugger, Albert Pena, Maury Maverick Jr., John Alaniz, Mary Beth Rogers, Henry B. Gonzalez, Franklin Garcia: these were just some of the people who invested time and energy in me; they helped me learn. They helped me learn not just to navigate San Antonio and Texas, but to think politically. Their generosity of spirit toward a young man just beginning to learn his way was incredible. Larry was my guide and mentor through this fascinating and extraordinary world.

# 3

## The Larry Way

JIM HIGHTOWER

Goodwyn lived and thrived as a maverick, not only because he was such an independent thinker, but also because it is derived from another non-conformist Texan, Samuel A. Maverick. Sam ran some cattle on the coastal plains in the 1840s, but unlike other ranchers, he refused to put a brand on his animals, so if anyone came across an unbranded steer, it was known to be "a maverick."

Even in the 1940s when he enrolled at Texas A&M (a quasi-military college that specialized in graduating engineers and agribusiness scientists), Goodwyn went off the beaten path to matriculate as, of all things, an English major! Back then, Aggies thought an English major was an officer in the British army. Yet even though A&M was hardly a natural fit, he made it fit him.

Goodwyn certainly bore no one's brand, nor was his work and personality easily categorized. He was at once an activist and an academic, a provocateur and a conciliator, both cocky and tender, a bare-fisted street fighter and a graceful writer. He could be impatient and even abrasive, but that was all tempered by his obvious passion for fairness and justice, as well as his delight in the democratic fight that must be made if there is to be any progress. Despite his seriousness of purpose, Larry was a laugher, finding great humor in life and even in the cause. In fact, he understood a truth that more of today's intense progressives should embrace: battling the bosses, bankers, big shots, bastards, and bullshitters is about as much fun as you can have with your clothes on!

And battle he did. The good professor didn't just teach and write about history, he experienced and practiced it—often on dangerous turf as a southern activist for oppressed African Americans, Latinos, poor whites, laborers, and other "outsiders." Indeed, the excellence of his academic work and his renown as America's best historian of people's movements are due in large part because he was actually involved in some of them, starting with an important political rebellion in the 1950s and 1960s against the "oilgarchy" of Texas.

In the mid-fifties, several leaders of various liberal groups in the Lone Star State did something drastic: they tried to unify into a pragmatic coalition and come up with an actual plan for winning elections. What a radical thought! The elements included:

A galvanizing political sparkplug—liberal firebrand Ralph Yarborough was a tub-thumping speaker who crisscrossed the huge state tirelessly in campaigns for governor and the US Senate;

An uncompromised medium of communication—the big newspapers ignored, distorted, or openly mocked progressive campaigns and ideas, so the now legendary *Texas Observer* was created in 1954 as a twice-monthly "Journal of Free Voices" to serve as "The Tyrants' Foe, The People's Friend," connecting the widespread community;

Door-to-door organizing in the big cities led by steelworkers and other unions that created such effective grassroots groups as Harris County (Houston) Democrats, orchestrated through a citywide network of block captains who regularly kept folks informed and engaged;

Hands-on voter registration of historically disenfranchised minorities—an especially onerous process, because of the infamous poll tax that required people to pay to vote (and it was no pittance, either, for it amounted to about fifteen dollars per person in today's money).

Young Goodwyn was in the middle of all this political tilling, planting, and nurturing. He was a feisty associate editor of the *Observer* with founding editor Ronnie Dugger; a staffer for Yarborough's dynamic campaigns; a field organizer in East Texas registering Black voters; and a strategist for the overall coalition of progressive Democrats. Such efforts over a dozen years produced Yarborough's victory in a special election for a US Senate seat in 1957 (reelected in 1964) and the election to Congress of such liberal icons as Henry B. Gonzalez, Bob Eckhardt, and Barbara Jordan.

In the early sixties, Goodwyn also became involved in the rise of a Chicano power movement in South Texas, La Raza Unida, and in civil rights protests by Black students in East Texas. He didn't just join a march or two—he literally studied the emergent movement, paying close attention to the interactions of participants and listening carefully to discussions among these groups of mostly poor, long-oppressed people of color. Thus began the development of his deep, empathetic (and rare) understanding of racial dynamics in political and social movements.

It was his genius to seek out, actually listen to, and bring forth the voices of marginalized people—either in contemporary movements or in his historical research. Through these voices, which most other reporters and historians didn't notice or didn't consider worth hearing, Goodwyn was able, again and again, to unearth the *real* story.

I compare his dig-it-out approach with another workhorse: the cowboy hat. Just as there is the working-class history of America and the sanitized "official" history written by the courtiers of the establishment, so are there two kinds of cowboy hats. Predominant today is the Show Hat—think George W. Bush strutting around in his spotless, perfectly formed, thousand-dollar white Stetson, probably bought at Neiman Marcus.

Then there's the real thing. Hollywood aside, there was nothing romantic about cowboying—it was hard labor, poorly paid, and backbreaking (sometimes literally). Likewise, a cowboy's hat was not a headdress but a utilitarian tool that no cowboy considered his own until it was broken in—meaning it had been in a hail storm, been torn by brambles, stepped on by a horse, and properly baptized in sweat, dirt, splotches of beer, and a few flecks of blood.

*That* is an honest hat.

And Goodwyn was an honest digger of history's real stories. One of his most important and lasting contributions was his initiation in 1971 of Duke University's superb Oral History Program. Through this innovative and extensive outreach, the memories of southern Black people were collected so their long-neglected perspectives, stories, and truths could finally be heard, felt, and given their due as the people's history of our nation's long civil rights struggle.

By word and deed—as an original thinker, progressive strategist, rebellious scholar, and inspirational teacher—Goodwyn gave us the gift of a bigger, bolder understanding of America's striving for our people's egalitarian ideals. Defying the contrived wisdom that power elites have placed at the center of history texts and classes, he used impeccable research and his academic credentials to upend the immobilizing, antidemocratic theory that the Great Men create history. Real progress, he revealed through all of his work, comes from the grassroots struggles of common workers, farmers, poor people, and other mavericks and mutts who dare to challenge the "great men."

In his 1976 landmark work *Democratic Promise: The Populist Moment in American History*, he bluntly corrected the gross historical errors and class bias of elitist academic interpreters of the revolutionary and remarkably successful Populist movement of the late 1800s. For example, none other than Richard Hofstadter, an Ivy League darling of establishment academia, had slandered the people of this mass movement in a widely used college textbook in which he basically branded the Populists as an incoherent and incompetent bunch of rubes and racists with nothing to say to modern democracy movements. In writing *Democratic Promise*, Goodwyn used his pen both as a torch of enlightenment for truthseekers and as a stiletto pointed directly at Hofstadter's astonishingly ignorant pomposity.

> When considered in their own time, and by their own standards of hope rather than our own, the Populists not only come to life, they send a very different message than we have possessed the poise to hear. It is difficult to hear people, however, when we are trapped within our cultural need to condescend to them. . . . The Populists spoke clearly enough; the burden of hearing them is ours alone. It is necessary, therefore, to hold the camera as steady as possible, letting events be recorded as they happen, letting the movement culture of Populism narrate its own flowering. . . . If we do not condescend too much to them we can hear what they say rather clearly.

All who knew Larry or have read his works agree that his influence will keep growing, thanks to his writings and to his hundreds of former students. I would only add that his impact was not campus bound—he reached and inspired thousands of us all across the country who were nurtured, informed, or even transformed by him into populist disciples:

> Like Ernesto Cortés, an innovative door-to-door organizer who rallied poor people into such powerhouse groups as COPS (Communities Organized for Public Service) in San Antonio. As a young agitator, Ernie was mentored by Goodwyn in the 1970s, and they remained close as Ernie went on to forge a national network of similar neighborhood coalitions, from Baltimore to Los Angeles.
> Like George Goehl, chief wrangler of important grassroots groups in fourteen states gathered under a hell-raising populist umbrella

called National People's Action. George tells me he never met Goodwyn, but he regularly rereads *Democratic Promise*, finding fresh insights and inspiration every time.

Like me—and my longtime coauthor and populist coconspirator, Susan DeMarco. In January 1977 I became editor of the *Texas Observer*, committing it to what I called "undiluted populism." Larry approved, Susan and I were adopted into the Greater Goodwyn Family, and regular advice flowed freely from him to us. Pushy, yes. But only because he cared and wanted our best, just as he genuinely wanted the best for us.

In April of that year Larry sat with us over coffee at our kitchen table for two or three hours discussing the possibilities of a progressive future, expressing some optimism for it. Before leaving, he inscribed our copy of *Democratic Promise* with his characteristic and endearing mix of the personal and the political:

To Jim Hightower and Susan DeMarco—Gentle people and good friends. You offer us in the new OBSERVER a look at the present . . . and a bit of yourselves.
Here, I offer a bit of the past . . . and of myself,
   With affection and shared promise, Larry Goodwyn
   Austin, Texas, April 5, 1977, in the kitchen.

# 4

## Calm Up

### Dr. Goodwyn's Workshop

DONNEL BAIRD

During my sophomore year at Duke I decided to try Lawrence Goodwyn's seminar on American history, with fairly low expectations. Our first assignment on Day 1 was to write a paper on "What Democracy Means to Me." I was nineteen, and not really in the habit of completing homework assignments. Amadou Diallo's four New York Police Department shooters had been exonerated the previous spring, in February 2000, and when I'd heard the verdict, I knew it meant that as a young Black man I could be gunned down at any time, for any reason, by cops, and that the loophole of probable cause meant that they would *always* be exonerated as long as they cited probable cause.[1] After discussing the verdict and ensuing hopelessness in a simultaneous Black Studies course, I shut myself in my dorm room for three days and cried, and emerged a cynical, depressed, and miserable young man. I was deep in despair, and I didn't really care about anything. Certainly not schoolwork. Certainly not what "democracy" meant to me.

When I returned to Goodwyn's class for the second session on Day 2, I'd forgotten to even bother attempting a draft response to Goodwyn's Day 1 assignment. All of the other students had brought typewritten copies of their papers on what democracy meant to them. I borrowed a loose sheet of paper from a classmate and quickly wrote a handwritten one pager on how democracy was like jazz, because there were different players all coming together, improvising, but performing one song. Some nonsense I'd read in a Cornel West book. And I handed in the paper. I have always had truly atrocious handwriting. I'd received a C+ grade in cursive handwriting in the third grade.

A week later Goodwyn handed back graded papers to all students, with one exception—mine. After class I asked Goodwyn whether he'd misplaced my paper. Goodwyn opened up a manila folder he had on his desk; in it was my paper. Without looking up from his folder, he snarled, "Is *this* YOURS?" "Why, yes, it was," I answered cheerfully. He slammed the manila folder shut and walked out. The next class, he handed me the paper, with a big D- at the bottom. This was session 4, and it was becoming clear by now that grades did not just concern what was on the page, but also in some fashion correlated with Goodwyn's comprehensive assessment of you as a person, as a *human*. The D- stuck in my craw. Goodwyn sent word via a classmate that he wanted to meet with me one on one in his office, if I chose to join him. Because I'd never been on the receiving end of a D-, I decided to show up.

As was his style, Goodwyn came over from behind his desk to sit across from me. He glared at me. I glared at him. He glared back. After about five solid minutes of silent glowering, Goodwyn finally said, "Well, you're just about the *laziest* motherfucking student I've ever *seen*."

The punches kept coming over the next five minutes, ultimately culminating in the line, "If you don't figure out a way to act politically on your anger and stop being so alienated, you're going to be dead of a drug overdose before you're thirty-five." I stayed silent. But I was intrigued.

That's where our relationship started. I could tell that he had seen my type before and cared enough about me to stage an intervention. It worked. He assigned us to read and respond to David Halberstam's *The Children*, about early civil rights activists in SNCC. I worked harder on the paper than any other assignment in college. I tried to understand Diane Nash's seeming fearlessness, John Lewis's doggedness, Marion Barry's subsequent spiral. I got my grade back: a goddamn B-. Plus, a reprimand scrawled on the assignment's last page. "John Lewis' strength was that he did not pretend to know things he did not know." Jesus.

I won some kind of research fellowship at the end of the year, and Goodwyn was faculty mentor to another fellow. At the awards dinner at the end of the year, I sat down at a table at the reception with Larry and Nell. The dean of academic affairs came over and complimented me on my project, and moved on to the next table. "His comment," Larry immediately informed me, "was EMPTY of CONTENT!"

When I showed up for the first day of another Goodwyn class the following spring, he asked each student to talk about why they were taking the class and what they hoped to get out of it. I was fourth or fifth to speak.

The first few students said they were in the course because they wanted to learn about social movements, or nineteenth-century American history, or the Civil War, or whatever the ostensible subject was. When it was my turn to talk, I said, "I took a class with Goodwyn last semester, and I thought he was totally full of shit. But I'm back." Take that for your goddamn B-minus, sir.

Goodwyn took my public jab in stride, without comment, and immediately moved on to the next student. By doing so, he was able to use my obnoxious comment to encourage other students to be more open and honest in that course, because they saw him accept my criticism without reacting. This became one of Goodwyn's favorite stories. He must have reminded me of this story fifty times over the next decade.

In this course, we were asked to analyze a Chalmers Johnson book on American militarism, *The Sorrows of Empire*. I dissected the text, and Goodwyn was quite pleased with my response. How, he asked me in class one day, was I able to deconstruct the way that Johnson positioned himself as a patriotic critic of the expansion of American empire? Well, I just spent the twenty minutes before the paper was due in the computer lab typing up what came to mind, and that's what came out. Goodwyn was annoyed and slightly offended by my flip process. But he appreciated my insight, so he awarded me an A.

Goodwyn would caution me over the next ten years about my tendency to be flip, to emotionally unplug from a situation, and therefore alienate myself from influencing the outcome. Instead, like SNCC, I had to find a way to "calm up." I had to channel my anger and perspective into a politically productive outcome. I wasn't to be resigned. I wasn't to calm down. I was to "calm up."

Well, how on earth do I do that?

So we spent ten years in consistent conversation, with Dr. Goodwyn offering feedback or sharing his insights on social movements, my dating life, and the lessons I was learning in my political career. I'll circle back to "calming up." In the meanwhile, here are a few of my favorite Goodwyn suggestions and life recommendations:

> Don't get married till you're thirty. You want to give yourself the opportunity to explore different political opportunities in multiple states, and get yourself fired, make some mistakes, be reckless, in order to learn. Social knowledge is experiential.
> Men like to put their feet up on the table and talk strategy. Often,

women will outorganize the pants off a group of men who are sitting around bloviating and showing off but not doing any real work. Don't get frustrated and waste too much time trying to persuade the men to work. The women will lead, if you're lucky.

Here's the advice Goodwyn gave me on how to get a job in a political campaign: Save up enough money to float yourself for a month or so. Drive over to the campaign office, walk in, introduce yourself to someone, and tell them you're here to work but are willing to volunteer for the campaign. Ask them for an assignment. Say, "I don't have a lot of experience, but I work hard, I'm smart, and I learn extremely fast." If they give you a confused look, move on to the next desk, and introduce yourself to the next person, and tell them that you're here to work but willing to volunteer for the campaign. Keep doing that until someone gives you an assignment. The person that gives you the assignment may have the workload and the authority to bring you on staff after a few weeks of good work.

Don't be flip. I'm still working on this one—Goodwyn wanted to flag for me my tendency to make dismissive jokes and under-communicate, particularly in times of emotional complexity. Being flip is the opposite of Talk, an important part of the Goodwyn philosophy.

After a talented classmate had written and premiered a play about how her mother's conception of appropriate southern white womanhood was a straitjacket, Goodwyn told me that a work of art, like music or a play, can create an *aura* that can offer a political opportunity. The play can create a chance to have the important conversations that follow, and the conversations can change how people see themselves and one another.

Talking was an important theme to Larry. "Oh," he asked, a bit surprised, "are you still trying to *impress* women in order to get them to sleep with you?" Well, what the heck else was I supposed to be doing, I asked. *Talk* to them, he helpfully suggested. Looking back, I think that this emphasis on folks coming together, dropping pretense, and talking about the things that really mattered, was one of the foundational pillars of the Goodwyn Doctrine. If you read through *The Populist Moment*, you will find Larry discussing the conversations farmers had among themselves about their exploitation by local merchants, eventually discovering that the explanation was structural. "Life under the [Communist] Party is crazy" was whispered at tables around Poland. Discussions of the humiliation of segregation, the challenges to exercising nonviolent direct action, and mustering the courage to act politically were dominant portions of the Nashville workshops in the civil rights movement. The civil rights movement, Larry used to say, thought *segregation* was the problem. We didn't understand that *white supremacy* was the problem. He told me that there was a break across racial lines—a withdrawal from interracial friendships, even important ones, for many civil rights movement participants after the movement. They needed time and space to grapple with white supremacy, and what it meant. There was about a decade of silence, he said. Then the letters started arriving. Years later, I would feel the need to write some of my own letters to white friends, explaining my own withdrawal from our relationships. White supremacy is tough. As an aside, I had the privilege of being trained by and functioning as a leader inside of an Industrial Areas Foundation organization, and I observed that power can transform racial hierarchies, in the short term and over the long term. I believe in organizing political and economic power to counter white supremacy in American institutions. Larry used to quote a closing line from the oral history of a sharecropper: "I look around the world, and I see the colored peoples coming up. But it takes many a trip to the water to get clean."

I was driving with friends from Durham to an antiwar march in New York City. "Well," Goodwyn said, "the useful thing about those marches would be if the people marching could start to see themselves as people who could actually change policy, and maybe participating in the march might help them understand that."

Goodwyn saw me go off to work for ACORN, and witnessed me take the beating that comes along with working for ACORN. On my first day, they laid a map of Newark, New Jersey, on a table in the near-abandoned building they called an office space, and drew a red circle around all of the worst neighborhoods. My job, my ACORN supervisor told me, was to drive into one of those red circles every day and knock on doors until I could talk my way into someone's home, discuss neighborhood issues with them, and sign them up to a ten-dollar-a-month bank draft for dues. I lasted six weeks, then I quit. (I'm still proud, perversely, that I did sign up some ACORN members. I was on track to an A, if I'd stayed!)

Goodwyn then sent me to the Industrial Areas Foundation, introducing me to inveterate organizer Arnie Graf—but only after he let me get my butt kicked at ACORN first. Arnie also became an incredibly important mentor to me. Goodwyn told me that I should consider working with John Edwards's presidential campaign in 2007. He might win, and then I would meet all of the Democratic bigwigs, the party elders and functionaries. And then, he and Nell said, down the line, I could run for president. This is still one of the nicest things anyone has ever said to me. I elected to work for Obama in the primary, because I thought he could win South Carolina and become Hillary's vice president, and therefore be a great example to Black children around the world. Both Goodwyn and I were wrong on that one.

So Larry was the first person I called with the internal staff numbers from the Obama campaign that said we were going to carry Iowa. We were floored, stunned. Once he digested the numbers, Goodwyn chortled with sheer glee and immediately flushed his prior support for Edwards from the recesses of his mind. I don't remember a transition period, or a period of grief like in the George Bernard Shaw quote that Goodwyn used to repeat, about how during times of change we always mourn what we lost. Goodwyn didn't waste a second mourning Edwards. I traveled to seven primaries and a general election for Obama, and I met thousands of passionate Obama supporters. Goodwyn had to be among the top percentile of Obama supporters in terms of depth of support and enthusiasm and admiration for Obama. Yep, I'm putting him right up there next to the African American eighty- and ninety-year-olds. I'm glad they all lived to see President Obama.

Goodwyn loved Obama after Iowa. LOVED him. Would not suffer a contrary word, as in, would not let you complete a sentence that was headed the wrong way on Obama. Goodwyn thought that Barack Obama was the greatest presidential campaigner of all time. "My God!" Goodwyn told me breathlessly as Obama was swinging through the Texas primary, "he looks good in a Stetson!" And, frankly, Goodwyn's assessment on Obama's campaign skills has to be credible, right? But, enthusiasm aside, Larry's shrewd political mind also pragmatically got down to the brass tacks of studying the politics of how Obama actually won Iowa. "Chicago UAW," he told me, matter of fact. The Chicago UAW locals called the Iowa UAW locals and got them on board, and the Iowa UAW brought their members out to expand Obama turnout to the Iowa caucuses.

One of my fondest memories is watching Obama's address to Congress on health reform with rapt attention in Nell and Larry's living room, and getting to see the pure joy on Larry's face as he devoured the speech and subsequent political commentary. There wasn't a lot of conversation—you could hear a pin drop—as Larry wanted to catch every single word. "Obama is large," he said in a 2010 interview with Alternet. "These are not softballs he's throwing. . . . [Obama] is larger than Jefferson."

Social knowledge is experiential. He told me that at least a thousand times. I can hear him croaking it at me now. For most of our relationship, I didn't understand what on earth he was talking about. I'm in my mid-thirties now, and I get it. I've triumphed, I've been defeated, I've stumbled, I've persevered, I've given up, I've embarrassed myself. But I've learned. The lessons I've learned cannot be taken away from me. My actions are informed by fifteen years of experience. Twenty years from now, I'll be further informed. Dr. Goodwyn knew that I didn't know what "social knowledge is experiential" meant—he told me that most young people didn't understand the concept—but he poured lessons and information into me nonetheless, in the hope that in my thirties I would turn into something.

I manage a Silicon Valley venture-capital-backed startup focused on bringing clean energy and jobs and economic development to low-income communities, for community residents to own and operate and control. It is not an easy task. We are building solar powered microgrids in New York City's poorest neighborhoods. We are working with mayors in Chicago and Boston and Detroit to think about what engineering and financial structures are possible to help low-income families benefit from the clean energy revolution. It's a different approach to building power in low-income communities of color. The idea is that if we can solve the demand problem for clean energy projects, by solving the financial and engineering problems of clean energy in inner cities, we will be able to generate enough jobs to hire large groups of men and women to green their cities' buildings and infrastructure. Goodwyn has a book out there that no one talks about, about how the wildcat oilmen of Texas were similar to the Populist organizers.[2] Way ahead of his time. The skills and lessons that I use every day, that I refer to as a touchstone, are Larry's, even in a field as seemingly unrelated as mine. Our company has an outside shot to do something serious.

Goodwyn knew from Day 1 that it was critically important for me to find a life partner to help heal me and get me emotionally reorganized. I brought my wife and her aunt down to Nell and Larry's house to go through a manuscript that we'd found from my wife's great-great-grandfather, who had served in the North Carolina legislature and helped to swing a group of Black legislators to support a North Carolina candidate for Senate named Pritchard. (You might recall that state legislatures appointed senators for some time). My wife's ancestor, Scotland Harris, wrote about hiding under the floorboards of his home as the Klan came by to kill him, as they sought to stifle Black political participation. Larry treated the manuscript like it was a golden treasure. He used the full weight of his professorial authority to arrange a meeting with the Duke Archives, to get them to assign a budget for the care and maintenance of the manuscript. When the meeting seemed like it might be running off the rails, Larry burst into tears over how important the manuscript was. The library staff was taken aback and immediately relented.

*   *   *

I loved Larry Goodwyn, and I am glad I told him that before he passed. I learned an enormous amount about how to live my life from him, through our relationship over the last ten years of his life. He liked to say that he was my representative of the older generation. He was incredibly patient with me, as he taught me politics. Groping blindly in the dark for a light switch, I called over to the house to help process my latest experience. Social knowledge is experiential, he would repeat over and over, and I harassed Larry over the phone for years to get his take on the lessons I was learning.

When I was young, he used to say, I was angry, walking around a light factory and turning off all the light switches. Democratic *aspiration* is what I'm looking for. And when I got a little too negative and angry for his taste, "Don't *poison* this conversation!" Part of the lesson there is: Yes, you're angry, and that's justified, and a source of power. But you've got to calm up. Not calm down, and internalize your anger, do nothing with it, and become alienated. Don't let your anger consume you. Or, don't let your unprocessed anger spill out and wash over others, because they will experience it as poison. It's your job to take the disapproving edge out of your voice, to make it easier for others to hear you without feeling judged. You're not going to lead the left or the Democratic Party by screaming at them about how stupid they are—even if you're right. Screaming at your democratic fellow travelers is as futile as turning off light switches in a light factory. Instead, search for those who have democratic aspiration, and recruit them to your specific action plan. Our job is recruiting, he used to say.

Chief among his lessons is the importance of people coming together to have sustained, serious, candid conversations about politics, and what can be done. In the case of the African American civil rights movement, my touchstone, we spent a great deal of time examining Reverend James Lawson's eighteen months of Nashville nonviolence workshops with Diane Nash, Jim Bevel, Bernard Lafayette, John Lewis, and other students who would become SNCC, the Student Nonviolent Coordinating Committee. The workshop allowed for the development of relationships through intimate and serious conversations about the tactics of nonviolence and their applicability to dismantling segregation in the Jim Crow South. The relationships forged in the workshop also helped SNCC students to organize nonviolent direct action, via sit-ins and Freedom Rides, despite their fear. My wife and I named our firstborn son Nash, after Diane Nash, the lead protagonist in *The Children*—the most important book I've ever read.

Dr. Goodwyn was running a workshop with all of us, his students. For years. And as students and participants in Dr. Goodwyn's workshop, what greater tribute could we pay to the man than to talk among ourselves and come up with a plan to take our country back.

## Notes

1. On Amadou Diallo, see Beth Roy, *41 Shots—and Counting: What Amadou Diallo's Story Teaches Us about Policing, Race, and Justice* (Syracuse, NY: Syracuse University Press, 2009), and Clarence Taylor, *Fight the Power: African Americans and the Long History of Police Brutality in New York City* (New York: New York University Press, 2019).

2. Lawrence Goodwyn, *Texas Oil, American Dreams: A Study of the Texas Independent Producers and Royalty Owners Association* (Austin, TX: Center for American History, 1996).

# 5

## Larry Goodwyn, Obama Volunteer

FAULKNER FOX

One Saturday in mid-March 2008, I was working in the new Obama field office in downtown Durham. My husband had taken our three children, including our two-year-old daughter, away for a week to visit his parents so I could work eighteen hours a day on the Obama campaign. Obama had just given his "A More Perfect Union" speech in Philadelphia, and I remember thinking: "I'll do pretty much anything for the man who wrote that speech," which I knew was a dangerous thought, but I had it anyway.

I loved that Obama had been a community organizer. This fact, more than any, made me think he genuinely had the interests of the poor at heart. Hillary, on the other hand, had been on the board of Wal-Mart, undoubtedly figuring out ways to squeeze more profits out of the oppression of its workers and customers. As the campaign wore on, my involvement became less about Obama the candidate and more about the empowerment of Durham's citizens. This might have been because I focused my own organizing efforts on voter registration. More people voting, being empowered to vote, is always a good thing, not entirely candidate-dependent. And yet, of course, someone needs to be running who is worthy of people's votes. Obama was that person in 2008.

We were going to beat Hillary Clinton, if it killed us. And then we'd win the general election with North Carolina, ex-slavery state that is is, going the right way in the election of the first African American president. Thousands of other North Carolinians, including my husband, seemed to feel exactly the same way I did.

It was late afternoon around four, and I was hoarse from teaching nonstop groups of people how to register voters. The scenario that day was an organizer's dream: people just kept showing up at the office, everyone ready to help Obama win. In past presidential elections I'd worked on—Kerry, Gore, Clinton, Dukakis, Mondale—it was like pulling teeth to get volunteers to show up. Not this time. People who'd never been politically active, some who'd never even voted, joined those of us who worked in every Democratic campaign. Volunteers came from as far away as Denmark and South Africa to spend their entire vacation in Durham, working for Obama. There was a palpable sense that this previously Republican state might go Democrat this time.

Amid the excited bustle of busy people, I heard a shuffling noise out in the entryway. Folks had already complained mightily about the long, narrow staircase you had to go up in order to get into the office. Someone even suggested the Obama campaign would be sued over this non-handicapped-accessible staircase. I'd helped the advance team pick this office a few weeks before, and we saw the stairs as a problem, but it was an available, centrally located downtown office—the best we could do on such short notice. I heard shuffling and looked out the door to see an old white man who'd come up the stairs, dragging an oxygen tank behind him, one laborious step at a time. I'm not proud of the thoughts I had at that moment. "Oh, no. It's an old white man. He's going to slow me down. I'm trying to teach hundreds of people how to register voters and get them out on the streets as fast as possible. I don't have time for this."

Sure enough, as soon as the man entered the office, breathless but still immediately talking, he peppered me with questions: "What are you doing? How many people go in each group? How did you pick the places you're sending people? How will people explain voting rights to ex-felons? What do volunteers do if people refuse to register?"

I listened as long as I could. Probably less than two minutes, as I was pretty impatient. "Sir, if you let me finish with this group, I'll answer all your questions. Just sit right there and wait for me, please. I can't answer you now because I've got to get this group out the door."

He watched the excited, urgent hum of Black, white, Asian American, and Latino people of all ages—paid staffers, volunteer organizers like myself, and hundreds of volunteers—working for Obama. Forty-five minutes later, I'd gotten two more groups trained and out the door, and I'd almost forgotten about the old man. When I entered the back conference room where he sat in a chair against the wall—a position allowing him to see everything going on in that room and in the adjoining halls—I didn't look at his face at first. I was moving fast, still working, fueled by grassroots adrenaline. "Oh, you're still here," I said. Then I stopped to actually look at him.

There were tears in his eyes, and he said: "I never thought I'd see the civil rights movement again."

Despite my busyness and hyper-efficiency, I teared up as well. "This really is something, isn't it?"

That's how I met Larry Goodwyn, as an old man who'd managed to stop me from rushing around, so I could feel the power of what we were a part of. Even if he'd told me his last name, it wouldn't have meant much. I hadn't read his books or studied with him. I knew that someone named Larry Goodwyn had previously occupied my husband Gunther Peck's office at Duke, and that he'd left a set of handwritten student complaints in a desk drawer.

After that mid-March introduction, Larry spent a lot of time at our house and around town with us as we went to parking lots, libraries, rehab centers, malls, grocery stores, nursing homes, and barbershops to register voters. Once Obama won the North Carolina primary in May 2008, the paid staff abruptly left, moving to work in other states. Everything in Durham—if there was going to be an everything—fell back to the local grassroots volunteer operation, Durham for Obama (DFO). We wouldn't stop voter registration just because the staff departed. Of course not. Too many people were too fired up. Plus DFO had formed back in February when there was no staff in town. Surely we could return to those self-directed days. Things pretty much moved to our house when the downtown Obama office closed in May. We had college Obama interns working full-time out of our dining room, and dozens of volunteers coming to our house most weeknights and all day every Saturday and Sunday.

Larry was one of them, coming over several times a week. Sometimes he phoned voters and potential volunteers in his raspy, gruff voice, rarely taking "no" for an answer. He was great on the phone. Even so, Larry felt bad about his limitations as a volunteer. He couldn't really go door-to-door, dragging that oxygen tank, but he could make phone calls, and he could recruit more volunteers who could canvass. He'd often ask what I wanted, what I needed. I always said "more volunteers," even though our house was full of volunteers a lot of the time.

One day he asked, "What do you need, to organize full-time? You're too good to be thwarted. What do you need, twenty-four/seven babysitting?"

"Larry, I have a two-year-old daughter, I want to raise her. Thank you, but no, I don't want babysitting."

He said, "Maybe you need an office so we can get this operation out of your house, and you can have some peace once in a while."

Again I explained why I didn't want that. "My daughter's too young to be away from me all the time. That's one of the reasons we're running things from the house. Gunther and I couldn't go to an office for this many hours."

Instead we had set up a babysitting co-op at our house with volunteers who couldn't canvass, or didn't want to, taking turns watching kids while everyone else went out door-to-door. Larry never struck me as the kind of guy who loved kids, but he would chat with the kids and the sitters, making sure the co-op was working while the parents were out registering voters.

Larry was endlessly supportive of me, always asking what I needed to keep going, keep organizing. In late May, I was elected as an Obama delegate. When Larry realized that we delegates had to finance our own way to the Democratic Convention in Denver—airfare plus a week in a hotel—he shook down his friends. "This woman has got to get to Denver, and she shouldn't have to pay for her own plane ticket, so give me a hundred bucks, goddamnit." That's what he told me he'd said to Peter Wood, Syd Nathans, and Bill Chafe, colleagues from his days as a historian at Duke, before he handed me a check for my plane trip.

Larry got upset when he saw me doing what he called "Jimmy Higgins work." He explained that Higgins was a loyal and enthusiastic but not-so-bright guy on a 1960s campaign Larry had worked on in Texas. Whoever was running that campaign made Higgins do all the shitwork no one else could be bothered to do—run errands, sort voter info, make copies. I appreciated Larry's concern, but I said, "Larry, I just want to get the work done. And I want to raise my kids, so I'm going to be tired. That's just the way it is."

When Larry arrived at our house some afternoons too worn-out to make calls, he'd say, "Give me some Jimmy Higgins work," and I'd hand him a basket of sign-in cards to sort alphabetically for easier data entry.

The Obama campaign decided over the summer that North Carolina would be in play for the general election. They sent a new set of young staffers to Durham in early September. One didn't have a car. "Larry," I said, "can you get someone to loan us a car for this Obama kid who just arrived?"

"Sure," Larry replied, and got the car. That's the kind of volunteer Larry was.

I was very busy in 2008, possibly busier than I'd ever been in my life. I know I was brusque with Larry many times. He always wanted to talk and ask questions about what was going on, our rationale, and I didn't always want to take the time to answer. Sometimes he said really problematic things, and I just tried to do damage control by shushing him. Once, he pronounced loudly from our living room couch: "The black people aren't working hard enough!"

Jesus. How was that helpful—or true? If anyone ever wasn't working in our house when Larry was around, it was only because they had temporarily stopped to answer Larry's endless questions about what they were doing. He was ceaselessly curious. And he was amazed—and thrilled—that he had nothing to offer, idea-wise, to the Obama organizing strategy in Durham, a fact he proclaimed as "nifty." He was very impressed with the 2008 ground operation here, remarking often that there was nothing, in forty years of experience studying and participating in democratic social movements, that he could offer, because the staff and volunteers had already thought of everything.

When Obama won the general election in November, he carried the state of North Carolina with fewer than 14,000 votes. Our work had paid off! People in Durham wanted to keep going, not lose the energy we'd built over nine months of organizing, so Durham for Obama (DFO) continued to meet at St. Joseph's AME Church, forming six postelection committees in early December 2008. People began to voice concerns at these early postelection meetings, though. When, exactly, would Guantanamo be closed? Why was no one talking about a single-payer health insurance option anymore? The largest committee DFO formed was health care, run by Rhonda Robinson, a fabulous speaker who had epilepsy and no health insurance. When would people like Rhonda actually get insurance?

Had we been naïve, foolish to believe Obama's campaign promises? I'd never placed this much faith in any politician before. Why had I lost my cynicism—or was it common sense—this time?

The Obama field staff kept throwing around a statement that FDR had allegedly made to civil rights leader A. Philip Randolph when Randolph tried to persuade FDR to take bolder action against racial discrimination. "You're right," FDR said. "Now go out and make me do it."

I got pretty sick of hearing this. We were exhausted from working so hard to get Obama elected. Now we had to fight with his staff to make them do what he'd promised during the campaign? Maybe this is how politics always works, but somehow I'd expected things to be different. I dealt with my frustration by focusing on a postelection initiative that had little to do with Obama per se: expanding the voting rights of formerly, and currently, incarcerated people. DFO wouldn't have to work with Obama's postelection

staff on this issue. I knew from recent experience that they wouldn't publicly touch the voting rights of the incarcerated with a ten-foot pole.

During the primary, I'd worked with the Obama staff to organize volunteers to go into local jails, register eligible people to vote, help them request
absentee ballots, then come back with the ballots so they could actually
vote in jail. The local press caught wind of this initiative and attempted to
make a big stink: "Obama Seeks Criminal Vote." It wasn't a good optic. I
told the Obama staff via voice mail (they weren't able to take my calls at that
point, based on advice from their lawyers) to cut me loose, portray me as a
zealous grassroots white woman who had acted independently. Whatever.
I didn't have anything to lose. Obama might. After the election, one staffer
admitted, "We really had to throw you under the bus on that one."

I took comfort, postelection, in working hard on an effort I knew would
be unpalatable to the Obama field staff. That was my thinking at the time—
they'd be less likely to interfere in something they didn't want to be associated with.

By the summer of 2009 I was questioning almost everything except the
importance of voting rights. On a personal level, I wasn't sure what to do
with my life. Soon after the election, I got fired from a job teaching yoga
at the downtown YMCA. "I must be the most stressed-out yoga teacher
in town," I'd told my students in October 2008. My very few regular yoga
students (all Obama volunteers) said, "We like that about you. If you can
do yoga, so can we."

But I wasn't doing yoga; I was teaching it (badly) as a part-time job. I was
doing okay teaching creative writing at Duke, but I was having a deep crisis
of faith about my work as a writer. How effective could writing be in making the world a better place? Couldn't I do more via politics? The energy I'd
used during the campaign—quick, efficient, aggressive at times—seemed
entirely different from what I needed as a writer. What mattered in a person's life? How should she spend her time?

One day I was sitting in the green chair in my office, looking out the
window, feeling utterly confused and unsure about how to proceed. I think
I maybe prayed a little—I'm not sure who I prayed to; I'm not formally religious—and this tiny, yet clear, internal voice said: "Call Larry Goodwyn
and Ann Atwater."[1] It took me about a week to do it.

Americans don't often turn to our elders for help. We're too proud, too
busy, too dismissive of old people. The Obama campaign had been uniquely
staffed by very young people. I remember a video clip of Obama thanking
his staff after an early primary win, saying: "Go out and celebrate, take the

night off, have a drink." Then he paused and looked at them. "Actually, some of you probably aren't even old enough to drink."

At forty-five, I was on the older side of people working for Obama. Larry and Ann, at ages eighty-one and seventy-four respectively, were at the far end of the spectrum, but certainly not alone. Plenty of people in their seventies and eighties—at least in Durham—volunteered for Obama.

I called these lifelong activists who had worked on the Obama campaign with me, and asked to meet. I wanted to know what they had done at my age, and what they planned now. I wanted to know if they were disappointed in Obama, if I should be disappointed in Obama. And I wanted to know, more generally, if they had advice about how to live one's life.

Larry and I met at a Durham coffee shop in June 2009. For the first time, I asked most of the questions. I recorded our conversation, a pretty wide-ranging and free-rolling dialogue. I still have the tape. Larry began by telling me not to be disappointed—or surprised—by the change after the election in Obama and his staff. As an historian, he said he knew "no example . . . of a movement that is more democratic in power than it was in the movement that brought it to power. There are no examples of that."

Larry didn't think this fact had to be depressing. People needed to understand that a shift had occurred and move forward, ready to negotiate hard with the candidate (now president) that they'd helped place in office. I didn't know if I was up for that. Why did we have to negotiate hard now? Why couldn't Obama just do what he said he would? I realized, of course, that this was naïve. So did Larry. He didn't dwell on my postelection disillusionment. He wanted to talk about his insights and idealism during the campaign.

"I was attracted by this candidate," he said, "the fact that the candidate himself seemed to know more about movements than any candidate, historically, since Thomas Jefferson." For Larry, it was marvelous that "in the course of eight months, from February to November, I was unable to make a contribution to the Obama campaign, in terms of something I knew that they didn't . . . not one contribution did I make . . . all you had to do was listen, nod, don't put anybody down, and then hit people with chores. There's nothing authoritarian about that, in itself. As long as your chores produce tangible results, people happily do them. They end up doing more than they had intended to. That's good." He explained that whenever he said anything analytical or historical, people would reply, "Yeah, that's true, but, man, we can't stop working."

Larry said I was the first person who actually talked to him. "Everybody else was busy doing one damn thing or another. And you actually talked to me. It was about what I needed to know, and so forth. And you kept doing it. I didn't know any of this stuff. It was just wonderful. I kind of just dazedly did it. Just like everybody else did."

I remembered the hard work of the campaign—of course I did—but I wanted to talk with Larry about the present. I asked, in a fairly breathless voice, "How much of my life am I going to continue to give to this thing [Durham for Obama], and/or am I going to switch careers and run for office or something like that? Or do I have more of a need to write about all of this, or do I need to pick up the pieces of not really taking care of my family for a long time?"

"You can take all the 'or's' out of it," Larry said. "You're not giving up anything not running for politics. What you do is you improve the quality of your life by—you organize as much as you feel good organizing. And it's not an either-or. You don't want to leave this thing right now. You know too much. Not because you have good character, which you no doubt do, it's because you have skill. You're just dripping with skill that's experiential. If you're going to give yourself a poor grade, how about the rest of us? How about the men that caused [all the problems] in the first place?"

While I had never organized as fully, or maniacally, as I did with Durham for Obama, I knew I had these skills. I'd learned them from my mother, a progressive activist in small-town Virginia. She could persuade anyone to do anything. She persuaded white ladies in an Episcopal church to give her all the money they'd raised for repairing their precious steeple bell so she could start an empowerment center for working-class women instead, a center that included child care. (Child care as a necessary part of women's liberation was a pretty radical idea in 1971 Tidewater Virginia.) Next, she made the racist women's club integrate the weekly dances they held for the town's teens. This action included forcing an embarrassed thirteen-year-old me to ask a Black classmate to join me in moving awkwardly to the Doobie Brothers' anthem "Jesus Is Just Alright" at the first integrated dance.

Larry made me see that, however tired and disillusioned I was in 2009, the kind of grassroots activism I'd been doing with DFO wasn't optional for me. I might teach yoga again (hopefully with more proficiency), and I might write a novel one day, but I would never stop trying to make the American South more just. That goal ran deep; it was in my blood. Larry got this, and reminded me of it, because the same was true for him.

Larry told me frequently that women make better organizers than men. Men simply have too much ego, he said, a condition he suffered from himself. "The worst thing about the inheritance of male domination is that . . . it's so ubiquitous. It's everywhere. It's been everywhere everybody's life, from the minute they became conscious they had a mother and a father. Mother is kind and attentive. Father is powerful. This means that it's very hard to engage, in terms of altering the dynamics [male authoritarianism] creates."

Still, he said, "An immense amount of progress has been made in my lifetime. Of all the things I've learned . . . women's rights had the effect of teaching me probably eighty percent of what I know about the dynamics of democratic movements."

He also said, "My contribution . . . was zero. People would ask questions that had never occurred to me. People would—when I got to know them better—[let me know] I was part of the problem. I was told about this in ways that were not condemnatory. They were critical, but mildly critical, supportively critical. What men did would cost money—rent offices, get desks so they could put their feet up—then they wanted somebody to write brochures, which would cost money. Whereas women would organize."

I thought about how powerful and effective my own mother was. More powerful than kind and attentive, to be honest. Even so, I understood the gender distinction Larry was making. Jimmy Higgins had been a man, but most men would never do the Jimmy Higgins work. This was partly what made women better organizers, according to Larry.

"I popped in your place one time really late at night, the place was empty, and you were sitting there correcting forms. . . . You looked exhausted, but you also weren't showing it, that is to say, it was not on display. It was just where your body and your mind was. And that was some operation you had. That's sweat, and knowledge. Knowledge and sweat. Drive. I met a lot of people with drive. Most all of them are women. Male drive is always about ego. It's tiresome after a while."

"Well, it gets in the way of—" I started to say.

"Of everything," Larry said. Then he continued, "But here's the worst thing about this. The fact that I can say these things, in no way means I don't do that. That's the most sobering discovery of forty years of studying social movements. Knowledge . . . gives you another window, in this case a window on yourself. It chips away microscopically at the totality of the authoritarian inheritance you represent."

Just because Larry understood male privilege didn't mean he didn't invoke it, inhabit it completely, time and time again. He'd just interrupted me, in fact, to make this very point. I tried to suggest that the same thing could be true for race. That I had wrestled, as a white leader, with a similar kind of dynamic—white people taking for granted our own importance. "When you feel that kind of urgency, like, this has got to be done and I actually know how to get it done, but you still want to be democratic, you don't want to tell people what to do—" I began to say.

Larry cut me off, saying that I had no choice but to "run over" Lavonia Allison, an old-school African American activist who had tried to stop Durham for Obama from canvassing in neighborhoods she said had always been controlled by the Durham Committee on the Affairs of Black People. In October 2008 she met pairs of DFO canvassers with a bullhorn, shouting, "Go back to Duke!" Two young women—one Asian American, one African American, neither with any affiliation to Duke—were reduced to tears by this welcome. Larry said he'd give me a B+ on the way I handled the Lavonia situation. "You cannot beat her by acquiescing to some kind of power sharing. You just run over her and go on."

But that's not what happened. I called Ann Atwater, and Ann figured out who would have influence with Lavonia, then called that person and explained the situation. The Black legislator Ann chose called Lavonia and persuaded her to let Durham for Obama into the precincts she was blocking. Within an hour we covered those streets with volunteers.

To me, this was at least an A- solution. Not my personal A- but a group grade for three people who all wanted Obama to win like nobody's business. Lavonia wanted that exact same outcome—of course she did. Ann and the legislator and I were fierce, yet practical: none of us thought running over Lavonia would be the most effective way to get canvassers in those precincts. It was odd that Larry suggested running over someone in this instance, because our conversation soon shifted to him giving me repeated advice to negotiate rather than deliver ultimatums. Wasn't running over someone akin to giving an ultimatum?

As we began discussing negotiating techniques, Larry talked about the value of making mistakes. He told me that the most important thing I could do—as an organizer and in life, overall—was allow myself to make mistakes and learn from them. He said men were often too caught up in their own egos to acknowledge that they were making mistakes. He recommended that I tell anyone I negotiated with: "I'm able to function because I give myself permission to make . . . errors . . . , and I recommend that you do the same."

Frankly, I had a hard time with this advice. I felt that women couldn't afford to make a lot of mistakes, that people would judge us harshly, that possibly they'd been waiting for us to fail all along. See, a man should have been leading this organization, not you. That's what I honestly thought someone might say if I made a huge mistake. Larry, on the other hand, wanted to probe the discrepancy between who he hoped to be and who he actually was, in terms of his own behavior. I understood what he was saying, and I admired that he embraced his own mistakes, but this strategy seemed way too risky for a forty-five-year-old woman. It was 2009, but I still felt judged on the old-school scale: work twice as hard as a man to be seen as half as good. I didn't agree that embracing failure would work for me, but I kept listening.

Our conversation moved to further strategies for effective negotiation. Larry understood my frustration with the postelection Obama field staff who arrived in North Carolina in early 2009. Were they here to keep the grassroots momentum going, or to co-opt us into supporting whatever watered-down version of campaign promises they now thought were po-litically palatable? (I ended up thinking they came to do both.) Larry coun-seled me not to make ultimatums, no matter how much the staff pushed.

"You've got to negotiate with Alex Lofton," he told me (Alex being the Southeast organizing director for Obama's campaign). "You have to have standards of negotiating. You have to improve the standards, and you have to learn to improve them because you're failing so much."

Larry was advising me again to let myself make mistakes, learn from them, and readjust. That was his definition of good negotiation. He said that negotiating, rather than delivering ultimatums, was even more impor-tant in intimate relationships.

"There's no marriage that's down the drain. There's no marriage that's all that healthy, either, so you just negotiate. I'm impressed with this guy that you married. He's the only professor at Duke I saw on the campaign. . . . He does not know what you know, and he does not have the problems you have, and he—I mean, you are a very rare person, but you have to negoti-ate with him." He noted that I couldn't deliver ultimatums to anyone in the family. "You can't do that with your daughter. . . . Each of the children, you can't just give them orders . . . you have to be softer."

I wasn't sure I wanted to be softer. I might end up doing all the house-work if I was softer.

"You said be softer when you negotiate," I responded, "but you don't want to be just putty, right? It's something in between—there's a bottom line you're not going to go below. You're negotiating, but you're not being stepped on, right? I think the difficulty is knowing when are you giving up too much and when are you being a good negotiator. What's the bottom line?"

"All negotiations are successful if you analyze them correctly," Larry replied. "You test and see—what did he say when I said this, what did he say when I said that? And you go to school on it. This is not being manipulative. It's being experientially intelligent. You're more impatient than [your husband] because you're more oppressed than he is. He's acting out authority. He doesn't even know it. If you are willing to blow it all, that means you're not really negotiating with him, that you've given up."

Huh. I just thought it would mean I was really angry.

"So, it's a question of tone, then," I said. "Part of what you're talking about is a question of tone and how significant that is?"

"Tone is the social verification of the presence of a negotiating posture. When you throw crockery, that's a bad tone, that means you've given up already on the relationship. So it's not really a negotiation."

Larry explained that he'd learned from his daughter and his wife how to negotiate at home. "I could forgo this stupid male indulgence every other Wednesday. I'm a noble and democratic person. Why can't I do that?" Yet even as he learned, his wife and his daughter always knew more. "I'm third. My daughter is first, my wife is second, I'm third. Is that the best you can do? Well, apparently. You're a cutting-edge democrat, and that's your contribution, being third place in your own life? That's pathetic. This just verifies that we [men], culturally, are the problem. It's worldwide."

I asked him to clarify how he was third place in his own life.

"I'm in third place in terms of my contribution to the growth and statistical gains of my own negotiating skills. Between me and my wife."

"So two other people helped you more than you could help yourself?"

"Well, I helped myself by being able to hear them."

"Well, that's good," I said.

"They have a lesser stake in it than I do," Larry returned.

"So you're saying, why couldn't you have figured it out?"

"Why couldn't I be 1A, and they could be 1B and 1C or something?" Larry said.

I kept trying to understand exactly what he was saying. "So [your daughter and wife] would be kind of like consultants, but you would have been the main instigator or something?"

"But that was an utterly unrealistic assumption, given the fact that I am the problem," Larry explained. "Well, it's very sobering. There are layers of male expectation that are just simply absurd."

"Yeah, I know," I said.

* * *

I did know. It struck me as pretty strange that an eighty-one-year-old man also knew. I thought I was going to talk to Larry about electoral and grassroots politics, and here we'd moved to the most intense gender negotiations that can happen inside a marriage. I was used to having this discussion with other fed-up women, not with an old man who called himself "the problem," yet kept analyzing, asking questions, and trying to change his own behavior to something more democratic. It gave me hope.

"Being a male is a socially programmed pathology," Larry said. "You do not have this disease, but you have it partly to the extent that this is what makes you acquiesce too much. As your own ability to negotiate gets better and better and better, you're going to start falling under the gaze of yourself. *You're not so hot after all, even though you're the world's biggest goddamn feminist, and the best organizer in the fucking American South,* and so forth and so forth."

Hey! I thought Larry told me not to throw crockery. Now he was saying that I acquiesced too much. Which was it?

"So you're saying negotiating is not rolling over, it's just negotiating. You start slowly," I said, "and you don't make ultimatums."

I began to see that Larry was advising me to negotiate with the Obama field staff and with my own husband because it was a strategy of strength, not weakness. Stronger, obviously, than acquiescence, but also stronger than unbridled anger. Negotiation is what had happened with Lavonia Allison, in fact. I wasn't privy to the actual discussion—Lavonia wouldn't have listened to me, someone she called "that white girl johnny-come-lately"— but she did listen to her friend the legislator. Ann Atwater had figured out the best negotiating strategy in this case. All I'd done was have enough sense to call Ann.

Larry ended our conversation by assuring me that I was now ready "to live the rest of your life on your terms. . . . You know enough now to shape it." I didn't quite believe him, but I wanted to, and I was heartened by his words. Maybe, just maybe, I could live my life on my own terms, more or less, in a world I viewed as still full of white and male privilege, of socially programmed white and male pathologies, to use Larry's terms. Maybe I could do this in my public life and my private life. It was a hell of a final wish—or blessing—from Larry.

## Notes

1. Ann Atwater was a prominent African American civil rights activist in Durham. She's best known for co-leading a set of intense meetings about school desegregation with C. P. Ellis, a Klansman whom she eventually befriended. A major film, *The Best of Enemies,* about Ann and C.P., based on the 1996 book *The Best of Enemies: Race and Redemption in the New South*, came out in 2019.

# 6

## Movement Culture in Durham, North Carolina

GUNTHER PECK

I first met Larry Goodwyn in the spring of 2003. I had just accepted a position at Duke University the previous fall and was attending a panel discussion at the Sanford School of Public Policy asking the following question: What role can the university play in making progressive change? I was struck by the eloquence and anger of one older man who, from the audience, denounced the academy as a trap for politically minded people, an institution that encouraged academics to substitute jargon for plain speech in their writings, replacing progressive intentions with career-minded calculations about how to succeed in "the guild." His critique was not new to me; in fact I agreed that many academics, including those on the left, suffer from a disease called self-commodification. But something about the totalizing nature of his critique, its dystopian mien, made me bristle. I countered with an impassioned defense of university employees' and students' capacity to build movements for social justice. The old man responded that I was deluded at best, a poseur at worst, naïve to the ways the guild corrupted democratic discourse.

Had I known I was arguing with Larry Goodwyn, whose book *The Populist Moment* I had named in my application to graduate school as the book I most wished I had written, I would have shut my trap. But I am glad I spoke up, even though the conversation unnerved me. I admired how Goodwyn explained with passion and purpose the ways ordinary people could become an extraordinary political force. The People's Party in the 1880s created a movement culture, not from some utopian fantasy about how democracy ought to work, but from their living, breathing wisdom as farmers and producers across the nation, whether they were white or Black. I also admired how Goodwyn explained that people miles apart politically might be closer to each other than they thought, capable of switching from the racist "populism" known as white supremacy to the truly democratic movement culture that might redeem the nation.

I conveyed none of that in my first encounter with Larry, but instead reflected on the relationship between teaching and democracy. I had been thinking about both things and Larry recently anyhow, as I had just moved into his old office. I realized it was *his* desk just a few months earlier because he had not, in fact, cleared it out. I found several letters addressed to Larry, had emailed several times about them, but he never responded. Initially I avoided reading them. He had, it seemed, left the academy without a backward glance. After our exchange at Sanford, I read the letters with a mixture of heightened interest and guilty pleasure. Here were documents that might vindicate my optimism, or perhaps prove his point.

The letters provided no such clarity, of course. But they did deepen my regard for Professor Goodwyn. Most came from adoring students who thanked him for opening their minds. The longest letter, however, berated him for "hammering your point over and over again onto the heads of your students" and "not LISTENING." This female student wrote as "the only woman in your section of the Civil War Class." I was moved that she had written such an honest letter and also that Larry had kept it, putting it at the top of a small pile, presumably reading it over and trying to learn.

I also found an "Anxiety Chart" that Larry crafted in the fall of 1992, detailing his thoughts about Bill Clinton's presidential campaign. It included no comments or analysis of Clinton's politics but simply a list of all states arranged into five columns, with states strongly for Clinton on the left and states strongly for Bush on the right. Most impressive about Larry's chart was not its accuracy—though Larry did predict the winner in Bill Clinton—but its abiding optimism. In his "ideal result," the only one he spelled out at the end of his chart, the South remained a united *Democratic* block, with every southern state voting for Clinton except South Carolina. Many southern states were not even close in his prediction, with North Carolina in the strongly-for-Clinton column. That electoral fantasy included candidate Clinton taking forty-four states and 501 electoral delegates. It was as if the southern strategy, the effort to recruit conservative and racist Democrats disaffected with civil rights victories, had never happened. Or perhaps it was 1892 instead of 1992, the Populist moment when Tom Watson, the eventual white supremacist, remained young and idealistic, committed to organizing Black and white farmers together in a new South. No wonder Larry described his number matrix as an "anxiety chart."

I soon began to realize that Larry's anxieties and my own were not that far apart. Like Larry, I yearned for a democracy that was real, that would not substitute a corrupt "populism" of white victimhood for the transformative vision of social justice that has lifted democratic struggle during all three of America's unfinished reconstructions. If only more people had read and taken to heart the powerful lessons of *The Populist Moment*, then perhaps his fantasy of a South not defined by racial reaction might have been realized. If people understood how the brooding class anger at the heart of Tom Watson's thwarted populism has policed and impoverished poor white and Black people simultaneously, then perhaps white victimhood could be unmasked and sundered.

The next time I saw Larry was in my house during the spring of 2008, in the midst of the mobilization to register voters for the upcoming Democratic Party primary that pitted Hillary Clinton against Barack Obama. I recognized Larry but was nonetheless startled to see him, wheeling an oxygen tank into my living room. He sat down on our couch amid thirty volunteers waiting to be sent out to Durham neighborhoods, part of a grassroots voter registration drive, Durham for Obama (DFO), a group that my partner Faulkner Fox and I helped organize, growing by leaps and bounds without any assistance from the Obama campaign.

Was the grassroots effort to elect Barack Obama in Durham a movement culture? In the choppy wake of the Obama presidency when notions of white victimhood motivated efforts by right-wing activists to roll back voting rights and a president's rhetorical war against women and people of color, it is important to remember how recently democratic activism nurtured idealism. For many activists in Durham in 2008, registering voters felt like a social movement to redeem the very fabric of democracy itself. DFO was, first off, what Goodwyn called in *The Populist Moment* "an autonomous institution," organized by citizens whose leadership was entirely voluntary and separate from the Democratic Party.[1]

Two key components of Goodwyn's definition of movement culture— "movement recruiting" and "movement politicizing"—were abundantly manifest in Durham County in 2008.[2] Every canvasser was trained to ask new registrants if they also wanted to volunteer, with better than one in ten becoming volunteers in the voting drive. By November, DFO had swelled to 11,000 members and registered a total of 26,500 new voters in Durham County and more than 10,000 citizens in surrounding counties. Durham not only had the largest expansion of its electorate of any county in the state, it also had the highest turnout for Obama.[3]

Many of these new voters were African American, but an even larger cohort were students. Obama won North Carolina by winning just one age group, 18-to-29-year-olds, taking nearly 80 percent of young North Carolinians, the most dramatic youth vote of any state in the nation.[4] On the campuses of North Carolina Central University and Duke, same-day registration at early voting stations dramatically expanded voting, with the number of students registered in North Carolina soaring from a few hundred to more than 4,000.[5] Countywide, new registrants were the most likely citizens to vote, with more than 80 percent voting. That translated into 23,500 *new* voters in Durham County in the fall of 2008, nearly double the state's razor-thin margin of difference of roughly 14,000 votes. Of more than 100,000 voters who cast votes for Obama in Durham, better than one in ten of them volunteered for him in 2008. To paraphrase moral Monday protesters in North Carolina four years later, "this is what Democracy looked like."

When Larry first came to our house in April 2008, however, I was anxious how an elderly man with an oxygen tank could help with the day's mission: registering voters in the parking lots of WalMart across Durham and Person Counties. Our efforts there had so far yielded spectacular fruit, up to seven new registrants per volunteer hour. But we also had been repeatedly chased out of WalMart's parking lots by security guards claiming we were disturbing the peace. At the WalMart in New Hope Commons, however, we registered the security guard on the two-to-four-p.m. shift, providing a small window for our work. I decided to take Larry there, bringing a small folding chair for him. Perhaps it was Larry's oxygen tank, or that gravelly voice, but few people passing by could ignore him. He buttonholed everyone who walked past, especially older folks, who did not seem put off by his age or the sight of his oxygen tank. He registered fifteen new voters during his shift.

Over the ensuing weeks, Larry became a regular presence at our house. Often he would not be up to canvassing but would sit in a corner of the dining room and call a long phone list of "sporadic voters," urging them to consider voting early. Our friend David Swanson had prepared excellent scripts for phone canvassers, but Larry never followed them. Fortunately, he was only occasionally petulant with the odd skeptic on the other line. On some days, he seemed happy just to sit in our living room, absorbing the energy of young people, Black, white, and brown, crowding through our door, many of them too young to vote but determined to make democracy and history simultaneously.

When Obama won North Carolina in 2008, Larry became one of the most doggedly optimistic people I have ever known. In the days leading up to the election of 2010, in which Republicans won both houses of the North Carolina legislature, setting in motion a dramatic rollback of voting rights, Larry was interviewed by Jan Frel of the online magazine *Alternet*, who insisted that Obama's policies were no better than George W. Bush's. Larry did not tell Frel she was wrong, nor did he predict a Democratic victory five days before the election of 2010. Instead, Larry embarked on a long lecture about transformational presidents in US history, comparing Obama favorably to Lincoln, Jefferson, and FDR. When pressed to explain that cheerful assessment, Larry pointed to Obama's remarkable speech on race in Philadelphia during the primaries, a moment in which Larry believed Obama demonstrated his capacity to transform the tragic legacy of racism and slavery in US history.[6]

In the face of mounting evidence that the movement culture he witnessed in 2008 had not generated a fully realized new South, Larry focused, at least publicly, on Obama's accomplishments as a wordsmith. At a moment of growing cynicism, he reminded readers why they had been so excited about Obama in the first place. In Durham, Larry remained attuned to the grassroots activist work that continued and even expanded in the spring of 2009. Just before Obama's inauguration, more than two hundred core DFO activists formed a series of committees charged with figuring out how to push for key policy changes in an Obama White House. "This movement was never solely or even primarily about Obama," one activist insisted. "We need to hold his and their feet to the fire."[7] A health care committee began organizing for Medicare for All. A new voting rights committee set its sights on expanding access to North Carolina's jails and prisons in order to secure and defend the voting rights of ex-felons. Each committee acted independently from Organizing for America, the official "grassroots" organization that President Obama began putting in place to secure his reelection.

This activism played an important role in shaping at least two political outcomes in North Carolina after Obama's election in 2008. DFO activist Rhonda Robinson, a student at North Carolina Central University and single mother, lost her health care because of a preexisting condition in the spring of 2009 and began a compelling personal campaign on behalf of universal health care coverage. Although Rhonda supported the public option, she organized an effective citizens' campaign, speaking at rallies, and personally persuading Senator Kay Hagan to support Obamacare. Other

DFO activists pushed back against top-down efforts to curtail DFO's independence. Just ten months after Obama's inauguration, DFO activists organized a forum for three Senate candidates who were seeking to challenge Republican senator Richard Burr in 2010. Just days before the forum, word came to DFO organizers that the head of Organizing for America was coming to town and that he wanted DFO to endorse Cal Cunningham, a white veteran that Obama higher-ups thought was "electable." Fox pointedly refused, reminding the caller that DFO was an independent, grassroots organization that would make up its own mind about which candidate to support. "This is what democracy looks like," she reminded him.

Such independence was dangerous in the view of Jim Messina, Obama's new chief of staff. Upon assuming his duties in the weeks before Obama's inauguration, Messina squandered one of the greatest accomplishments of Obama's election: an engaged citizenry ready to enact a progressive agenda without reliance on big money. Instead, Messina began using OFA to discipline the activists who elected Obama by focusing their energy around one purpose: reelecting the president in 2012.[8] Messina's efforts to transform millions of awakened activists into foot soldiers meant radically changing the way groups like Durham for Obama performed their work during the 2012 reelection campaign.[9] When Obama's young organizers returned in 2012, gone was any sense of collaboration with local actors. OFA organizers insisted that Durham volunteers only canvas local neighbors and pointedly refused to allow voter registration activity to be organized across precinct lines or in places where lots of pedestrian traffic occurred. One OFA organizer in Durham County wept if volunteers who lived in her "turf" canvassed outside of it, fearful co-organizers would get the credit and she might be upbraided for failing to deliver her quota of door knocks. More interested in metrics than movement, OFA organizers made many volunteers feel anxious and demoralized rather than empowered. A similar obsession with door knocks informed Hillary Clinton's campaign in 2016, which also disastrously ignored rural Democratic voters, opening field offices in just 27 of 100 North Carolina counties.

One of the consequences of these top-down efforts in North Carolina has been a decline in voter turnout in key counties like Durham.[10] Durham has become one of the bluest counties in the nation since 2004, but the moral and political energy unleashed by citizens registering thousands of new voters in 2008 has not been repeated, as national campaigns have ignored the insights of local actors who often know where the unregistered live and why they don't vote.[11] Larry did not predict such an outcome in *The*

*Populist Moment*, but the parallels to the People's Party's struggles *after* they won statewide offices in 1894 are striking.

Larry was not surprised by these developments in Obama's organization as he learned of them in 2010 and 2012, nor was he demoralized. Rather, he remained deeply idealistic about citizen-led democratic action, focusing on ways of nurturing new generations of multiracial activists. He believed, passionately, that ordinary citizens, you and me both, could become extraordinary historical actors: that we could fight bigotry, corporate greed, gender injustice, and still win. Larry was no saint, a beneficiary of many of the same privileges he decried. But in the fall of 2008, Larry had an answer for even the most anxious and betrayed citizen he encountered. To the Black Vietnam veteran who cursed the country that made him kill "yellow men" and then abandoned him like "a piece of broken furniture," Larry simply listened, initially not saying a word. This was Larry's most powerful answer: respectful silence, while looking the man in the eye and providing a moral witness to his anger and betrayal. After a beautiful pause, Larry broke the silence with three short words: "I hear you."

The veteran paused, sized up Larry's oxygen tank, and then took Larry's registration form, for the first time in his life deciding to vote. This is how I will remember Larry—not as an angry curmudgeon or a hypocritical moralist but as a radical democrat, a citizen-canvasser who could in fact listen and empower. He was, in the end, an imaginative believer in movement culture, one that emboldened ordinary people to speak truth to power and transformed their imagining of what is possible in this thing we call democracy.

## Notes

1. Lawrence Goodwyn, *The Populist Moment: A Short History of the Agrarian Revolt in America* (New York: Oxford University Press, 1978), xviii.

2. Goodwyn, *The Populist Moment*, xviii.

3. Data on the number of new registrants in Durham County and statewide were gleaned and researched by Durham attorney Stephen Gheen, who during the fall campaign used data from the North Carolina State Board of Elections to send weekly emails to canvassers and voting rights activists updating the total number of newly registered voters within each county across North Carolina.

4. The data for Durham County's turnout was gleaned from the official election returns found at the Durham County Board of Elections.

5. Calculating the precise percentage of Duke students who were registered in Durham County and who voted has been an empirical challenge because students are not

listed as such on county voting rolls. More challenging still is the fact that Board of Elections officials do not purge the voting rolls every time Duke students graduate, meaning there are scores of *former* Duke students on the active voting rolls in Durham County at any one moment. To calculate turnout in the 2008 campaign, I took the then current list of registered Duke students and cross-referenced it with the county registration lists to see how many current Duke students were registered in Durham County. From that number, I then checked to see how many of them had voted. I focused on the two precincts that cover Duke's campus, the second and the fifth. Turnout was highest—at 93 percent—for current Duke students registered on East Campus in the second precinct, the Duke class of 2012, while students registered on West campus in the fifth voted at about 81 percent, giving us the composite rate of 84 percent. Duke students who lived off campus, for example in Trinity Park in the seventh precinct, were excluded from the calculation.

6. Jan Frel, "Lawrence Goodwyn: The Great Predicament Facing Obama," *Alternet*, October 30, 2010.

7. Rhonda Robinson, DFO activist, Healthcare Committee meeting, February 21, 2009, Durham Public Library, Durham, NC.

8. Ari Berman, "Jim Messina, Obama's Enforcer," *Nation*, March 30, 2011.

9. On reasons why President Obama did not organize for the public option in his campaign for health care reform, see Ari Berman, "Herding Donkeys," *Nation*, September 29, 2010.

10. All county election results were found at the Durham County Board of Elections website. No historical records are visible on the current website, but inquiries about county returns can be directed toward the BOE superintendent of Durham County.

11. For a more detailed analysis of why Clinton lost North Carolina in 2016, see Gunther Peck, "Learning the Right Lessons from Defeat: Organizing a New Democratic Majority in North Carolina," July 2017, Scholars Strategy Network, http://www.scholarsstrategynetwork.org/page/learning-right-lessons-defeat-organizing-new-democratic-majority-north-carolina.

# 7

## A Democrat for the Ages

BENJ DEMOTT

The *New York Times*'s respectful obituary covered Larry Goodwyn's "authoritative" work on American populism and his role in the civil rights movement and Texas politics (where he once served as an advance man for Senator Ralph "Put the jam on the lower shelf where the little man can reach it" Yarborough) as well as his career in the academy. I was struck, though, by the obit's next-to-last paragraph, which invoked *Breaking the Barrier*, Larry's gripping study of the rise of Solidarity in Poland, and then left readers hanging. It had a one-off quality that hinted the book was a sort of an outlier: since much of Larry's life-work had roots in the American South, what's Poland got to do with it?

I'm probably projecting—the *Times* man may just have been squeezing in one more fact before he faded out. Still the obit left me ruefully thinking about how I'd failed to pick up on *Breaking the Barrier* when it first came out in 1991, even though my mind had been blown when I'd read *The Populist Moment* at the University of Rochester in the 1970s. (*The Populist Moment* was assigned by Christopher Lasch, who once told Larry he considered him *his* Engels—a notion that amused Larry, though he thought it a bit rich for Lasch to equate himself with Marx.) Larry's work on populism not only revived a disappeared American democratic tradition, it offered a fresh approach to political economy that transcended dead-end antinomies between corporate capitalism and state socialism.

*Breaking the Barrier* was another great refusal of dry, quiescent political discourse. Goodwyn not only caught the heated rush of the Polish August but broke it down, telling the truly revolutionary story of how Solidarity happened. My failure to follow up and read Larry's thrilling "Polish book" back in the day was my bad. But I and other potential readers didn't get much help from New York intellectuals: *Breaking the Barrier* was reviewed dismissively in *NYRB* by Timothy Garton Ash, who failed to mention Larry had repeatedly (if gently) cited Ash's own book, *The Polish Revolution*, "as an urbane example of the simplistic conventional interpretation of Solidarity, i.e. the presumed causal role played by Warsaw intellectuals in its origins and development." Larry nailed Ash in *NYRB*'s letter pages, pointing out the review amounted to "damage control."[1]

But that unfair deal went down. *NYRB* reviews have weight, and Larry's work on Solidarity never got its due. An outcome that didn't shock him. His book, after all, upheld the idea a people's politics may hustle and flow beneath the noses of urban intellectuals (who presume to know better whether in New York or Warsaw).

I'm reminded, on that score, of a story he once told about meeting C.L.R. James—another radical thinker at home with folks who lived below what a genteel voice once termed "the men who make up your mind." Larry encountered James in the early 1970s at a university conference on the theme "The Year 2000." The meeting hall was filled with academic stars who sat up front in a sort of inner circle. Larry was placed in the back, and his sense of distance increased as he listened to the certified "geniuses." He wasn't all alone, though, as he found out when James scribbled a note to him suggesting the only thing the assembled mandarins knew about 2000 was that each hoped to be president of Harvard by then. James kept quiet for the first day or two of the conference. When he finally opened up in public, he began by recalling modern instances when striking steelworkers destroyed machines in British factories and farmworkers in Trinidad fired cane fields that provided their livelihood. He pondered aloud if such heavy expressions of alienation might be worth a thought or two as conference panelists tried to project what life might be like in the next millennium. There was a pause; the silence resonated promisingly until . . . the discourse picked up where it had left off before James posed his question. Larry caught James's eye and they walked right out of the room to the nearest bar.

Larry told that story when he was having a beer with the crew from my publication *First of the Month*, whom he was meeting for the first time in 2000. He'd just given a short talk (at a postelection City College conference on third parties) where he'd tried to flip scripts of leftist politicos by passing along the key lesson he'd learned from studying American populists' methods of recruitment:

> There wasn't anything in my culture that taught me that to build a movement one has to create social relations among people that would

cause them to be in a room where politics is the center of discussion. I'd been taught that what mattered is what people said in the room. But the key question is how to get people into the room to hear—and respond to—whatever is being said there.

Larry was out to connect with would-be political organizers, not editors. But his talk had collateral benefits for *First of the Month*. It gave me the democratic logic to back up my once inchoate faith that our writers' collective must let argument breathe.

I came to lean on Larry to help explain our rejection of consensual wisdom: "*First* provides one answer to a question posed by (one of our most important mentors and contributors) Lawrence Goodwyn: 'Is there a graceful and constructive device by which we can come together and, in ways that enhance all parties, *disagree*?'" (When Greil Marcus, responding to our last annual volume, affirms: "I love the complete absence of a line," he's endorsing a principle that's long been foundational for *First*, thanks in part to Larry Goodwyn.)

Larry got a little too fragile to enjoy the *frisson* of disagreeing with a friend in his last years. So I'll allow I'm glad we were almost always on the same page in the Age of Obama. He understood Obama's elections as large democratic achievements—triumphs of the organizing tradition he'd traced in his work on populism and the civil rights movement. As a southern liberal, he'd seen enough to know (what he noted "every card-carrying white supremacist in the Republican Party knows"): "those are not softballs Obama is throwing." Yet Larry never forgot economic relationships have a "causative bearing on democratic possibilities" in America (as in all societies around the world). And he realized as long as bankers rule, the party of hope is living on the creative margins. I think he got Obama time's mix of forward motion and stasis exactly right in an interview he did with Jan Frel for *Alternet* in 2010. That interview comes close to being his final testament.

Larry didn't have energy to compose anything new for the 2013 annual *First of the Month* volume. (He'd been a regular contributor to *First* since we reprinted excerpts from *Breaking the Barrier* in our earliest issues.) But his prophetic side is represented in *That Floating Bridge*, which includes an out-of-left-field *First* piece he wrote in 2004, before Obama's epic convention speech, that called attention to the Democrats' rising star in Illinois and to the passing of another exemplary democrat, Poland's Jacek Kuroń.

Larry dug the young Obama because the candidate broke rules of spin: "he does not see political recruitment as requiring the fabrication of constant agreement." Obama's liberal-minded readiness to hear and respond outside the box linked him to Kuroń in Larry's head, since the Pole's "enduring democratic legacy is his commitment to candor as an instrument of politics and his belief one worked with anyone who was willing to help one deal with a persisting social malfunction inherited from the past." More than a decade on, it seems Obama is still in Kuroń's tradition.

Larry extolled Kuroń for being willing, unlike most intellectuals, to cop to what he couldn't comprehend. Kuroń famously said about Solidarity's rise: "I thought it was impossible. It was impossible. I still think it was impossible." Goodwyn noted that this "unsolicited burst of Kuroñesque candor" distanced Kuroń from more vainglorious Polish intellectuals who imagined themselves as Solidarity's vanguard, though they were just as clueless as Kuroń when it came to understanding the movement's self-organization. Kuroń's comment endeared him to Solidarity's working-class heroes like Lech Walesa who, Larry wrote, "thereafter relied on Kuroń, among others, to interpret the utility of Warsaw types. Indeed, upon hearing of Kuroń's death, Walesa used Kuroñesque language for repayment. Kuroń was indispensable, he said. Solidarity was 'impossible' to imagine without him. Polish speak."

Let us now praise famous Poles!? Larry realized Solidarity's "Polish speak" wasn't that far gone from southern accents of down-home folk in America's provinces. His faith in democratic conversations was founded on a feeling for the dignity of everyday people everywhere. He credited his father, a military man and New Deal fan, with nurturing respect for self and others. Along with advice on *First*, Larry passed on parenting tips he got from his pop. I valued, in particular, a lesson he'd been taught after he'd screwed up one time as an adolescent. Larry had come home with his buddies in a trashed car that he hadn't been supposed to drive in the first place. He expected his pop would chew him out. But it didn't happen. When Larry asked his pop why he'd kept cool, his pop said: "Never embarrass your son in public." Good counsel I've tried to live by with my son.

I'm reminded just now of my own dad's responsiveness to Larry's example. Back in the 1980s, Larry's work on populism informed my dad's review of Ronald Steele's fine biography of Walter Lippman, enabling him to zero in on the antidemocratic nature of Lippman's template for mainline political commentary. About twenty years later, I told my dad to check *Breaking the Barrier*'s "Critical Essay on Authorities"—a brilliant summative appendix analyzing how/why intellectuals have misinterpreted social movements—since it was relevant to what he was writing on at the time.

My dad read that appendix and immediately went back and read the entire volume (though he was deadlining himself). When he was done, he mused to me in a voice that took in the wackness of it all, *how could there have been no prizes for that book?*

I told him the tale of Ash. But—let that go—prizes are ashes.

Larry Goodwyn's work is alive and burning.

## Notes

1. Lawrence Goodwyn, "Solidarity's Sources," *New York Review of Books*, October 24, 1991, https://www.nybooks.com/articles/1991/10/24/solidaritys-sources/.

# 8

## Nell's Kitchen, Larry's War Room

PETER H. WOOD

"Do you need a cup of coffee, comrade?" The offer was generous, the home welcoming. "Open up that thermos," Larry would say to the visitor, tapping his pack of cigarettes on the kitchen table, with its littered ashtray and open books. "Nell just made a fresh pot," he'd announce, gesturing with a Styrofoam cup. "Clear off that chair. Have a seat."

Years later, the cigarettes would disappear, a personal victory over the cancerous southern-based tobacco industry, a win that added decades to his life before his lungs gave out. It was not his only battle with the insanity of his beloved South—far from it. "We have lots of snakes to kill," he'd say, ever the Texan, even on Tobacco Road.

Tobacco gone, the coffee cup remained, as did the pile of books, new and old, by friends and foes—underlined, dog-eared, highlighted, marked with coffee stains. "Have you got a minute," he'd say. "I need to read you something, if I can find it." He'd flip through pages, adjusting his thick glasses. "See what you think of this part here."

Whatever the passage, it would unlock a storehouse of insights and recollections, cross-references and asides, digressions and bull's-eyes, anecdotes and observations, tirades and questions. To read a well-chosen page was to buy a ticket on the Goodwyn roller coaster. Off you went, strapped in beside Larry and sharing his emotions—the agony and ecstasy.

Some telling statistic or apt quotation would sweep you high up, where you could see beyond the horizon; then a key line or a hidden footnote plunged you both down into a valley of despair. As time passed on this huge circular track, you might pause to hear a ball game or an NPR story, attend to the dog and cat, or admire some new backyard garden project.

When the conversation ended hours later, maybe days, you'd heard three old Texas stories and two new ones, all framed to show how democratic movements grow. You had, in Larry's military imagery, "stockpiled serious ammunition," "laid out a battle plan," "exploded those myths," "blown that ship out of the water." You had "seized the cultural high ground."

"Amazing, isn't it?" Larry would end, shutting the book. "Reminds me of a piece I wrote for the *Texas Observer*. He misses some key points, but we can fix that. He's young, and he's never seen a real movement. But this is *heavy* artillery. Lord knows, we need all the help we can get. I'll call Dirk Philipsen and Bill Greider too. We're going to win this battle."

\*    \*    \*

With Larry gone, Nell moved from the friendly Goodwyn house on Welcome Drive. The battles all around us continue, unfolding in strange ways that Larry might not have predicted. But he was always full of advice and predictions and questions, so I miss the kitchen conversations more than ever. Often, when I need to talk politics and history, I play out fresh discussions with Larry in my own head. And sometimes I miss those long rides on the Goodwyn roller coaster so much that I even sit down and write him a letter, just to share an idea or a story.

I did that again yesterday, though I am not sure what prompted it. Perhaps it was reading Jacquelyn Dowd Hall's latest book, *Sisters and Rebels*, a stunningly penetrating, wide-ranging and graceful saga that will be especially haunting for white southern activists who each wrestle with their own tangled regional roots. Or was it this week's anniversary of the bombing of Hiroshima (in the war that put Larry's brother in a B-17), or the second anniversary of the deadly white supremacist turmoil in Charlottesville, or the passing of Toni Morrison?

Maybe I wrote just because I was renewing my order with Duke for the Blue Devil basketball season tickets that we shared with Larry and Nell for many years. Whatever the reason, I scrawled a provocative title across the top of the page in the hope of getting his attention. I trust it reached him, wherever he is. If so, I suspect it reminded him of a story.

**Blood at the Depot**

Lawrence Goodwyn
Out There Somewhere
August 7, 2019
Dear Larry,

You have a better vantage point than I do on what's going on for humankind these days, and perhaps you even have an inkling of how it may turn out in the long run. Given your time with the *Texas Observer* covering oil barons and blustering politicians, I know you could reassure me that the festering political landscape your friends are facing these days is hardly a novelty. You told me long ago that race-baiting, voter suppression, false advertising, and the posturing and deceptions of faux-populists and white supremacists are not new inventions.

Two things are uppermost in my mind these days, and both relate to our country's deepening and toxic political swamp. For one thing, I am belatedly consumed with trying to understand climate disruption and consider what historians can do to help inform, and support, the next generation of activists. I am fascinated by how slowly individuals and groups react to crisis conditions when there is no sudden shock or wake-up call, like Pearl Harbor or 9/11. (You don't know it, but you sharpened my interest in the environment years ago, when you discovered that I had never heard of the Balcones Fault. You insisted that I accompany you to Austin, so I could get a clearer sense of why East Texas and West Texas are so different!)

So I thought I would be spending my post-teaching, post-Obama years helping to address global climate issues. Instead, I find myself still immersed in African American history after half a century. Through 150th anniversaries, the culture is in the midst of revisiting the realities of Reconstruction, with all its highs and lows, in ways that would have been unimaginable fifty years ago. But many Americans continue to seem stumped by the question of whether "Black Lives Matter." And most, especially west of the Mississippi where I now live, still have no sense of how, when, and where American racism put down its tenacious roots.

Therefore, I continue to give occasional talks about my book called *Near Andersonville*—though I have not found anyone who has read it as closely as you, or seen so many of its intended implications. (Your son Wade gave me the copy you marked up so copiously, and I keep it beside my desk!) In my silent conversations with you these days, I often thank you for sparking my interest in—among many other things—the American Civil War and Reconstruction. So let me pass along a story that I came across while exploring life and death near Andersonville Prison. It's vivid and true and revealing—the kind of stranger-than-fiction southern tale that you always enjoyed sharing and discussing at length in your kitchen.

Remember Rebecca Felton? No, she wasn't one of our students at Duke, though in some ways she could have been. A century before us, when old Mr. Duke was just beginning to sell tobacco, she was a complicated and opinionated Georgia feminist, activist, white supremacist, and champion of the Lost Cause. Much later, in 1922, she became the first woman appointed to the U.S. Senate, at age 87! (That made her the last member of Congress who had owned slaves.) She took the place of Tom Watson, the Populist-turned-nativist-bigot, when he died suddenly; she only held the post for 24 hours, as a symbolic gesture. She advocated the vote for white women, but she also opposed spending on Black education and even defended lynching. I first learned about her in 1979 through *Revolt Against Chivalry*, Jacquelyn Hall's eye-opening book about Jessie Daniel Ames and the "Women's Campaign Against Lynching."

Anyway, Rebecca Latimer Felton lived through the Civil War as a twenty-something in Macon, Georgia, raising small children while her older husband attended to wartime duties. (William Felton had been the impressive speaker at her graduation from Madison Female College in 1852, and she married him the following year.) As a widow in 1919, she wrote a memoir about her experiences, *Country Life in Georgia in the Days of My Youth*. She comes across as articulate and myopic all at once, still unable—despite all her passion and cleverness—to confront her own demons, and eager to help others indulge in stilted nostalgia. It's no surprise that in 1893 she pushed for a special exhibit at the World's Columbian Exhibition in Chicago, "illustrating the slave period" with "real colored folks" shipped in to spin cotton and strum banjos, proof of "the ignorant contented darky—as distinguished from Stowe's monstrosities."

Thinking back to the 1860s, the octogenarian gives moving descriptions of the dire lack of food supplies that gripped southern Georgia late in the war. "After Stoneman raided from Atlanta towards Macon, in July, 1864, I knew a nice family," she writes, "who had nothing whatever to eat unless they chewed bushes or dug up roots to quiet hunger. After the raiders had passed them they gathered up the scattered corn left by the cavalry horses, washed and rewashed it and boiled it into hominy and kept going cheerfully." Salt and coffee were virtually absent, "flour was scarce," and even corn meal was in short supply. "It was a serious time," she recalls, even in planter homes "where hunger had never entered before." But then, as she reminisces about white fortitude, she tells this story. It might be called, "Blood at the Depot."

Late in 1864, Felton traveled east to Crawfordville, near Augusta, to visit her sick mother, who feared for her only son at the front. When Sherman's Union troops burned the Georgia Railroad's bridge across the Oconee River west of Greensboro, her return trip was diverted south to Savannah. From there, she took the Georgia Central Railroad, traveling 190 miles back to Macon. The train followed the Ogeechee River up to Millen, and then turned west, pausing at each little railroad town along the way: Cushingville, Herndon, Sebastopol, Spiers. . . . It was a sleepless night in dark, uncomfortable cars, as the steam engine struggled from Davisboro to Tennille to Oconee to Emmel, occasionally passing trains on sidings heading east. Though not one to empathize with Union soldiers or enslaved Georgians, Felton still remembered vividly, half a century later, what happened next.

Somewhere along this route—perhaps between McIntyre and Gordon, as the train chugged slowly past Friendship and Solon's Mills—the sleepy passengers suddenly found themselves staring through the train windows at sickly ghosts. Outside, they saw "car-loads of Andersonville prisoners being removed to another camp" due to Confederate fears "that Sherman would strike for Andersonville," just as General George Stoneman's U.S. Cavalry had done unsuccessfully in July. In late fall, thousands of emaciated prisoners of war had been loaded onto trains at Andersonville Station and shipped east to Camp Lawton, the newer, less vulnerable stockade at Millen. Those too sick to travel had been left behind. "The night was gloomy," she recalled, "as our train rolled along beside passing flat cars on which those Federal prisoners were guarded, with torch lights illuminating the faces of those ragged, smoke-begrimed, haggard and miserably filthy men."

Though inured to the shocks of conflict, Felton had never seen anything like this nighttime tableau. "I had a glimpse of war conditions that was new to me," she confessed. "Prison treatment of such men has always been a disgrace to Christianity and civilization," the activist observed in hindsight, recalling that in those days, reading wartime papers, she had justifiably "been angered at the treatment of our Confederate prisoners" in northern prisons such as Camp Chase and Johnson's Island in Ohio. Nevertheless, "that sight of train-loads of Federal prisoners on that wild night in Southern Georgia" seared her consciousness: "when I could look into their faces within a few feet of the train," Felton lamented, "I became an eyewitness to their enforced degradation, filth and utter destitution and the sight never could be forgotten."

But the shocking nightmare did not end there. Felton also remembered what happened next, as her train halted at the small station where the prisoner convoy had just departed. "Nor can I forget," she recalled, "seeing a dead negro man who had said something offensive to an Andersonville guard and he had been shot a few minutes before our train pulled in." The gaping passengers must have averted their eyes, and then stared furtively and repeatedly at the brutal scene, piecing together from train-side chatter why an unarmed Black man was bleeding to death on the dimly lit platform. Soon it was time to reboard the train and push on into the night, leaving the murdered Georgian behind. "The quivers of dying flesh had hardly subsided in his stalwart body," she remembered, "as we rolled away."

Years later, old Mrs. Felton wrote down her vivid account of witnessing these two horrific scenes in one night. The recollection appears in her 1919 memoir, *Country Life in the Days of My Youth,* and it makes clear, as she put it, that the awful sights "never could be forgotten." Yet it also seems obvious that throughout her adult life, she effectively pushed these nightmarish scenes to the back of her mind and refused to reexamine them. Each repressed image challenged the narrative of life that she inherited, embraced, and then perpetuated, at great cost to herself and others. Felton went on to craft a long and influential public career during some of the most depressing and hate-filled decades in the South's troubled history. That career, despite all its progressive aspects, was characterized by repetitiously waving the bloody shirt and fanning the flames of white racism.

Reading this story took me back to the exciting undergraduate class that you used to teach on three "Southern Insurgencies," highlighting

the complexities of the Reconstruction struggle, the Populist moment, and long Civil Rights Movement. How much this next cohort
could use such a course now, getting in touch with how previous generations have fought for and against meaningful change in a society
built on white male privilege. I was also reminded of *Educated*, an
enthralling recent best-seller that gives a striking firsthand account
of a young woman's difficult battle to break out of the intellectual
straitjacket that her upbringing had imposed.

Am I crazy to imagine that Felton, this smart and pious woman,
was only inches away from following a different track, if only she had
processed these events differently? She came so close, and she would
never have a better chance. I know—close is not enough, and anyway,
it takes more than a mind-shift by one shrewd person to change the
course of history. Still, epiphanies and aha moments do happen. I
wish I could share this true tale with you over a beer, Larry. That way,
I might hear you exclaim, "My God, where did you find that story?"
Then we would go on to explore all the ideas it opens up, starting
in wartime Georgia and moving outward. I miss those long, intense
conversations, spiraling into the unknown.

Can you believe that while I was at Harvard in the 1960s, that
august college never taught classes on the Civil War? (Did it seem
too divisive, or too unimportant? I don't know.) It was not until we
met in the 1970s that I heard someone speak in a passionate and informed way about that conflict. I remember the moment, over lunch
in a coffee shop, when you realized my ignorance about the Battle
of Chancellorsville. This had to be rectified immediately! Turning
over your placemat, you drew the winding Rappahannock River and
diagrammed how General Hooker divided his Union forces, sending
two corps and most of George Stoneman's cavalry across the river,
hoping to surprise and envelop General Lee's outnumbered forces.

Now I know, from writing about him, that's the same George Stoneman who, during Sherman's later siege of Atlanta, led an unsuccessful
raid to liberate the Union prisoners dying in Andersonville. He failed
and was captured (no doubt to the delight of Mrs. Felton). But I knew
nothing about any of this at the time. Instead I sat dumbfounded,
watching you map out Chancellorsville using salt shakers and coffee
cups, as you explained how Lee's astuteness—and Hooker's timidity—turned that encounter in May 1863 into a Confederate victory,

paving the way for the Confederate advance into Pennsylvania. I suspect you drew similar maps, for other uninformed listeners, when you took students on those memorable field trips to Gettysburg.

In the coffee shop, as if confronting a magician, I asked, "Wait, how did you do that?" I had seen your play-by-play diagrams of basketball games, and I knew that came from years as an undergraduate sports reporter. But a detailed reenactment of Chancellorsville, on a placemat? You explained that as a boy you had read Douglas Southall Freeman's four-volume biography of Lee, in part to impress your Virginia-born father who knew the war backward and forward. You inherited your parents' fascination with southern history, but somehow you developed an abiding commitment to uncovering a clearer and less whitewashed version of the region's past.

Since the African American experience is central to that past, I recall asking, over another cup of coffee, how you explained your involvement with the civil rights movement. You noted in an offhand way that your father, as a white cavalry officer, had been placed in charge of African American troops in France during World War I. Then later, during the 1930s, he was sent to Fort Huachuca in Arizona to train Black soldiers. Since you were born in 1928, this means you spent formative years at a spot that had been a base for Buffalo Soldiers half a century earlier. I suspect some of your earliest passions about justice and equality were ignited there. Living amid a large Black community on that isolated post, you and your older brother must have asked your parents some hard questions about our segregated country.

Talking over Rebecca Felton's nightmare, I know these themes of race and region would reappear, along with the horrors of wartime violence. Your father had seen it in France, and your brother Cary saw it all too clearly in Germany as the navigator on a B-17 Flying Fortress. The "Ritzy Blitz" was hit by enemy aircraft and crashed in flames near Hanover in November 1944, killing half the crew. With four others, Cary survived, but his long months as a POW left lasting marks. Turns out that I too have a POW in the family, but I didn't learn about George Butler from Winthrop, Maine, until *after* I finished the Andersonville book. As a member of the 3rd Maine Infantry, he was captured in the Peach Orchard at Gettysburg, confined to Belle Isle Prison in Richmond, and then shipped to Andersonville, where he died in March 1864.

Like you, I never cease to marvel over all the unlikely ways that personal stories intersect with huge political eruptions and vast social movements. And now that I live in the West, I have a greater appreciation than ever for the South's rich storytelling habit, which you helped me appreciate. Am I being too optimistic to hope that this venerable tradition, so long used to disguise the region's tangled heritage, is now finally being used to look the real past and future more clearly in the eye? I can't answer that, but the deep well of southern history still contains an endless supply of surprising, meaningful, and revealing moments. Rest assured that your friends continue to work—often with you in mind—to haul these stories up to the surface as rapidly and as well as we can.

As ever,

Peter

# 9

## Goodwyn Taught Me How to Live in 2019 Two Decades Ago

ADAM LIOZ

To say that our country is at a crossroads, our democracy on the brink, is a cliché at this point—which doesn't make it any less true. I write these words in 2019, with a clear and present danger front of mind; but without significant structural changes they will likely ring true in five or ten years as well. To push through this moment, to get to a future where we don't just restore our republic but forge a new, more inclusive democracy that reflects and embraces our growing diversity as a nation, we'll need millions of people to find and maintain purpose in civic engagement; and we'll need to be clear-eyed about the role of race in American politics. This is a story about how Larry Goodwyn taught me both of these lessons twenty-two years ago.

I arrived at Duke University in the late summer of 1994 with a vague sense that life isn't fair—that some people get the short end of the stick—but without any strong sense of why, no sophisticated political analysis to accompany my gut-level discontent with the status quo. After some low-level racial tension in my wealthy, mostly white suburban high school and a disturbing *60 Minutes* episode depicting Duke as a segregated campus, I thought I would come to Durham to tackle the issue of race-based division. But I was soon largely preoccupied by my frat-driven social life and a bit disillusioned when I realized that my ideas on race were, shall we say, oversimplified.

I meandered through college without any real direction or purpose. I did what it took to get good grades but felt a bit fish-out-of-water in the lacrosse- and prep-driven culture I chose to inhabit. I was pretty sure I didn't want to be a consultant or an investment banker, but I had no idea what I did want to do. I even decided to take a semester off in part because graduation loomed as a scary day. The backup plan was to take a year off to ski out West and then go to law school. What I lacked in direction I made up for in privilege.

Then, the first semester of my senior year, my good friends and roommates Dan Kessler and Andrew Keats told me that I absolutely had to "shop" a history class they were taking. I wandered into an East Campus classroom and came face-to-face with Professor Goodwyn, a craggily sixty-nine-year-old Texan who promptly announced that "we are all white supremacists. We were born, raised, and educated in a white supremacist society, and that makes us white supremacists." I immediately thought, well, this won't be a typical Duke class, and I was in.

Over the course of the semester in Comparative Social Movements, Larry urged us to speak truth to power—to tell him "what you think you think," and even to critique his award-winning book, right to his face. He urged us to question the presumption of progress and exposed us to the idea that our democracy is in fact not working that well for most people. We read about the agrarian revolt and the civil rights movement; we dug into William Greider's *Who Will Tell the People*, a powerful tale of special interests' capture of our political system. The "white supremacy" point wasn't a throwaway line, but rather an essential lesson in how structural power works in our society.

All of a sudden I had language and a political analysis through which to channel my emerging sense of injustice. That same semester, the State Public Interest Research Groups (now U.S. PIRG) came to campus to hold an information session on job opportunities. As I listened to the presenter talk about the organization's work against "special interests" and for the public interest, the discussions in Larry's class rang in my ears. I made the radical discovery that someone would pay me (not very much) to fight "the man."

I, of course, went to Larry for advice. He said, yes, PIRG is a good organization and they'll train you well. He also picked up the phone while I was in his office and called John Richard, Ralph Nader's right-hand man. (This was pre-2000 when Nader was a revered hero on the left.) His call got me an interview at Nader's Center for Responsive Politics—but the interviewer actually advised me to take the PIRG job for the best possible training. So I did.

But Larry wasn't done helping me. Before I left campus I decided it would be wise to set myself up to get into law school if I ever did decide to go. I took an LSAT class during my semester off, and I needed letters of recommendation. Back to Larry's office. I was afraid he would scold me for wanting to go to law school, like I would be betraying the higher calling of organizing and advocacy. But, to my surprise, Larry was in favor. Again while I was sitting across from him, Larry typed out a short recommendation letter—just a few paragraphs—and handed it to me (no sealed envelopes here). I must admit I was a bit concerned; it couldn't have been more than three hundred words. I took the letter across campus to Dean Gerald Wilson, my pre-law advisor. "Um, is this OK?" I asked tentatively. Dean Wilson read the letter, picked his head up, and said in no uncertain terms, "Any student would be lucky to have this letter." I was relieved and grateful.

As organizers or advocates for social change, we are constantly telling our own stories. Larry is a key part of my personal story, of how I became the person I am today. My life has continued along the course that Larry helped set. I worked for U.S. PIRG or affiliated organizations for thirteen years, and for seven-plus more have been with a progressive think tank called Demos promoting voting rights and fighting to curb the influence of big money in politics. I did go to law school, and legal work has—to my surprise—become foundational to my activism.

I'm grateful to have found meaning and purpose in my life through this activism. And I'm especially fortunate that I've been able to build a career out of it—to wake up every morning and get paid to fight for a democracy in which the strength of our voices does not depend upon the size of our wallets. Research suggests that happiness inheres not so much in achieving objectives but rather in the progressive pursuit of worthy goals. It's another way of saying "it's the journey not the destination." But the destination matters in a key way: if the endpoint is material, or self-focused, the pursuit often feels empty.

Another way of looking at this is that our satisfaction in life is a vector of sorts, with one arrow representing the worthiness of our ends (direction) and the other the efficacy with which we pursue those ends (speed). Many people struggle with both arrows: am I making enough money . . . and is making money even a worthy goal? I have plenty of struggles with the speed prong, but thanks in no small part to Larry I feel pretty confident in the direction. I feel like this has mitigated a key aspect of the struggle for a satisfying life. Maybe I would have found this purpose, this confidence in my direction, without Larry's intervention at a critical time. Maybe . . .

It took many years for the second seed Larry planted to fully blossom.

I appreciated reading about late civil rights icon and congressman John Lewis's formative years preaching to chickens, and I found Larry's labeling me a white supremacist arresting, but I didn't actually *believe* him. I was liberal and enlightened, surely not an active player in a system of race-based oppression. In law school my friends and I spent a whole semester digging deeply into the central role of race in America, and I . . . didn't get it. It took another decade for my eyes to begin to open, when Demos engaged in a deep program of racial equity learning and training right as the Movement for Black Lives was highlighting the realities of police brutality and continuing as neo-Nazis were marching openly in the streets of Charlottesville. I began to appreciate for the first time how in the United States our workplaces, our cities, our cultural and physical spaces are constructed with me—a cis straight white male—in mind, and how little energy I put into navigating them as a result. More important, I began to see how economic and political elites use racism strategically to divide and conquer, breaking apart class-based solidarity among Black, brown, and white people so they can hoard money and power—and how this has not been a side story in American political history, but rather the central plot. Turns out Larry was more deeply correct than I was able to see as a twenty-year-old in 1997.

More than twenty years later, many of Larry's lessons are sadly prescient. He taught us to question the presumption of progress at a time when the continuing expansion of democracy across the globe seemed inevitable; now it is in retreat. He taught us about structural racism and how our democracy pushes people of color and those without money and lobbyists on retainer to the sidelines; now an authoritarian, white-nationalist administration is tripling down on strategic racism to divide working people, concentrate economic spoils at the top, and erode the very foundations of our democracy.

But Larry also gave us a roadmap for renewal. He showed one directionless kid drowning in race and class privilege how to find purpose and passion in viewing this privilege as a profound responsibility; he surely did a similar service for countless others; and his wisdom and example apply even more broadly. Right now we need more people than ever to conclude that engaging with society to transform our democracy into the truly inclusive and equitable place we know it can be is a good path to a satisfying life. It doesn't have to be a full-time job for everyone—in fact there isn't enough funding in the nonprofit space for that, and those of us who get paid to pursue activism as a career should never forget how fortunate we are. But getting involved with a local Sierra Club chapter to help fight climate change could be the most satisfying piece of "work" one does, regardless of one's career.

Larry also taught how race is not an incidental factor but a central through-line in American history and politics; and now we are at a moment when failing to confront race head-on could literally cost us our democracy. Once you see—I mean really see, which took me years—the picture of power that Larry painted, you can't un-see it. This makes you want to go out and fight for change, and it opens the door to finding profound meaning and satisfaction in fighting the good fight, even as the struggle is slow, and long, and anything but linear.

# PART II

★ ★ ★ ★ ★ ★ ★ ★

## "The Point of the Entire Thing"

### Teaching inside Democratic Relationships

★ ★ ★ ★ ★ ★ ★ ★

"Teaching," as both term and category, is too small to contain the material in this section. For Goodwyn, relationships of openness and trust lay at the foundation of learning and teaching. The phrase "all learning is experiential" was an article of faith in Goodwyn's discussion seminars, whether those discussions took place in an actual classroom or a bar or at a voter registration workshop. He both learned and taught through relationships. The idea was simple: each person brings a different set of experiences; for real interaction to happen, two people had to relate to each other's experiences. Activist and artist Julius Lester captured this idea succinctly. "I taught for thirty-two years, and each semester when I walked into a classroom for the first time, I was overwhelmed by the fact that each student represented a story," he reflected in 2004. "How could I be a good teacher if I did not know their stories? Their stories determined what they heard and how they heard it."[1] Goodwyn was thrilled when he was told by a former student that the major topic of discussion between the great intellectuals C.L.R. James and Edward W. Said during their one and only meeting had been: "What makes a good teacher?" That, to him, was the right topic of conversation.

Larry Goodwyn, as person, as citizen, and as intellectual, cared deeply about teaching. It was a craft, he felt, that was not practiced very well in the academy. What stood in the way? Hierarchy, condescension, and a false sense of superiority on the part of too many faculty members. People who thought they knew the answers were inherently suspect. And teachers who thought learning is a one-way street—instructor teaching students—were downright hopeless. Learning was about interacting, and doing so in a way that included the whole person. Movement organizer and teacher Ella Baker was a model for him. Her dictum was: Meet people where they are.

In this vein, relationships are the foundation of knowledge, not disconnected "expertise." Institutions of higher learning often suffocate inquiry based on experience and relationships. Instead, the university tendency is to calcify knowledge in data and archives, plumbed only by highly credentialed researchers. At Duke, Goodwyn tried to bend the university to his view of how to build "best available knowledge," by working with Bill Chafe, Peter Wood, and others to form the Oral History Program, by nurturing young community and labor organizers, by helping to keep Richard Nixon's museum off of Duke's campus, and by supporting pockets of movement building and resistance everywhere else. As the interview with Thelma Kithcart demonstrates, he knew enough to bring in experientially knowledgeable people, like Kithcart, to build institutions he simply did not know enough about to build alone. In the last two decades of his life, he saw the emergence of email and social media provide unparalleled abilities to communicate.

Throughout it all, he encouraged student groups and young organizers to make sure they continued to develop face-to-face relationships as well as a social media presence. When arguments happened, he echoed Ash-Lee Woodard Henderson, codirector of the Highlander Center, in noting that people must engage in face-to-face dialogue, no matter how painful, if they are to build freedom movements.[2] "The only way to fight organized money is with organized people," Goodwyn's son Wade recalled from Larry's lifelong teaching. "It's an awful political truth, because the ramifications are so dire for those yearning for a more democratic society." Money is relatively easy to organize. People aren't. Yet, as Goodwyn saw it, it's the only pathway worth pursuing.

Wade paints a vivid picture of how his father's attempt to create an open and candid learning environment played out. Subsequent contributors provide additional layers to show how this relationship-based learning worked best, or didn't. The stories here show ways to nurture young people like community leader Wendy Jacobs or historian Chuck Bolton and, by doing so, enable them to create their own independent work. On the other hand, we also learn about the wounds he sometimes inflicted. Larry could be excessively judgmental and he was especially hard on students who he felt deferred too easily to him. At times, students, colleagues, and comrades felt insulted or misunderstood. Too many never measured up, or simply failed to gain his attention. Several look back at a raucous, intense, and discordant relationship to Goodwyn.

Through well-known freedom movement teachers like Septima Clark and Ella Baker, we know about this mode of how people learn best "inside relationships." Few, at least those outside of social movements, ever get to experience people power directly. They never see it play out, conversation by conversation. Curiously, the scholarship is still thin on the intricate dynamics of political relationship building—of movement organizing, of teaching as a liberatory and self-empowering effort. As Larry and many of his students learned through their own experiences and scholarship, anyone who approaches life with humility, candor, patience, and self-reflection can be an organizer. For Goodwyn, it always started out with a recognition. He put it in his usually linguistically abstract and highly theoretical language: "We all fuck up." Indeed, it is necessary and important that we do so. For if we don't give ourselves permission to make errors, we never try anything new.

Goodwyn was unapologetic about his right to make errors, though at times only variously tolerant about the errors of others. He had considerable disdain for people who denied their own errors behind a shield of titles, positions, and status.

Perhaps one can be happy that Larry Goodwyn did not live to see yet another era of heightened fear, deception, and denial. On the other hand, he would have been thrilled at the global sweep of the Black Lives Matter democracy movement. Today we face the need to engage in tough conversations, confront our own mistakes, allow the other person to make errors, and build new ways through and past it. Communication is always a two-way street, but the person with more power always has a greater responsibility. As Staci Haines, an organizer and cofounder of Generative Somatics, notes, it's an essential skill to learn: how to deepen trust when people work through conflict in ways that align with their values.[3] Goodwyn talked about this as needing to find ways to "walk through the fire" with your comrades if the organizing effort was "to have a chance in hell of making it." He maintained, front and center, that we needed not one theoretical intervention but a multiplicity of paths. He would likely ask us today: Why are we so timid in pursuing such deep mutual engagement, keeping sight of the relationship as a "both/and" engagement, at a time when it is so clearly required for new political and social forms to bloom?

## Notes

1. Julius Lester, *On Writing for Children & Other People* (New York: Dial, 2004), 76.

2. Ash-Lee Woodard Henderson, "Grassroots Organizing," panel, March 24, 2018, North Carolina Central University, Durham, NC, https://vimeo.com/270135809, min. 44–51.

3. Staci Haines, *The Politics of Trauma: Somatics, Healing, and Social Justice* (Berkeley, CA: North Atlantic Books, 2019), 30.

# 10

## Family Politics

### Son of a Little-*d* Democrat

WADE GOODWYN

Growing up Larry Goodwyn's son was like being dunked in a whiskey barrel of storytelling and coming up soaked in democratic political theory. It started in the car, on the way home from basketball or track practice when I was twelve. But the teaching began in earnest in my teens. I'd come home at ten or midnight or one a.m. and Dad would be sitting at the little white table in the kitchen. He had an Irishman's way of engaging you in a conversation, friendly, interesting, and before you knew it my mother would call down the stairs, "Larry, it's four in the morning, y'all need to come to bed!"

My father taught at Duke University for nearly thirty years, but nobody had more classes with him than I. Thousands of hours, I essentially earned my PhD before I graduated from college. It started with the idea of democratic social relations.

Relationships between people must be democratic to thrive. No power playing, no coercion, no deception; anything one gained that wasn't given freely by the other was tainted. And it didn't matter if the relationships in question were friendships, love relationships, public relationships—teacher/student, boss/employee, the same rules applied. It was both simple and radical: "Do unto others" broken down into specific social and political acts. And, as I was to discover, so very difficult to practice and achieve. It's like hitting a golf ball long and straight, damn near impossible to do with much consistency. If you want to find me, look to the right of the fairway, over in the woods, deep in the shade. My father explained that these conversations, the ideas, were "culturally unsanctioned." And I learned it was true. Even in the mid and late seventies, after the civil rights movement, in the midst of the women's rights movement, the ideas my father was talking to me about I didn't hear anywhere else, not from teachers, coaches, friends, friends' parents. It was a way of understanding both the world around me and my place inside it. These lessons of self and mutual empowerment clashed intensely with the world as I experienced it in Durham in the mid-1970s and beyond. There was no hint of democratic social relations when football coaches grabbed your facemask and screamed in your face. And white supremacy was ever present without a whiff of subtlety about it. Hierarchy ruled the day, it was ascendant, and its ubiquity lent power to my father's theories. "Culturally unsanctioned," you didn't have to tell me. In 1978, at the direction of the federal government, my best friend Jeff Kline and I went to the downtown post office together to register for the draft. The Vietnam War was over, but it had been waged for nearly all of our lives. Registering made us nervous, disco was king. We spent our nights dancing in Chapel Hill. Ronald Reagan was about to change the country forever.

Larry Goodwyn grew up the son of an army colonel, Carey, born in 1881 in Georgia, a descendant of the Bloodworths and Pounds, families that had come from English gentry. Sir Thomas Bloodworth, one of our forebears, was Lord Mayor of London from October 1665 through October 1666. When part of the city caught fire, he stopped by on his way to the theatre, turned up his nose at the size of the blaze, and announced, "A woman might piss it out." His inaction was widely blamed for the city burning to the ground and has forever served as a warning to anyone in our family considering elective politics or management as a profession—remember Sir Thomas.

My parents' experiences of the Great Depression could not have been more dissimilar. My mother grew up in South Texas in a German family whose men made their living with their hands as farmers and carpenters. My grandfather on my mother's side ran an ice cream store, built caskets, bought and sold used cars, and did whatever else he could to get his family through the 1930s. There were chickens and roosters in the backyard, and the enormous extended family would get together every Sunday; during bad weeks, some hadn't had enough to eat.

My father on the other hand grew up in a life of privilege. In Arizona and then Virginia, Grandmother Goodwyn had a housekeeper and a cook, and the colonel had a driver. Every two years they bought a new car. My father remembered a procession of men coming to the back door on the army base to beg for work. The cook was instructed to invite each one into the kitchen to be fed. While my mother experienced the Depression in a way that would never really leave her, my father witnessed it as it paraded through his family's kitchen.

Growing up in Virginia and then Austin, my father was short and smart, and his parents, perhaps eager to get him out of the house, enrolled him in school two years ahead of his grade level. That meant he was eight years old in fourth grade. He also wore glasses. And being an Irish lad, he was loath to back down. He fought a lot. When it was time for fists, my father would take off his eyeglasses and put them in his back pocket so they wouldn't get smashed when a punch to the face landed. But being five feet tall and practically blind without his glasses often meant he'd end up on his butt and his frames and sometimes the lenses too would be smashed. The colonel would reprimand young Larry for breaking another pair of expensive glasses. His mother tried to keep an old pair in her dresser for post-fight emergencies.

These school years formed in large part the foundation of my father's character, his politics, and his way of regarding the world. He saw himself in league with the little guy, he remained undaunted, and he learned to strategize so as to have a chance at winning. Until his last breath my father was up for another go.

In some ways my childhood was an echo of his. We both had stints in Austin. I was born there and grew up going to University of Texas football games at Memorial Stadium. There used to be a section in the end zone for kids called the Knothole. They were bleacher seats, and they were low and you couldn't see much of anything. When discussing political ideas, my father was big on the concept of "received knowledge," which meant ways of seeing the world absorbed through one's surrounding culture and life experiences. In this case it was how to successfully sneak out of the Knothole into good seats at halftime. At the end of the first quarter you would carefully scope out a group of empty seats, no earlier, you had to be patient to account for late arrivals. Then just before halftime you made your move. First, you hit the concession stand to buy two cups of Coke. Now your hands were full, signaling to all ushers not to bother you about tickets. This next part was key: as you passed the ticket takers at the stadium portal, you had to look like you knew exactly where you were going, turning the corner heading up the steps, frantically but calmly searching for those seats you'd spied. You learned to identify multiple landmarks—the fat guy wearing the hat with giant longhorns sticking out the top, the five guys all in white T-shirts. There was no sweeter reward than your butt in a seat fifty rows up on the 30-yard line. By God, you could watch the Texas Longhorns crush the poor Rice Owls 63–10 like a boss!

It was a subversive moral lesson—if you were clever about it and did your homework, defying authority could work out to your gain. My dad taught me how to game the system, and I loved him for it. One of my favorite pieces of my father's writing is about his experiences as a boy in the Knothole Gang—"Wonder and Glory in Another Century."[1]

My father's political education began in 1956 when he worked as an advance man for Ralph Yarborough's campaign for Texas governor. Watching Yarborough campaign up close day after day was a revelation. They would drive into some tiny Texas county seat and go to the courthouse, and hundreds of Democrats would be waiting to hear Yarborough speak.

Yarborough was in his fifties and my father was twenty-nine, and at the end of the day Dad would be dead on his feet but Yarbrough was still raring to go. Campaigning, meeting farmers and working-class Texans revved Yarborough up. They flew in private planes with my father sitting behind the seats in the luggage compartment (luckily, he fit). Twelve speeches a day starting with breakfast were common. After Yarborough was elected to the US Senate, my dad went to work for Ronnie Dugger, writing for the *Texas Observer*. This is where the first glimpse of my father's future could be seen. Even after writing books for major publishing houses, Dad often told me that Dugger was one of the best editors he'd had. Dad had natural writing talent, but he said Dugger knew how to take a good writer and make him clearer, cleaner, more powerful.

It was my mother, Nell, though, who became his most trusted sounding board, beginning with his first book, *The South Central States*, for a Time-Life series. If my mother didn't like it, if she didn't understand what he was trying to say, he'd protest a bit and then redo it. For the Populist book, he was trying to tell a story that hadn't been written before, a tale of a democratic movement grounded in political ideas that were so radical and unsanctioned that readers were going to have difficulty internalizing them even, or perhaps especially, in the modern era. My father's writing could be thick with implication, and my mother was ever vigilant for professorial tone. She'd beat it out of the script, if not my father. Two days later he'd hand her ten new pages and say, "Okay, how about this?" "Much better," she'd say with a smile, and away he'd go, back to his Royal manual typewriter. The clapping sound of keys hitting roller would resume like a World War I machine gun.

*    *    *

One day when I was about six, I was playing catch with my friend across the street when a car pulled up and four young Black men hopped out and went inside. This was not an uncommon occurrence, as dedicated civil rights workers and organizers were often at the house. But my friend's father was from Mississippi, a white used car salesman who sold mostly to poor people of color on credit. He was not a fan of what was going on at the house across the street from him, and he was there that day in his front yard where we were throwing around the baseball. "Big Jim" walked over to me and leaned down, grabbed my arm tightly and hissed in my ear as the four African Americans disappeared in our house, "Better watch your mama, son, one of these days one of those boys is gonna git her."

I was too young to understand exactly what he meant, but I very definitely got that I was being threatened. The angry grip on my arm was explanation enough. In Big Jim's world in 1966, you were either on white people's side or you were against them. The Mississippian let go of my arm and went inside his house, and his son and I returned to playing catch. Austin was different from other parts of Texas and the South, but then again, it wasn't. The civil rights movement of which my father was a part was overtopping Jim Crow's banks, gouging a new path across the South, right through our next-door neighbor's front yard. Blacks and whites were dancing in the Goodwyns' living room, "Lay Lady Lay" blasted from the console stereo, my father made gin and tonics and Rob Roys while cigarette smoke and raucous, hopeful laughter filled the rooms.

In 1971, after four years of graduate school at UT, family along for the ride, my father was hired at Duke University. Our lives would never be the same. My father had stumbled upon what would become the great work of his life, the history of the Populist movement. He recognized from his reading that he was looking at a precursor of the civil rights movement, only it was impoverished southern and midwestern farmers at the base.

He told me a story of how he'd come across one of the first newspapers of the Farmers' Alliance, called the *Rural Citizen*, espousing "A Government by the People and for the People." He drove up to Jacksboro, Texas, and found the offices of the *Rural Citizen*, still going after nearly a hundred years. The paper was completely staffed by women. And they had every back issue of the *Rural Citizen* all the way back to those very first days of the Farmers' Alliance.

The nice ladies let my dad sit there with them and read those newspapers from beginning to end about the creation of the Farmers' Alliance in Montague County. The emergence of its activist wing. The discovery of who the leaders were. People who were unknown to history, but were vital players. They were the Martin Luther Kings of that era, these were the Freedom Riders of the 1880s in Texas that were pioneering what would eventually come to be known as Populism. It's in newspapers, and you just have to go everywhere the papers are. And so he went.

At Duke my father created what he called the Oral History Program with colleagues like Peter Wood and Bill Chafe, who became close friends of our family in the process. The nights Peter would join us in raucous board games like Lie, Cheat & Steal (about American politics) were many. The 1970s in Durham felt to me very much like the 1960s in Austin, full of hope, of optimistic joy. Our family's love of UT and Dallas Cowboys football now had a new baby brother, Duke basketball. We got our first season tickets to Cameron Indoor Stadium in 1973, and not long afterward I had my first kiss after a Duke game, my date and I freezing on a marble bench outside at night in February, waiting for my father (late again) to pick us up.

My conversations with my father were steeped in this brief promising moment in history, the beginning of the end of this progressive striving. The ideas we discussed remain deeply radical. My father explained the concept of "democratic social relations" as the ideal to shoot for in one's interactions with others. It was kind of like "Do unto others . . ." but really a lot harder to pull off. It's hard to be democratic. Another radical idea was that "all social knowledge is experiential." It took me years to understand just how far-reaching this concept is. At its core it's about confronting power, whether it's your boss or your mayor or congressman. But the awareness encompasses more than just confronting power—it's about one's relationship with and to power in all its complexities. It is the foundation upon which rests the ultimate awareness that no social or political change is possible unless it's organized. Good journalism doesn't do it, raising consciousness doesn't do it, the economy getting so bad that "people finally wake up" won't do it either. The only way citizens become political actors is simply by being political actors, and since that is a scary and mostly impossible thing to do in this day and age, you need to be trained by professional organizers. Leaders must be trained to develop followers. This is the way political organization is built, and this is the way political experience can become internalized political knowledge. The only way to fight organized money is with organized people. It's an awful political truth, because the ramifications are so dire for those yearning for a more democratic society. Change is too hard won, filled with the drudgery of relationship building—it's the only pathway to power. If only a Pulitzer Prize or an Ellie or a Peabody would do it, then by God, times would change. As we saw after the shootings in Charleston in 2015, Twitter can't do it either.

*   *   *

When I left New York City and my position as an organizer for the Queens Citizens Organization and the Industrial Areas Foundation in exchange for a job as a reporter for NPR in Austin, I had no illusions that I wasn't abandoning the good fight. I knew I was. While journalism is a profession that allows me to live in political peace, I've never tried to kid myself that I'm changing the world by raising consciousness, plowing political ground through storytelling so that the country might hear and understand and thus be moved to action so we'll all reap a bountiful crop of economic and democratic change. Those kitchen conversations taught me that political revolutions don't happen through reading or watching TV or listening to NPR, or because so many Americans have fallen into economic ruin that the collective political light finally goes on, spurring them to action. If only it were that easy.

In the world as it is, political transformation occurs as a result of broad-based, interdenominational, multiracial, grassroots organizing. It's a fact that professional organizers grasp that professional journalists, even leftist journalists, generally don't. To my dismay, I annoyed the hell out of Molly Ivins in a couple of conversations on this topic. Of course, she may have been the exception to this rule. Molly, wherever you are, please don't blame me. Blame the organizers like Ernie Cortés and Ed Chambers, Tony Mazzocchi and, most of all, Larry Goodwyn.

What I'd give to have one more night on Welcome Drive in Durham, leaning on the edge of the counter at three a.m. while my father opines from behind the little white kitchen table.

God knows we'd have plenty to talk about these days.

"Sorry, Mom, we'll be up in a minute."

## Notes

1. Lawrence Goodwyn, "Wonder and Glory in Another Century," *Southern Exposure* 7.2 (Fall 1979): 42–47.

# 11

## You Already Know Everything

WENDY JACOBS

The interview between Wendy Jacobs and Wesley Hogan took place in Durham, NC, on December 16, 2015, and has been lightly edited.

I had a pretty traditional type of upbringing, growing up in New Jersey in an upper-middle-class Jewish family. I went to a public high school. I wanted to try and challenge myself and be in a different environment, and I had gotten into some good schools in the Northeast. A part of me subconsciously wanted to put myself in a different environment. I thought Duke was pretty. I am the oldest in my family. I have a memory of driving down to Durham in 1979 and staying in the Heart of Durham Hotel. I remember going to the vending machine the night before going to the Duke campus. They had fried pork skins in the vending machine. I thought, "Oh my gosh. What are these? I am really in a different place." That feeling when you're traveling in a different country or a different culture. That was the first image I had: this was really going to be a different environment.

My freshman year was probably similar to a lot of freshmen: confusing and overwhelming, trying to figure out where I fit in. The history department was fantastic. I had placed out of some of the lower-level classes; I knew I wanted to be a history major. I was in Jack Cell's European History class, one of the only freshman, a small seminar. It was fantastic—reading primary sources, doing primary source research. With upperclassmen, I was absolutely intellectually stimulated. I loved it. Socially I was trying to find my place. I lived in Trent, an all-freshman dorm. I joined a Jewish sorority and went through the initiation and dropped out the next day. I felt so uncomfortable, and I realized it just wasn't something I could be a part of.

Sophomore year I lived in Wilson House, the alternative living situation on East Campus where the nontraditional students lived.

One of the biggest influences on my life growing up in high school was reading the *New York Times*. I loved reading the second page of the *Times*, focused on things going on in the world. My dad was a frustrated history professor—he had wanted to be in the foreign service, had gone to Franklin & Marshall, Phi Beta Kappa, the smartest person I've ever known. He was told at that time that "Jews won't get into the Foreign Service—just forget about it." So he ended up going to medical school. He would work until seven o'clock at night, then we'd have dinner as a family, and he would go back to work at nine o'clock. He worked all the time. We lived about ten minutes from the hospital. But those dinner hours he would quiz us on things going on in the world. We had the *World Book Encyclopedia* sitting in our den off the kitchen, and he would ask us questions. We would get a quarter if we got it right. But if we didn't know the answer, we had to go look it up.

So I grew up with that, and had this feeling that I hadn't blossomed yet. I didn't know who I was going to be or what I was going to become. So sophomore year I took Larry Goodwyn's class, The Insurgent South, in the fall of 1980. He had just started teaching the class. Larry's class was absolutely pivotal in my life. I met two really important people: my future husband, Michael Meredith, and Judy McDade, an anthropology major. I thought she was the most amazing person I had ever met. (Mind you, I was not focused on my future husband at this point.) I had never met anybody like her, and so immediately she was a role model, a self-actualized woman. I ended up reading Sara Evans's *Personal Politics* the second semester with [Professor] Bill Chafe. This was the time of the women's movement, and that's what Judy represented to me. She became one of my best friends and an entree into this group of seniors at Duke. Judy was going into the Peace Corps in Kenya, and I met a lot of other people following different paths that I really respected and was fascinated by.

The relationship that developed between Judy, Larry, and me was all connected. And at the same time I met my husband Michael Meredith, in this class of probably a dozen people. Michael was the only person in the class actually from the South—Charleston. He had only come to the United States five years earlier when he was fourteen years old from New Zealand. Poor Michael, every time that Larry would refer to anything about the South, Michael became the scapegoat or the focus [*laughs*] as the symbolic white southerner in the class. And he would try to say, "Well, you know, Larry, I'm not a southerner. I'm a Kiwi. I'm really from New Zealand." Larry really did not care. He refused to acknowledge that. Michael had gone to Porter-Gaud High School, a historic private school representing aristocratic southern society.

Larry was so revolutionary as a professor in so many different ways. One of the most fundamental was the way he treated his students. I remember when he invited me to have a beer with him at the Student Prince Hofbrau House on Broad Street, where Whole Foods now is. I was just flabbergasted at that concept: to sit down and have a beer with my professor. He told me to call him Larry. That was just turning that whole relationship completely on its head. His ideas about democratic relationships, that's the most fundamental thing. You are empowering your students, you are trying to, as much as you can, put yourself on an equal footing with your students by sitting down and saying, "Let's have a beer, let's talk, I'm interested in what you have to say, I'm interested in getting to know you as a person." That was transformative for me. The other thing was that he would say to me and Judy, "You already know everything. There is nothing that I can teach you." It had very direct consequences for me. It influences the way that I live my life today. I don't think I really knew exactly what he meant at that point. What it did was give me a sense of self-confidence.

Real things that happened as a result of Larry saying that. During that time, the fall of 1980, the verdict [arrived] related to the Greensboro, North Carolina massacre—the year before, in 1979 in November, the Greensboro Massacre. The Klan showed up with guns and opened fire and a number of people were shot and died.[1] There were the allegations of complicity with the police department in Greensboro. There was a video going around of the shooting. I was absolutely blown away when I saw that. I couldn't believe that in our day and age that something like this could happen and people would be found not guilty. The Klansmen were acquitted. There were no charges, no complicity, nothing.

At the same time, in Larry's class, we were studying democratic movements and he was teaching us to question authority. When we were studying the Populist Movement from an academic perspective, the other thing he would tell us all the time: "Remember to always question the lenses of who is saying what. Where is the evidence coming from? Always question your own lenses."

This idea of bias, and protecting power—and beyond that, questioning everything around you, the narratives you're given. So the parallel is the

Greensboro incident. There was a rally. I started taking this video around to the common rooms in the dorms and showing it to people. I especially remember showing it to Black students at Duke and trying to educate people and have conversations about it. In a women's dorm on East Campus, I was showing it to a Black female student, on what's happening and the fact that the Klan still exists and is alive and well in Durham, North Carolina, in 1980. The police came and arrested her in her dorm room because she had a bounced check at the grocery store. That was a shocking experience for me. I helped organize [the rally] because I was now, through Judy, connected to all these seniors who were active on campus. My memory was of walking up to the quad and Larry was speaking. Larry literally handed the microphone to me. It was literally giving me a voice. The rally went on for hours. I ended up being the emcee for the entire rally. I didn't know that I could do something like that. I didn't know that I had something to say. I enjoyed it. All of a sudden I was leading this rally.

It became the catalyst for ongoing events throughout the year. I ended up becoming the point person for a lot of the events around the Greensboro Massacre. We had [antiwar activist] Philip Berrigan speak at Duke. We had [the wife of one of those killed] Marty Nathans come and speak at the chapel. We had members of the Wilmington Ten come.[2] This was really an outgrowth of what I was doing in Larry's class—understanding how you create popular movement or democratic movement. We started trying to do that on the Duke campus around the Greensboro issue. I joined together with Brian Fair, a leader with the Black Student Alliance, the BSA, who was also the Duke student body president. We called a meeting for all organizations on campus who were concerned about social justice. And we had our first meeting in Flowers Lounge and people showed up from all different organizations. We decided to call ourselves United Duke Students, UDS, and our goal was to create an umbrella group of all the organizations on campus concerned with social justice. We were specifically focused on the Greensboro incident. This was happening through the fall of 1980 while I was in Larry's class.

There were students interested in the antinuclear movement during the arms race. There were women on campus who were involved with the Women's International League for Peace and Freedom. The BSA. Some environmental groups were just starting at Duke. These were some of the major groups that were coming. We were having our meetings in the Flowers Lounge. We realized that we didn't have any place to meet. There were only certain hours we could meet there, we had to sign up. It wasn't ideal—it was literally sitting in some hallway. We all of a sudden realized this parallel with what Larry was teaching us. Not only do you have to build a coalition of different groups of people, then you have to create your own space and create your own institutions. So we decided that we needed a place on campus that was run by students, controlled by students, where students could meet and express themselves. That's how we started the idea for the Coffeehouse.

Larry knew about this because I was consulting with him and he was telling me who I needed to talk to. I started meeting with Bill Griffiths, who was the vice president of student affairs, and a few representatives of UDS. We want[ed] something nonalcoholic, just a place of our own. For months I would meet him with a small group. We were told, "We just don't have anything. We just don't know where we can do that."

By the second semester, early 1981, I'm taking Bill Chafe's class, Civilities and Civil Rights. Terry Sanford was [Duke's] president and had something called Breakfast with Terry. You could sign up and have breakfast in the CI with the president. So I signed up. I sat down in the CI with Terry Sanford and told him what we really wanted and that we'd been meeting with Bill Griffiths. He proceeded to tell me all these things that he knew about me: "Well, I know what you're up to, Wendy. You've been doing this, you've been doing that. If we're going to have students plotting the revolution, then we want you to be in our front yard, not in our backyard. So here's the card for the university architect. And you'll get your coffeehouse." [laughs]. And that was it.

The Dope Shops, those were my favorite places, the West Campus Dope Shop and the East Campus Dope Shop—which were the remnants of the old Duke, with the soda fountain and the ladies with the beehive hairdos. I lived in Wilson House on East Campus. Right behind that was the Dope Shop. Often I would go there and study, eat. That was the only place I could get a bagel. I was very familiar with the East Campus Dope Shop. So we met [with the architect] over there with some other students. He says, "Well, we have this storage room." And he opens the door and there's a huge room. There is a big mural on the wall, a collage made out of magazines filling up the whole back wall. It had been made by Duke students in the 1960s when the space had been a coffeehouse. He said, "This space is here, but you have to prove that there's a need for it, because in order for you to use it, we have to make it ADA accessible, we have to put in bathrooms, we need to put in water, but we're not going to put any money into renovating this for you until you can prove the need."

So that spring we had a Coffeehouse two nights a week in the Dope Shop. We had speakers and all kinds of programming in the Coffeehouse. We had to document how many students showed up and prove that there was an interest and the need. And that was the first incarnation of the Coffeehouse.

Before we got permission for the space, a lot of students were at the Nelson Music Room trying to make the case for the Coffeehouse. I was infuriated, because Larry was there and didn't say a word. I was so angry. I thought, "Here's his chance to advocate for us. To speak up for us. And he's just standing there." I can see him in my mind. He is standing against the wall on the left-hand side, standing there and not saying anything. Now I understand why he did that. He did that purposefully. He wanted us to speak up for ourselves. Him being at that meeting and not saying anything was a challenge to me, saying, "I'm not going to get up here and speak for you. You have to speak for yourself. You have to advocate for yourself." It took me a while to understand that.

Over the summer the space was renovated. The Coffeehouse officially started spring of 1981. And then the real opening was in the fall of 1981, in the space that it is now. I changed very dramatically [during this time], and I can say, "My poor parents." [laughing] Because the Wendy of sophomore year of college, as soon as I would get in the car with my parents, would be engaging my father in a conflict about something. Some conversation from Larry Goodwyn's class. My family and my father became the symbol of what Larry called "the received culture." Doing battle with my received culture. I think my dad did read The Populist Moment. It was such a big deal that when I got married in 1989, my father mentioned Larry Goodwyn in his speech at my wedding.

In that context, my father never forgot the first car ride, picking up me from the airport with Michael, my future husband, in the car. I started to launch into some Larry Goodwyn–inspired tirade. Michael intervened and told me to tone down [laughing] my vitriol towards my father. My father decided that he liked Michael. "This is going to be a good influence on Wendy's life." [laughing] This was the story my father told at my wedding. It's part of the internalizing and personalizing the message and the impact it had on me, and my whole way of looking at the world, my relationships. It was that fundamental.

I spent the summer of 1981 in Durham, working at the Salvation Army Thrift Store on East Main Street. I worked two projects, one in the West End of Durham with a Vista project teaching children. At the same time, I ran a summer program with Operation Breakthrough in the Saint Theresa neighborhood, now called Rolling Hills or Southside. Two very poor neighborhoods. It was a big deal that I didn't go home, but [was] imbedded in the community and focusing on poverty and children. [My friend Marcie] came to tell me that Judy had died. It had happened while I was gone—I had missed the funeral because I was away. I was in shock and devastated. She and another good friend, Bennett Johnston, had been working at Yosemite National Park, had gone hiking off-trail. Bennett had slipped, fallen, and was hanging, and Judy had gone to him to help. Instead she fell herself. Bennett had been able to get onto a ledge and stay there for hours until he was rescued. The idea that she died trying to save Bennett. I never had a friend die. She had an incredibly bright future ahead of her, off to the Peace Corps. When I came back to school junior year, I was a different person. I focused on the Coffeehouse but underlying things for me was feeling very depressed. We ended up dedicating the Coffeehouse to Judy. Her family had blown up some pictures she had taken in Kenya, they gave us these beautiful photographs, and we had a plaque saying it was the Judy McDade Coffeehouse. Now the mural the students had made in the 1960s is gone. The photographs are gone, the plaque is gone.

Nineteen eighty-one, 'eighty-two was an exciting time for the Coffeehouse because professors were using it for classes and it also became a place for student activism. I was involved in starting the Central American Solidarity Committee, organizing against US involvement in Central America. The antiapartheid movement started at Duke. The [opposition to the proposed] Nixon-Duke Library. We had [environmentalists], we had the Migrant Farm Workers solidarity work. All of these different groups met in the Coffeehouse. There was all the interrelatedness as well, we all could support each other. There was a community. I lived in a group house by that time on Urban Avenue. Mikel Taylor, a graduate student in anthropology, headed up the antiapartheid movement at Duke. Ruffin Slater led the Nixon-Duke Library effort. We had this sense of community, definitely connected to the Coffeehouse space. [From Larry's classes] I learned that I actually could do those things, that I had the ability, that I enjoyed the process. That gets back to the mantra of Larry. "You already know everything." Then it becomes the process of learning, "What do I know? What is that I know? What is it that I can do? What can I make happen? How can I make change? How can I be the change I want to be?" My life has been a journey related to that.

[At Duke] there was so little support for not going to law school, not going to work on Wall Street, not going to work at some corporation. We created that space and support for students to come together and explore: "What are some other things that I can do with my life when I graduate from Duke, live the kind of life I want to live, and have the type of values that I want to have?" An outgrowth of all of this was that Ruffin Slater went on to start Weaver Street Market and led the fight against the Nixon-Duke Library. Ray Bunnage and David Kirkpatrick, the two of them went on to start Durham's first recycling program, named Sun Shares. And then Grace Nordhoff went on to open Mad Hatter's Bake Shop. They and my future husband Michael bought a house on Wilkerson Avenue right after they graduated for $15,000, each chipped in $3,000. They formed the Wilkerson Partnership, learned how to do plumbing, carpentry, wiring, and they renovated this house. It was a cooperative living arrangement. Everybody called it the WilkerZone.

I went on to become an elementary school teacher. I've lived in a co-housing community. I sent my kids to public schools, been very involved, always been a huge volunteer in the community. I led a neighborhood effort ten years ago to create a park, New Hope Preserve, now named the Hollow Rock Nature Park. Even my reason for becoming a county commissioner, it all comes out of the same values and ways of looking at the world. The way I conduct myself as a county commissioner, the way I try to partner with people, the way I see myself in relationship with people in the community, it is all connected back to Larry Goodwyn and that class.

In the spring of 2015, the Durham Women's Commission had a panel inviting women leaders in the community to come speak about their lives. We were asked to give a few minutes' speech reflecting back on our lives, to share lessons with others on how you got to be where you are. I mentioned Larry Goodwyn. I talked about the comment "You know everything," and I talked about my parents. Those were the people I mentioned.

The last time I saw Larry was in 2008 or 2009. Right after Obama had been elected. I was with [my daughter] Eliza in Target. I ran into him near the concession area. I was excited to introduce him to Eliza, and I filled him in on what I was doing, serving on the Durham Planning Commission and heading up this [New Hope Preserve] Master Plan Committee for Durham County, Durham City, Orange County, Chapel Hill. I told him how I had led this neighborhood effort and we had raised $200,000. He said, "I told you—you already know everything." He just came out with that line again. He said to Eliza, "I always told your mother she knew everything. She already knew everything." He then launched into this analysis of the Obama presidency. In one statement he was able to explain the importance of this moment in time within our entire history. The significance and what it meant and what was so great about Obama and what was going to happen. He had this amazing ability to put things in perspective, make sense of history, provide insight in an accessible and understandable way. And be completely positive and optimistic at the same time. That optimism—he just had not lost it at all. His warmth, his humanity. I have a wonderful last memory of seeing him.

What other people may say about their values and who they really are as people—there's [often] a disconnect. I learned there are people who espouse revolutionary ideas and talk about things like democracy or respect for all people. But then they don't treat people like that in their everyday lives. I experienced this firsthand when I went to China—some experiences with [Duke faculty] that were very devastating. I contrast that with Larry, the way he treated people. His optimism. For me personally there wasn't a contradiction. I think it should be a reminder to teachers [of] the impact they have on students.

## Notes

1. On the Greensboro massacre, see Greensboro Truth and Reconciliation Commission, *Final Report* (Greensboro, NC: Greensboro Truth and Reconciliation Commission, 2006); Sally Avery Bermanzohn, *Through Survivors' Eyes: From the Sixties to the Greensboro Massacre* (Nashville, TN: Vanderbilt University Press, 2003); Signe Waller, *Love and Revolution: A Political Memoir; People's History of the Greensboro Massacre, Its Setting and Aftermath* (Lanham, MD: Rowman & Littlefield, 2012).

2. On the Wilmington Ten, see Kenneth Robert Janken, *The Wilmington Ten: Violence, Injustice, and the Rise of Black Politics in the 1970s* (Chapel Hill: University of North Carolina Press, 2015).

# 12

## "Can I Buy You a Beer?"

### Goodwyn's America

ANDREW NEATHER

As soon I heard the gravelly Texan accent down the phone line, I knew that Larry Goodwyn would be very different from any teacher I'd experienced in England as a Cambridge University undergraduate. And when he asked me, "We'd like to fly you over—can you come next weekend?" I realized this could be a hell of a ride. What I didn't know then was how much Larry would change my view of America, of history, and indeed of who I was, too.

It was early spring 1987; I was twenty-one. I'd applied to Duke University solely because of reading *The Populist Moment* the previous year. I'd never been to America, had only studied its history for one eight-week term, and wasn't even sure I wanted to spend years on a PhD. But I'd been intrigued by Larry's brilliantly counterintuitive history of a radical yet very American insurgency that seemed so at odds with the Reagan years. I also hoped that the US South might offer me a more idiosyncratic window onto modern American life.

Both these instincts were confirmed when I arrived in North Carolina a few weeks later and climbed into Larry's battered red Ford Mustang. We spent what seemed like much of the next few days driving around Durham and sitting in bars, as he attempted to explain to me the tragedy of the American republic and of the South in particular. It was something we did a lot over the ensuing six years.

I was charmed and energized: Larry was unlike anyone I'd ever met. He was refreshingly skeptical about what he dismissively termed "the academy" in general and Duke—"the gothic rockpile"—in particular. He was irreverent about liberal historical shibboleths: "The Progressive Era? Hell, one more progressive era like that and we'll all be on our backs."

And his views seemed as much rooted in actuality as in history: he attempted to explain the racial and social inequalities of the South by driving me around East Durham.

We got lost several times. "We need a beer," Larry declared, pulling up next to a heavily fortified liquor store (the kind with a grille between customer and clerk). Opening our cans of Budweiser back in the car, Larry conceded that it was technically illegal to drive in North Carolina with an open alcohol container. "But I'm from Texas! Of course you drive with a beer between your legs—it's hot!"

The rest of the Duke history faculty seemed pretty laid back too, at least compared to their Cambridge equivalents. Larry took me along to a lunchtime talk by Natalie Zemon Davis, at that point still a leading exponent of the vogue for [Clifford] Geertzian anthropological approaches to history (how long ago it seems). I was surprised that not only a good third of the faculty but the speaker herself were in shorts (it was late April), and at the informality of the discussion afterward. Davis was enthusing about poststructuralist approaches she'd just heard aired at a conference; Larry and others were firmly skeptical in their response.

I went home to England via Harvard, where I also had an offer: it was impossibly stuffy by comparison. I realized I couldn't study with anyone but Larry. So it was that I arrived in New York that August, staying with Larry's son, Wade, in Brooklyn before getting the bus south the next morning. I had almost no money and felt terribly small and alone trying to find my bus in the New York Port Authority that day. The warmth of Larry and Nell's welcome—I lived in Wade's old room at their house for the first week, until I found a place of my own—made me feel a lot better.

What theirs and others' generosity didn't dispel was America's sense of foreignness for me. Britons often tend to assume, because of the shared language and our saturation with American popular culture, that the United States is more familiar and comprehensible than nearer European nations. That's just a surface effect: it isn't. Larry was my greatest guide to the new country, from my puzzlement at drive-through banks to my incredulity when my healthcare package was explained to me. "Welcome to corporate America!" he laughed.

He also set me thinking in earnest about why the United States' history was so different from Britain's. Larry would have objected to being branded an American exceptionalist. Yet while his theories of movements and his belief in popular democracy were universal, Larry did believe there was something special about America: the fact that Americans regard freedom as a right, and the way that belief—that individuals can determine their own destiny—is ultimately what the country stands for. Larry's radical politics stemmed from that tradition: they were organically, unmistakably American.

This is in no sense to downplay the fierceness of Larry's left-wing radicalism. His frustration with liberals sometimes seemed almost greater than his dislike of the Right. He delighted in Jim Hightower's dictum that "there's nothing in the middle of the road but yellow stripes and dead armadillos," dismissing a variety of academic and other institutions as "wall-to-wall liberals." And he was always unequivocal in condemning white southern power especially, calling it what it was: white supremacy.

Yet while Larry acknowledged the Left's debt to Marx—"the great German," as he called him—he never felt much real affinity with Marxists. And he never had much time for the post-structuralist and Marxist cultural theory that I for a while embraced. Partly it was an anticommunism sharpened by his time in Poland and studying Solidarity in the 1980s. But more than that, such theorizing frustrated his empirical and political instincts, both as a historian and as a former journalist and political activist. He was primarily focused on power, money, and local democracy. It was a problem-solving approach that made him more interested in the mechanics of insurgent movements than in simply recovering the past, let alone in historical or theoretical arguments for their own sake.

Despite the injustices of history, he was remarkably uncynical, even when up against a supremely cynical political and economic elite. And he was optimistic: he had faith that democracy and movement building were practically possible, even if they were difficult, the bigger they got. He loathed "You can't fight City Hall" defeatism.

This approach to democracy—more widely, perhaps, to the very potential of the future—was personal as well as political. Larry liked young people and hated the academic establishment's institutional arrogance toward them—"cuffing the young," as he called it. One of his mantras was "Give yourself permission . . ."—to think, to challenge, to take risks, to screw up and start again. It's some of the best advice I've ever had—and when I now share it with twentysomething friends and colleagues, I realize from their expressions how "unsanctioned" (to use a favorite Larry word) such an idea is.

At the same time, this freewheeling style didn't always make Larry the easiest of PhD advisors. His disregard for the conventions of the academy, which I'd found refreshing on arrival, wasn't so helpful later in my graduate career. And his legendary personal disorganization could be infuriating. Not completely flippantly, he justified this politically: his refusal to live and work more tidily was an expression of his anarchic ideals. He was at least consistent in excusing others' personal chaos in this way: indeed he once exclaimed to me of his cute but barely trained sheltie, Travis, "He's all dog!" Travis scarcely knew it, but his erratic toilet habits were a private insurgency against suburban bourgeois manners.

Larry shared his knowledge with me largely via long discussions at his kitchen table—"Sit down, lad!"—or in Durham bars, usually Val's Upstairs on West Main Street, and after its closure the Ninth Street Bar and Grill. But much of the same approach was evident in Larry's undergraduate classes.

He was sometimes provocative—but when he had provoked undergraduates to challenge him, the discussion about the nature of power could begin in earnest. I remember in one seminar toward the end of my first semester watching what looked like the lights going on for several students. "So we're having a democratic discussion here now," said Larry. "How far could we extend that—to the whole building? The whole university? Just how big can a democratic conversation get?"

Which is not to say that Larry was a perfect teacher. In a graduate seminar on social history in my second year, Larry compounded his tendency to talk too much by rashly assigning his history of Polish Solidarity, *Breaking the Barrier*, while still in manuscript. He wasn't ready for criticism of it. After one evening where he'd defended the book without interruption for most of the class, I stopped him in mid-flow, telling him that he was silencing us even as he taught a class about hearing silenced voices. The atmosphere was electric: one fellow graduate told me afterward that she was shaking when I finished speaking.

Larry accepted my challenge with equanimity: he welcomed such conversations about the reality of power. My phone rang within fifteen minutes of getting home that evening: "That was quite a performance, my friend. Can I buy you a beer?" Of course he could: I hurried down to Val's, relieved that we could continue the argument.

Larry simply believed passionately in the radicalism of grassroots democracy, which he knew was potentially the most dangerous and systematic challenge to power. So without any of the tedious nostalgia for the 1960s so common among middle-aged radicals in the 1980s and 1990s, he was always on the lookout for the start of the next movement. During the movement against the drive to war in Iraq, in December 1990, several hundred Duke students staged a march from East Campus to the downtown Durham post office, followed by a "die-in" there, with thirteen arrests. It was an intense and charged moment—the Duke *Chronicle*'s student reporter, standing next to me, was in tears—and an impressive piece of organizing. Larry was riveted: in one photo he stands, cigarette in hand, watching intently as the drama unfolds.

Not that the campaign ultimately did much good: the movement shrank to a hard core of activists as soon as US forces went into action the following month. It didn't do me much good, either: I frittered time organizing and teaching, belatedly settled on a research topic, and eventually completed a sprawling, overambitious PhD dissertation.[1] I couldn't find a job—nobody could really figure out what my specialism was, possibly including me—so I moved to Detroit to work as an in-house journalist for the United Auto Workers, then to a political job back in England and a different career. In the end, even Marxist historians' lives are as messy as history itself. But Larry was always sympathetic to such moves, driven primarily by the imperative of having to make a living: "You need dignity."

Returning to North Carolina the week of Obama's inauguration in 2009, I had lunch with Larry and former fellow graduate student Tim Tyson. Larry, by now carrying around an oxygen tank to manage his emphysema, was electrified by Obama's triumph. Race had always been at the core of Larry's radicalism: he rejoiced in the fundamental challenge a black US president—and a former community organizer, at that—presented to the status quo. He reeled off polling figures and tales of the local grassroots campaign for Obama that he'd been involved in. I remember thinking: *Damn, I hope I'm still as sharp as this when I'm in my eighties.*

A newspaper journalist by now, I covered the next US presidential election from the UK for the *London Evening Standard*. By the time I rose at 5 a.m. on November 7, 2012, to news of Obama's victory over Mitt Romney, I felt more connected to US political debates than I had in years. I felt the pull of the South—and I thought of Larry too. I emailed a mutual friend, who told me: "I don't think he'll last more than a year now. You should come soon."

And so in January 2013, amid the ritual chaos of North Carolina's annual snowstorm, I sat across a bar table from Larry in Durham. In my mind's eye he still has a Bud Light longneck in front of him and a cigarette in his hand, an illusion of memory created only by his undimmed political passion, for as he faced me that day, he was very frail and using his oxygen machine most of the time. Yet he was as sharp and as engaged with the fate of the republic as ever—and as big an Obama fan, despite the president's shortcomings.

Back at his home after lunch, he read with delight an op-ed piece I'd written for the *Standard* in the previous November's election week.[2] There I talked about America's seductive optimism, and about how, the antics of Capitol Hill and the rest aside, I wasn't going to give up on the United States' democratic promise. Those are American lessons that only Larry Goodwyn could have taught me.

## Note

1. Andrew E. Neather, "Popular Republicanism, Americanism, and the Roots of Anti-Communism, 1890–1925" (PhD diss., Duke University, 1994).

2. "For All Its Faults, US Democracy Is Rooted in a Dream," Comment, *London Evening Standard*, November 5, 2012, http://www.standard.co.uk/comment/comment/for-all-its-faults-us-democracy-is-rooted-in-a-dream-8282009.html.

# 13

## Mentoring as Community-Building

THELMA KITHCART

Thelma Kithcart worked between 1972 and 1981 as the administrative assistant of the Oral History Program (OHP). Goodwyn frequently noted that she was essential to the spirit as well as the functioning of the program. The interview took place March 31, 2016, in Durham, NC, with Wesley Hogan.

When I first met Larry, I was working at the bank downstairs in the old Student Union. It was a SunTrust bank, on the Duke campus. A young teller with me, Suzie Boughton, was a very good friend of [Duke history professor] Bill Chafe. So when she heard that they were looking for someone [for the Oral History Program], she mentioned my name. I had met [Bill and Larry] in the bank and so we struck up a friendship and started talking.

When [Larry] really got ready to do the program, he said he wanted me. I explained to him that I didn't have the background. I had gone to school, but I did not finish. I was married and had two of my babies, and I was pregnant with Celena. But he said he wanted to have lunch. So he, Bill, and I met in a cafeteria dining room over on West Campus. The discussion was about the grant that they had just received from the Rockefeller Foundation to develop an Oral History Program, and they were looking for a person to run the office and intermingle with potential graduate students. I told Larry I didn't have the educational background that was required for the job, and he said quite frankly, "You can learn, can't you? You are who I want in this position." I said yes. He said, "Oh, you can do it. I know you can do it. We can send you to school." He made it possible for me to attend Durham Technical Community College.

I started to work part time and started school in the evening. Transcribing was part of what I did in the very beginning—transcribe some of the tapes from Larry and some of his students. I went to Durham Tech, finished the course, and Larry went back to [Duke] Personnel and said, "This is the young lady that I want. Do whatever you have to do to hire her." They talked about titles. He said, "We really don't care what you call her as long as you give her the money that I want her to have." I think they put me in as a Research Technician I or II even though I performed as an administrative assistant because I helped with all the office work.

Then I started to help with the students as they came in when they first started at the [Oral History] Program. Larry and Bill would bring in students—Larry wanted me to be a part of that process. He thought if I couldn't relate to new students, then they didn't need to be in the program. He wanted it to be a multicultural kind of exchange. Primarily he assumed that the Black students and I—we would relate. He wanted to make sure that [non-Black] students were going to be able to relate without having a problem with Black students and with other black people when they went out to interview, because a lot of the places he sent them was dealing primarily with Blacks. They wanted to get this history because most of us had not recorded our history. That was why he thought it was significant. If they could relate to me first, then he thought that they would be okay.

Our students [in the Oral History Program] were sort of separate from the Duke environment. There were a lot of times when we would meet in the office and then we spent too many hours at the Down Under Pub after work. He called it his "unsteepled place of worship." We would talk about everything. At the time, I was also typing his book, *The Populist Moment,* over and over and over again. (It was before computers.) I typed and he would come back to me after reading it on a given day and say he had a paragraph to add. When I got through, that paragraph would be five or six pages. So it all had to be retyped. I dreamed about *The Populist Moment!* It [went on] forever and ever and ever!

Bill Chafe was known as the organizer, bringing people together. Peter Wood was the financial back for us. We all had to keep Larry on target as far as what we needed to do because we had to report back [to Rockefeller]. They wanted to make sure that the monies were spent the way that they were supposed to. It was me, Bill, and Peter Wood who would get Larry to do his part. I would be in the office to help the students along to know what they needed to do in order for us to do what we did. They too were receiving money and they had to get things in on time. It was a multitasking position, and half the time I didn't know what I was doing, but I did it.

People came from all over the country, predominantly Black graduate students, and subsequently it worked out and we became a cohesive group. There were two young ladies that I became friends with, and we took it beyond the campus. Donna Benson is now [professor of history] at Winston Salem State. Donna became my friend. When I left Duke, I went to work for her. She was the interim chancellor at North Carolina Central University. She called me and said, "What are you doing?" I said, "What do you mean what am I doing?" She said, "Well, I got the appointment and I need an administrative assistant." She said, "I want you to come with me." So I did, and I had my first two grandbabies while I was with her.

The other lady was Aingred Dunston, [working in 2016] at Eastern Kentucky University. Aingred was one of the older students. We became friends. After work there was a little place where we would go for happy hour. They watched my children grow up, because when Donna met [my daughter] Celena, she was in the ninth grade and then she graduated and had her first baby and Donna said, "Gee, I can't believe I watched her grow." Those were the two that I really got close to. The others, I was more like a mother or big sister maybe because they were really young. They were right out of undergrad.

There were so many Black students in [the Oral History Program], and some were having a hard time adjusting to being at Duke. The university didn't know what was going on as far as oral history was concerned. The program centered around our Black students. Yet Duke was not receiving them well. In housing, a lot of [our students] stayed off campus because there were problems, especially for the Black young men. Even one of the professors when he first came here said the Duke security was not very friendly. Sometimes they would stop a Black student even though he was a student and would show that he was a student. It was a little difficult. Two or three or maybe four students would talk about that in the office. Most of the time they called me T. "T, so and so happened." Eugene Walker—he was the very first [student in the Oral History Program]—he would come through in the mornings on his way to the library and sit there for a few minutes, and then he would go over to write his dissertation. He would stay in the library for three or four hours and he'd come back through because he had to go home for his children to come home from school. Almost every day he would come through in the morning, say "hello," and then come back through in the afternoon. I was so glad to see him at the [Goodwyn] memorial service. I met his wife and I watched his children. They grew up with my children.

What I learned from Larry was that he was just such a personable person and it taught me a lot for him to say to me, in the very beginning, that it didn't matter whether I had all of the background that they thought I needed. He was willing to give me a chance, and that meant more to me than anything. It really impacted my life, because it was at a time where I was going through changes with my ex-husband who is deceased now. At the time, I was struggling with three children and Larry gave me the opportunity.

Even after I started to work for him at the Oral History Program, I went to cosmetology school. I thought if I'm only going to be working part-time, I'm going to need some more money because I've got three children that I've got to raise. So I went to cosmetology school at night and started to do hair on a part-time basis. After a couple of years, they offered me the full-time position. Even though I finished the cosmetology course, I continued to work. Working with him and typing, I did both.

Some days he would come in from class and I'm typing and he said, "Just wait a minute." Then he would start to talk; it may be [about] the book or what he used to do. He would allow me to share stories about me and my children. He watched my son grow up as a basketball player and he would give me pointers on that. Sometimes of course Junior got difficult, and then he would talk to me about [his children] Wade and Lauren, and some days I would pick [Lauren] up. We just established a friendship. Anytime if I needed to I could say, "Larry, I need to do such and such," and he'd say, "Do what you need to do." We just had a really good relationship.

He would also stop sometimes and ask me what I thought about such and such or one of the students: "Do you think she will be okay or should we do something to help her through this process?" There was one other student who didn't leave. She finished her degree, got her degree, but she had such a difficult time through the process because I think she was on the verge of a breakdown. She pushed on through. He would stop sometimes and just say, "What do you think we need to do?" I can't get into the specifics, but we got her through.

When our relationship really got funny is when they merged the history department [offices]. We were on East and West. The history department main office was in the Allen Building, we were in the Old Chemistry Building, [both] on West Campus. The Oral History Program [eventually] dissolved, but I was kept on. That's when the relationship changed, because there were so many other professors [and] we didn't have that kind of close relationship. [After the whole department moved to East Campus,] one professor I ran into—that's when I had to retire, because he got under my skin. It was not worth it anymore. I was not enjoying what I was doing, so I took early retirement. But I stayed in touch with Larry. And when he retired, he made sure that I was at that retirement party. We stayed in contact. Sometimes he would call and say, "Kithcart, what are you doing? Do you want to go to lunch?" And we would go to lunch. I need a tissue. It's making me cry.

Another time, I was in Target and bumped into Larry, he told me he would come there to walk, after he became ill. He said he could rest on the shopping cart and walk around the store for exercise. He said, "Why don't you join me for a cup of coffee?" and we ended up spending an hour or so catching up on children, and current events. [In 2007–8], he said he wanted to talk about the election. So I said, "Okay, when?" He told me the day and time. We met and he had his chalk and told me how [the election result] was going to happen. We sat in TK Tripps restaurant from twelve p.m. to almost two p.m., and people were walking by like—because it was an odd couple—"What?" We sat there and he explained to me what he thought was going to happen, and it happened! It was really amusing to me, the fact that he wanted to do that and that he had all of his material ready to show me how Obama was going to win.

When [Obama] won, he called and said, "I told you!" I said, "Yes, you did!" I told the kids about that because they thought it was just crazy. They said, "What?" I said, "I'm going to eat lunch with Larry Goodwyn," and I would. He was just a good person to me, and of all the people that I've ever worked with, if I had to pick the best person, it would be him. It would really be him. I enjoyed the relationship that I had. Larry had a tremendous impact on my life, his insight on current events as well as life issues helped me as I worked, went to school, and raised my children. I treasure the wisdom I gathered from our friendship and working relationship.

Oh, we had our moments. When I was doing *The Populist Moment*. He knew when he had stepped over and was pushing. He would make a comment like, "Okay, maybe I need to back up." I have a look. People still talk to me about it now. "When Kithcart gives that look, we know that it's time to back up." He knew: how many more times do you think I'm going to type this before you're done? Enough is enough is enough! I typed that introduction twenty-eight times, and I'm not exaggerating. He would know when it was time to back up and go away. Even though we had a good relationship, we both knew when we were on the other's [nerves], because it happens.

I learned from that time that you don't give up. Even when things look like there is no hope, you can make it through, because I never would have thought five years before I got the job with Larry that I would have been able to accomplish the things that I had as a result of having that job. Not only did I meet all kinds of historians, people from all over the world. Because of the influence that I had, I never would have been able to sit across the table from [historian] John Hope Franklin if I had not met Larry Goodwyn.

John Hope Franklin would come through some days after we got up on East Campus and he'd say, "Thelma, we're going to lunch," and I would go to lunch with him. Do not count yourself out because you think that you're not qualified—because if you keep pushing, you can accomplish all those things.

I keep telling my grandson now who is getting ready to graduate from Virginia Episcopal School. He's an exceptional basketball player, and he had a contract to go to University of Pittsburgh. He signed a letter of intent and will be attending the University of Pittsburgh this fall. Those are the kinds of things that I talk to them about—you've got to hang in.

I don't know how much credence [the Oral History Program alumni] would give to [the program], but I think it had quite an impact. Because he was just there, nudging them along. Most of the time he did not expect them to give him credit for the fact that he was there. I really feel like he had a major impact on all of those students that came through.

Larry was not like anyone else. He acted like "I'm a human being, you're a human being." Immediately he said, "Thelma." It was no "Ms. Kithcart" and "Dr. Goodwyn." "I'm Larry, and this is Bill and this is Peter." Peter Wood, he was the benefactor, but he said, "This is Peter Wood." At the time in that program, it was just so personable because we were a cohesive group and we got along.

That's important to me to be a part of, because it's not that I'm trying to make him be any different than what he was. That's what he was to me.

# 14

## Why Is Your Voice So Small?

ELISE GOLDWASSER

In May 1982, when I was twenty-three years old with a brand-new college degree, Professor Goodwyn and I set off for Boston to dig through primary sources related to his research project on Shays' Rebellion, an agrarian revolt in western Massachusetts in 1786–87. Those days set the tone for our decades-long relationship and illuminated the complexity of a mentorship inevitably damaged by sexism: a mix of miscommunication, understanding, paternalism, and the lopsided power dynamic that can exist between a female student and her male mentor. Our time together highlighted his simultaneous frustration with and generosity toward me, my desire to impress him and learn from him.

There is a lot I don't remember about the trip. I assume that Thelma Kithcart, the history department administrative assistant, must have made the flight arrangements and coordinated our logistics. I don't know if we flew up together. I know we stayed with a family in Jamaica Plain—a couple, a man and a woman, both community organizers. Larry called the couple "young" and I thought they were very worldly at thirty-five. My memory of what we did in Boston is hazy—research time in Houghton Library at Harvard University and local Boston archives. I was on this adventure into new archival territory and unfamiliar emotional landscapes in Boston all because I had shown him a footnote from a primary source in David Szatmary's *Shays' Rebellion: The Making of an Agrarian Insurrection.* Larry implied that I had shown promise as an historian.

My clearest memory of our Massachusetts trip, in a neighborhood bar near our host family's house, is a perfect metaphor of my complicated, messy, and multifaceted relationship with Goodwyn. I think we were there for supper, and their daughter, about six years old, was with us. The bar itself was homey and dimly lit with dark wooden tables. Larry pointed out a huge portrait of John F. Kennedy. He saw a man of Irish descent with a very red nose and said, "That's an alcoholic." And I pointed out that the bar only had a men's bathroom.

We finished off pitchers of beer. My hosts told me that they were impressed that I was able to outdrink everyone. While I don't know what anyone ate for supper, I do remember that during the middle of the second or third pitcher, the woman and I had gotten involved in a political discussion with an undercurrent of clashing perspectives. In a tone that made her daughter upset, we argued about whether race or economic class is a bigger divide when it comes to organizing women. At that point in my life, I was not able to reframe a conversation with someone older and more experienced who pressed her authoritative advantage. I was unable to ask, cowed by her authority, why the question needed to be either/or. I assume, however, that as a southerner, I argued for race as the more intractable barrier.

Later that night, Larry stood outside the men's bathroom so that I could go in. In retrospect, this simple act suggested the much larger roles Larry played in my life. He was my personal gatekeeper to what in the late 1970s and early 1980s was a male-dominated field, he acted as a guardian of the values of the proper place of women and the chivalry of men, and at times he was a genuine caretaker and nurturer.

On occasion, I tried to adopt Larry's characteristic mannerisms, including making blanket declarations of truth that made many uncomfortable, and they failed me miserably. Saying things just because they were true when they were hurtful didn't sit well with me after they came out of my mouth. I did not get positive reactions from my audiences: fellow undergrads, grad students, and adults. Particularly Larry—I felt like I was disappointing him, possibly even failing him, and I could not put my finger on why. I didn't understand at the time that in the sexist environment of the academy, I would be judged negatively for bold, firm statements. At the same time, when I called Larry on his sexism, he did not like it. He preferred that I analyze other aspects of the dominant culture, rather than our personal power dynamic—which was, it goes without saying, quite lopsided in his favor. I felt inauthentic all the while envying my male classmates who, like Larry, could practice this bravado and be rewarded for it, even captivating large groups.

Larry expected me, as a woman, to respond to adverse situations with grace and patience. His sexism typically meant he gave credit and praise to male students while diminishing my contributions. The dynamic went something like this: In the course, I would make a comment. Either Larry would respond dismissively or he would not respond at all. A few minutes later, one of my male classmates would say word for word what I had said. Larry would tell the man how insightful he was. Again, I felt invisible and on the margins, in class with my classmates and even with Larry.

On the other hand, I think of that image of Larry outside the bathroom door is a demonstration of his truly caring, protective side. For the most part, my memories of Larry as a nurturer come from my senior year and the years before graduate school. I have snapshots in my mind of conversations and times he helped me write. There were times Larry defended me from myself. Certain phrases that I use with my own students now stand out in my mind. I remember one time in his West Duke Building office when I was comparing my own uncertainties to the confidence a good friend projected. He told me, "We're all just a pile of jello inside." It never occurred to me to ask if he included himself in that statement, even as I imagined my friend as a puddle of lime green. Or when he told me to read a book by Willie Morris, *North Toward Home*, because my behavior reminded him of his friend's resilience and perspective from the margins. It was reassuring for a twenty-three-year-old to hear him say to me, "You are resilient."

Larry's nurturing and protective side came out most clearly when he helped with my writing. At those times, I felt like we had a body of knowledge to discuss, whether we were editing over the phone or in person. I have a clear memory of sitting on the main floor of West Duke on a bench to work on my essay for graduate school. We took my examples about cooking collards with kosher meat to a different level. As a southern Jew on the margins of southern and Jewish culture in the United States, I had a unique perspective on the study of history. I remember how astonished he was when I pointed out C. Vann Woodward's description of Ben Tillman's patrician good looks. "You think that means something?" he asked me. In second grade, Rabbi Eskowitz taught me that every word in a text has significance. I explained to Larry what I imagined was Woodward's implication—that being good-looking gave Tillman extra power, and being patrician set the standard of what was good looking and therefore deserving of extra privilege.

One of my other significant memories of writing with Larry was the semester before I started graduate school in the history department at Duke. I was taking two classes at UNC. I felt out of my league. None of the readings dealt with power struggles head-on, the way I had encountered them in my history classes as an undergrad. I remember calling Larry in tears and then showing up at his house to pet [his dog] Zoey or his office to rewrite what I thought were the most disastrous essays of my life. He reassured me that I was not losing my mind even as I read *Marxism and Literature* by Raymond Williams or essays by Peter Gay, neither of which showed me what I wanted about how to craft arguments about images of race and empire in popular culture.

The last time that Larry and I engaged productively over my own writing was when I took his Oral History seminar as a graduate student. My topic was the immigrant Muslim community of Durham in the late 1980s. I interviewed people from several countries and continents whose work ranged from blue collar to white collar. I read immigrant and labor histories, a novel that Larry suggested, Henry Roth's *Call It Sleep*, and found that what I learned about the Muslim immigrants in Durham turned the dominant paradigm of assimilation on its head.

He told me that he was very happy with my argument and my ability to marshal evidence in that work. I was pleased that I figured out how to write about a multicultural community without a male-normative framework by using women and men equally as models for adulthood. I wrote, for example, about how pregnant adults do not fast during Ramadan, without making pregnancy only a women's issue.

There is always another turn, though, and there were times that, as a young woman in an environment full of implicit sexism, I was still looking to Larry, who did not appear to be aware of his own contributions to the situation in our department, for support even as I challenged his perception of what he called the dominant culture in my research. For example, he was not pleased with the slide show I presented to our Oral History class as practice for an American Studies Association conference. He didn't have many comments about the Grand Ethnological Congress (Barnum & Bailey, 1895) or the Pilgrimage to Mecca (Sells Brothers, 1893.) He agreed with my analysis of the racist images. Where we clashed was over only one slide in particular that hit too close to home for him. I showed a poster from the 1913 Ringling Brothers' presentation of pale harem girls, acrobats and equestrians from the Great Balkani Troupe. When I pointed out that in the center of the poster, the harem girl with a handful of throwing knives standing above a man who looked exactly like her just with a beard. While she was aiming at a target, I traced the lines how if she dropped her knife, she would castrate the man. "I don't see it," Larry growled at me. "Sir, do you want me to show you with a yardstick instead of a ruler?" I asked him.

That was the end of the exchange, and I moved on to the next slide of "Oriental Splendor."

There were times, however, when Larry thought I was useful. I taught him, for example, that copying a chapter from the end to the beginning is the most expedient way to use a Xerox machine. I found his reading or distance glasses, whichever ones were under papers on his desk and not on his face. Plus, he indicated that my perspective from the margins—Jew, socially awkward, southerner, opinionated—was helpful to him in understanding what was happening in his classrooms and in certain areas of campus culture.

He asked me questions about students in groups and as individuals. I could explain to him what was going on with different organizations on campus, and I had opinions about how the dynamics between them worked. In these situations I was articulate, concise and clear, in my element, not trying to prove myself in a male academic contact. In other situations I was not poised or sophisticated or witty or clever. I fumphered.

Often Larry asked me about pretty young women's personalities. Once he asked about a certain group of young women and commented that he thought they had "built their own corporation" by espousing radical beliefs and simultaneously establishing an exclusive hierarchy in their clique. I never felt like one of the pretty young women.

I didn't know what to call Larry. Usually I settled for "Sir" and others times "you." Never Larry. He did not call me "comrade" or "lass" or "Elise." I think that I too was "you." Particularly painful was that I could not explain clearly to him that my interest in the Middle East expanded to studying visual images of Arabs and harem girls and their relationship to empire. To me, the meaning was clear and it was inherently political according to the Goodwyn definition. I applied analytical skills I developed under him to a body of knowledge that was important to me and alien to him. I felt like a failure in his eyes, even though I knew I was onto something important. And yet because we had our history, I asked Larry to write one of my recommendations for a PhD program. He did not submit it. I do not know if he forgot, or if he did not want to write it and did not tell me to find someone else. I never asked him why. Again, my desire for his attention was so fierce that I could not bear knowing either that he forgot or he didn't want to support me. As a grad student, I was scared to call Larry at home. As I rang him by phone, my heart beat hard enough for me to hear it in my ears. I worried that he would be angry that I had called and then my cascade of talking too fast and not explaining what I needed would start.

When I was young, in many ways I did not do a good job of resolving issues with Larry. I have a litany of regrets about my relationship with him. I wish that I had called him, gone to visit, introduced him to my daughter, let them sit oxygen tank to oxygen tank as they discussed politics across the generational chasm. I was afraid that he did not remember me, even though every day when I walked into my building on campus, I wondered if he was still alive.

The last time I know that I saw Larry was over the summer of 1999 or 2000. At first I didn't know if he knew who I was. I introduced myself to his graduate student and told Larry that if he had quit smoking, I wanted him to meet my daughter. She had cystic fibrosis, so I didn't want her around his cigarettes. (Again, all in one fast breath, unsure if he got my entire meaning or knew what CF was.) "I quit cold turkey," he said. But I have an image of Larry with an oxygen tank and a nasal cannula. So maybe I did see him again. I don't know if I did see him with it or if I imagined him with it after one of my classmates told me how sick Larry was. I think my thoughts were that the tank would scare my preschool daughter. (Little did I know how soon Corey would need her own oxygen tank and nasal cannula.) I am sad that Corey and Larry did not meet. He would have appreciated that even by age ten she was feisty, articulate, and able to read political situations in a very sophisticated way. I think she would have helped him understand millennials and the LGBTQ movement from personal and systematic perspectives.

Today I have a stronger sense of self than I had in graduate school, and I trust my intuition more. I am willing to disagree in a polite and firm manner. ("Well, I don't see it that way.") I know how to share what is important and let what is not important drop from the conversation. I know that it is okay to express anger to someone who matters to me.

Now it's 2015 and I'm looking at the door to my office in the Sanford School of Public Policy. In comes one of my students for office hours. Larry is hovering above my desk. I hear his craggy voice as I pepper the student with questions, "What do you mean by this?" "Why is it in passive voice?" "What are you trying to say?" "How can you make this sentence clearer?" Along with Larry's staccato is my own smoother, quieter rhythm: "I understand why you want these two lines in your personal statement/cover letter/ resume. I suggest you write one version with 'dismantling the patriarchy and disrupting the racist, capitalistic culture.' And then you keep another version where you leave out those two lines, depending on where you plan to apply."

It is obvious to me that these conversations start out about grammar and wind around to forays into students' personal aspirations and their own emotional landscapes. Such vital exchanges are part of the legacy Larry left me. I raise my head and look at this student: "That whole section is in passive voice and you're using a subterranean thought process that you can fix with a better topic sentence." And here we are, the three of us—-Larry's essence and my colored markers, just no cigarettes and none of his sexist attitudes. I don't mean to conjure him, but Larry is suspended over this scene, like brides in a Chagall painting. He seared himself in my critical consciousness. Now I pass this inheritance of listening, challenging, and writing to another generation.

## Addendum

I have developed a set of loose rules based on what Larry did well and did not do well as my mentor:

Let students know they are not bothering you or if you are not available.

Tell students what you want them to call you.

Let students know you see and hear them as individuals, not just as a mass in the classroom.

Respond quickly to email and voice mail messages.

Take time with documents.

Be meticulous word by word.

Tell stories about your own struggles/being vulnerable.

Ask students if you are repeating a story you've told already.

Raise your voice only if necessary.

There are several colorful phrases I appropriated from Larry that I use to discuss writing with my students. These are some of my favorites.

How did you parachute that in from Mars?

No more subterranean thought process. (What I teach students as a remedy is a topic sentence that moves an argument forward.)

You know more about this topic than anyone else does.

Why is your voice so small?

# 15

# From the Bottom of the Mud Hole

CHARLES C. BOLTON

I got to know Larry Goodwyn by pure chance. I entered the Duke PhD program in 1984 as undoubtedly one of the greener students ever enrolled. I knew little about the Department of History's truly excellent faculty. When I went for my first advising session with the director of graduate studies, Russian historian Warren Lerner, he asked me what I wanted to take. "I don't know. Can you tell me more about some of these classes?" A bit exasperated at my lack of preparation, Professor Lerner dutifully went down the list of courses. He got to Larry's Oral History Seminar: "Goodwyn is kind of a maverick." I immediately selected the class, not even really sure what oral history was. I quickly learned, however, that Goodwyn was one of the modern pioneers of oral history methodology, and in the early 1970s he had started an innovative oral history program at Duke that sought to bring together Black and white graduate students to work on the history of southern race relations and the civil rights movement.

The first lesson I learned from Larry came during the opening weeks of that yearlong oral history seminar: he helped me recognize an attribute about myself that I already possessed but had not really understood. Larry had us interview each other in class and then report back to the group on the biography of the person we interviewed. None of Larry's classes ever came with anything resembling a syllabus, but I believe he used this exercise not only to help us hone our listening skills but also to get us to think about how we represented another person's story. For this in-class training exercise, I paired with a student from California; I grew up in south Mississippi, and as the only white student from the Deep South in the class, I remained self-conscious (even embarrassed) about my home state and its history. In my mind, I found myself sitting in the Allen Building's stately Boyd Seminar Room with students who seemed to have much better pedigrees than me, and with perhaps less suspect backgrounds. In our conversation, I tried to convey to my interview partner some sense of my home place and what I saw while growing up there in the 1970s, including something of the complexities surrounding the changes and continuities in race relations. My colleague's report on my story, however, seemed to bear little resemblance to what I told him—indeed, to me, his presentation came through as something of a cross between *Birth of a Nation* and *Deliverance*. This account disturbed me, but I offered a fairly timid rebuttal.

Larry, however, sensed that the episode had bothered me, and about a week later we had a long discussion about it—over a couple of beers at Val's Upstairs on West Main Street, of course. Larry told me that the student who interviewed me, because of his own background, did not know how to get beyond a condescending characterization of my narrative. He also pointed out that, precisely because of where I had come from, I would likely not have that problem. "Bolton," he said, "you've come from the bottom of the mud hole; it's very hard for you to condescend to other folks. And that is one of your strengths. Not just as a person but as a historian."

That conversation transformed my outlook and bolstered my confidence. I began to trust my judgment about what was important about the past, even when others disagreed. In an Old South class I took the following year, I decided to do a research paper on poor whites in North Carolina, even though my professor told me he doubted I could learn anything about "those people." He (and pretty much all historians at the time) referred to them simply as "poor white trash": they were lazy, no-good, drunkards, beyond the pale. That sounded like one of those condescending characterizations, and I resolved to see what evidence of these people actually existed. As it turned out, the poorest group of whites in the antebellum South did leave behind a fairly limited documentary record, but enough remained to construct a story of actual human beings that moved beyond the oft-repeated but never-proved caricatures.

I discovered that the impoverishment of many of these white southerners stemmed largely from the fact that their work had little value in an economy that relied primarily on the forced labor of African Americans. Despite the claims of southern proslavery advocates, the bondage of Black people did not ensure the economic independence of all white men. That class research project became my dissertation, and my first book, *Poor Whites of the Antebellum South*. Larry became my mentor for the project.

Even though he had no particular expertise on the antebellum South, he remained open to the idea that I should search for evidence on a topic that few had bothered to explore.

After leaving Duke, I returned to my old stomping grounds and took a job directing the oral history center at the University of Southern Mississippi, a job I held for ten years. Other lessons I learned in that yearlong oral history seminar profoundly shaped how I ran the oral history center and how I used oral history in my own research and writing. Larry required that all students in his oral history class, no matter what their specific project, get oral sources from among both Blacks and whites (a nonnegotiable requirement), even as he preached how a difference in the race of interviewer and interviewee would affect and shape the outcome of our conversations.

The first interview I ever conducted certainly confirmed his insights. My topic was school integration in Durham. Terrified of having to talk to anyone, never having done an oral history, I initially focused on the tried-and-true method of archival research. During my labors, however, as I had to get oral sources, I searched for potential interviewees, and I ranked them in what I thought would be some kind of order of difficulty.

I placed my Black sources at the bottom of my list. Better to start with the white folks. More specifically, I began with a white woman whom I had identified in my search of local newspapers and school board records as the most progressive white person involved in the Durham school integration process. After I arrived at her house, a mansion in one of Durham's toniest neighborhoods, I set up my equipment, but before I could ask my first question, she had one for me, "Where are you from?" I replied with the only answer I could give, "Mississippi." She said, "Oh, well, you know how things are," and then she proceeded to offer a narrative of Durham's school integration that would have made members of the white massive resistance crowd proud.

She freely admitted that she had favored the maintenance of segregated education because she believed that Black students had "inferior" intelligence and "could not keep up" with the white children. She indicated that she had supported changes to Durham's education system only when forced by the federal courts to act. Even then, she and the other white board members had focused not on dismantling segregation but on limiting the impact of any changes for the white children of the school district.

After the interview, I immediately drove to Larry's house. As I recounted my encounter to him, I told him that I thought I had somehow tricked this woman into telling me things she would not normally have discussed.

Larry pointed out that I had merely told her where I was from; she made assumptions about that information that affected how she shaped her story.

Larry reminded me that an interviewee's perception of me would always profoundly affect the testimony I gathered; at the same time, anticipating the exact nature of those opinions would remain virtually impossible. He also pointed out that her reading of me based on the simple fact of where I was raised allowed me to gain insights into her position on Durham race relations that would not have been possible had one of my white colleagues from New York or California, not to mention a Black student, conducted the interview. Needless to say, this interview with the "progressive" white woman dramatically reordered my understanding of the story of Durham, North Carolina's, school integration.

When I returned to Mississippi, the question the woman from Durham asked me in my first interview—"Where are you from?"—would be repeated numerous times as I interviewed Mississippians, both Black and white. After initial greetings, that question often emerged as the first words out of the mouths of the informants I visited. I always remained unsure whether the knowledge that I was a fellow Mississippian conveyed trust or wariness or some other attitude, although I knew that the meanings my interviewees took from my answer varied as much as their individual histories and personalities. The people I interviewed also made a whole variety of other assumptions based on the knowledge that I was a college professor, was white, was a man, and on and on. Each encounter created a unique memory of the past, something I first learned in Larry's oral history seminar.

Larry also showed me the importance of utilizing oral history to understand the twentieth-century South. As Larry often emphasized, because of the racial caste system that existed in the region for much of the century, the written record preserved tended to reflect a white perspective. Collecting oral memoirs from Black southerners provided a chance to somewhat equalize the documentary record. And it turns out that the Black account of much of this history did not just differ from the perspective offered by white observers, but in many cases, as Larry would say, it remained "wildly different."

That insight became important as I worked on my second book project, a study of the battle over school integration in Mississippi. Among the many conflicting accounts of the history I uncovered as a result of the biracial interviews I collected for this project was how communities perceived the transformation to integrated schools that occurred around 1970. The written record did not contain key parts of this story. Local newspapers, most owned by whites, generally just bemoaned the fact that the federal government forced school integration on Mississippi, conveniently ignoring the role Black protest played in the transformation. The minutes of local school boards, administratively obtuse to begin with, typically explained only how local, almost always white, school officials made the necessary changes to follow the directives of the federal government.

Overall, white sources tended to suggest that school integration would never work because the federal government imposed an unwanted change on the state. Interviews with Black informants revealed a much more important reason for the difficulties surrounding the implementation of school integration in the state. To actually achieve integrated schools, whites needed to share power with Blacks in making decisions about how communities would move from dual schools to unitary school systems. Despite Black efforts to contribute to those discussions, in almost every case, whites made all the judgments, typically in ways that barely satisfied the letter of the new federal laws—and that rarely embraced the spirit behind the Black struggle to eliminate segregated schools. As a result, achieving school integration in Mississippi proved exceedingly difficult, and for Blacks it came with a cost in terms of a loss of employment for Black teachers and principals, a loss of control over Black education, and in some cases a loss of extremely important community institutions.

The final lesson I learned from Larry was perhaps the most important: he was a generous and supportive mentor, a trait I have tried to emulate with my own students. I remember him spending hours—many hours—talking with me about something I had written. He would always acknowledge at the outset that it "was my work" and I needed to write "what I wanted to say," but then he would give his critical and typically brilliant suggestions about how "to make it better," both the content and the prose.

Larry took his role as mentor so seriously because he believed that the young represented likely agents of change in any society, an insight no doubt gleaned from his analysis of a variety of social movements. He understood that his interactions with his students offered an opportunity to transform their lives and, in the process, reshape the future.

His classes often seemed an exercise in deliberate chaos, as if he were continually searching for the best way to shake us free of the "received wisdom" we carried into class. If he could accomplish that feat, he could get us to look at the past in ways we had not yet imagined; to understand the dynamics of power, class, and race; to appreciate the struggles people had always waged for principles such as democracy and justice; and perhaps inspire us to act in the present. For Larry, this work as teacher and mentor represented the essence of what he did, a belief that no doubt placed limits on how much he could produce as a historian. On more than one occasion, I recall Larry summing up the nature of his job by simply stating: "I get paid to talk to young people." Larry's many students were the beneficiaries of those conversations (in class and beyond), which were intense, and indeed often transformative.

Not long before Larry died, I went with Jim Bissett—another of Larry's students, now a professor at Elon University—to Durham to have lunch with Larry and Nell. After lunch, Larry and Jim and I sat talking around that tiny table in his kitchen where all those discussions about "my work" had taken place years ago. Just as thirty years earlier, various papers and books cluttered the table. As Jim and I started to leave, Larry dug through the pile and found an article evaluating the Obama administration. The piece was "seriously flawed," Larry said, and he gave us the citation and invited us to take a look and let him know what we thought. Basically, he gave us some homework.

# 16

## Goodwyn 101

SCOTT ELLSWORTH

It all began, late one afternoon, with beer.

A lot of beer.

As a Texan, Larry was, of course, well familiar with the stuff. It had been the preferred lubricant during his poker playing college days in the early 1950s, and it is what one drank after a long day on the campaign trail canvassing for Ralph or Don Yarborough or other liberal Democrat candidates in Seguin, San Angelo, or Port Arthur a decade later.

More important, during his years at the *Texas Observer* in Austin, Larry had been a regular at what was arguably the greatest bar in the Lone Star State, Scholz's beer garden. The Germans, of course, had brought beer—and accordions, and abolitionist sentiments—to the Hill Country in the years before the Civil War. But it was at Scholz's, which was established in 1866, that Texas beer hall democracy would eventually soar the highest.

Almost everyone went to Scholz's.

Your friends, your enemies, the cigar-chomping boys from the back room, union organizers, loose-fingered lobbyists, burned-out political hacks, LBJ partisans, bone-dry cattlemen, wide-eyed wildcatters, former Dixiecrats, and future SDSers. Here, amid endlessly flowing taps and clouds of cigarette smoke, was where the great issues of the day—Coke Stevenson's campaign for the US Senate, the Civil Rights Act of 1964, whether the Longhorns had a prayer against the Sooners on Saturday—were parsed and dissected, debated and run ragged. Here, beneath the shadow of the state capitol, was the Texas version of Parisian streetcorner cafes, Munich beer halls, the blue-collar pubs of the Industrial Revolution in *The Making of the English Working Class*. Larry knew it well.

That afternoon, however, we were a long ways from Scholz's.

Instead, Larry and I were sitting at a table in a nondescript, and now long gone, basement bar—called, depending on which of its two signs you believed, either the Student Prince or the Hofbrau House—located in a small strip mall across the street from the East Campus of Duke. Knots of students gathered in nearby booths, huddled over frosty mugs of Budweiser and baskets of potato chips, while the jukebox churned out the latest hits from this, the last weekend of the summer of 1976. Carter and Ford were neck and neck in the presidential election polls, Soweto had exploded, the Bicentennial had come and gone, and *Rocky* and *Taxi Driver* were cleaning up at the box office.

Larry, meanwhile, was in fine form.

"I'll buy, and you fly!" he'd announce.

Then he'd peel off another five from his wallet for a fresh pitcher. Our other companion, Marcellus Barksdale, a third-year history graduate student and a Morehouse grad, was equally happy. Marcellus had just returned from doing interviews in Monroe, North Carolina, a onetime Ku Klux Klan hotbed that was also the home of Robert F. Williams, a World War II vet who urged African Americans to arm themselves during the civil rights days. But he also talked about how local Blacks would cruise the main drag in town in pickup trucks and muscle cars. "Man, in Monroe, even the Blacks are rednecks!" Marcellus said, sending Larry into a fit of laughter.

I, on the other hand, wasn't feeling quite so chipper.

While I had arrived in Durham only two weeks earlier, I had already concluded that I had likely made a huge mistake in deciding to attend graduate school. I'd picked Duke, sight unseen, on the recommendation of Herbert Gutman, a New York–based social historian who was about to rattle the worldview of both the American historical establishment and Washington-based policy wonks with his new book, *The Black Family in Slavery and Freedom, 1750–1925*. John Strawn, my undergraduate advisor at Reed College, was a Gutman PhD student. And when Strawn asked him where a student interested in studying southern race relations should go to grad school, Gutman pointed squarely at Larry Goodwyn and the Oral History Program at Duke. I applied, and got in.

Only now I was having second thoughts.

My first meeting with the chair of the history department had been less than encouraging. And the handful of graduate students whom I'd met seemed mainly interested in how this or that professor behaved, how many books you had to read in one class or another, how many essays Dr.

So-and-so assigned, and how such and such a historian was now passé. It was as if studying history was a job to be endured. Nowhere, at least at first, did I detect much passion for history for its own sake. Only that, as it turned out, was about to change.

While the jukebox rambled on and the beer continued to flow, Marcellus and Larry and I started to get to know each other a little better. We talked about the civil rights movement and how its story needed to be told, and we talked about slavery and lynchings and race riots, and we talked about Elvis and Memphis and rock 'n' roll. Suddenly Duke was looking a whole lot better.

Then it happened.

Somewhere along the line, I made an offhand comment about race relations in mid-twentieth-century America. Something like "After all, life was much better for Blacks in the North than it was in the South." It was as if I'd just shot one of the barmaids. Larry and Marcellus jumped on me immediately.

"No, no, no—"

"What are you talking about?"

I gamely tried to defend my position, one that was accepted as the gospel truth by white folks in the West as it was in the North. I brought up the Great Migration and the Second Great Migration, Jim Crow buses and Jim Crow drinking fountains, Pitchfork Ben Tillman and Theodore G. Bilbo. But it didn't matter. As they countered with abundant evidence of their own, it was soon clear that I was cooked. Larry and Marcellus carried the day, and I quickly folded my tent. But in that moment, my world had suddenly shifted. I had a *whole lot* to learn about the South, and I had finally found the passion that I'd been looking for. Here, in this basement bar, with the Allman Brothers and James Brown blaring from the jukebox, was history that mattered.

An hour or so later, the still rollicking conversation moved to the Goodwyn family home on Welcome Drive—and to a cacophony of kids, dogs, a blaring TV, and a hungry Siamese cat walking in circles on top of the refrigerator.

"Hi, Scott," Larry's wife Nell greeted me in the kitchen.

Then she handed me a paring knife and a bowlful of potatoes. "Would you mind peeling these?" Dinner, more beer and more talk followed, as did the appearance of Bill Chafe, the co-director of the Oral History Program. I don't think I got home until after midnight, incredibly happy but also bombed out of my gourd. And while I didn't know it yet, I'd found what would be my home away from home for the next thirty-seven years.

A couple of days later, classes began.

Only it didn't matter. For my education had already begun.

To say that Larry Goodwyn was a breath of fresh air compared to most American historians during the middle of the 1970s is an understatement of massive proportions. Clear writing and provocative historical insights aside, it was also the way that he engaged young people, especially students, and encouraged them to find their own voices.

Part of it had to do with his personality. Lively and engaged, boisterous and direct, when Larry was on, he was not easily ignored. But another part had to do with the particulars of his background, which both informed his arguments and armed his debates in uncommon ways. To put it bluntly, there wasn't anyone quite like him.

To begin with, Larry was a southerner.

True, he had been born in Arizona, he'd lived in Hawaii briefly as a child, and he was once squired around New York City as the next big-deal American novelist. But he was raised in a southern home and spent nearly his entire life below the Mason-Dixon Line. It both confounded northern liberals and raised the blood pressure of white southern conservatives, but it gave added weight to his insights. It was also completely authentic. For Larry, the South wasn't some exotic place of study. It was home.

Some parts he knew exceedingly well. As a teenager living in San Antonio, he had schooled himself on Confederate military history, carefully poring over all three volumes of Douglas Southall Freeman's *Lee's Lieutenants: A Study in Command.* Taken with Freeman's work as an undergraduate at Texas A&M, he wrote a paper on *Lee's Lieutenants,* for which he received an A. Larry's roommate, one of the other handful of English majors on campus, however, got a B on his essay and went to their professor to complain.

"But Larry didn't even follow the assignment!" the roommate said. "We were supposed to write about an American novelist. Not about a bunch of Civil War generals!"

"I know," the professor replied. "But it was a really *great* paper."

There was more to his southern identity than that. Throughout his life, Larry always rooted for southern sports teams—the Washington Senators, Dallas Cowboys, Atlanta Braves, the Duke Blue Devils—while his everyday speech was peppered with more than a few southern fried expressions. "It beats poking yourself in the eye with a sharp stick." "She'll do to ride the river with." "That's a bird's nest lying on the ground."

That said, his South was anything but sacrosanct. His own father, a Georgia-born career US Army officer, was no apologist for Dixie ways and means. "Southerners act the way they do," he'd tell Larry and his siblings, "because they don't know any better." Even as a young man, Goodwyn's critical eye was far more attuned than those of many of his contemporaries. He once told me about a spur-of-the-moment car trip one night to Appomattox in the company of some other young southern writers, including Willie Morris and William Styron. Fueled by whiskey and maudlin sentimentality, some made teary-eyed toasts to the soldiers of the Lost Cause. Larry didn't. He thought it was all a load of crap.

Being a Texan helped to mold Larry in other ways as well. Parts of Texas are most definitely southern, other parts are not. During his years in Austin, he and Nell and their children literally lived on the dividing line between the two. At their house on Rabb Road, Larry managed to successfully plant a magnolia, that most southern of trees, by drilling into the limestone with an electric drill. But only a couple of miles to the west, the western-feeling Hill Country began. It was on this edge that Larry found freedom, first in liberal Democratic politics, then the *Observer,* the Movement, and the Texas Coalition.

By the time that he launched his second career as a historian, Larry was already a seasoned political operative. He knew that political movements did not arise because an intellectual gave a speech somewhere, or the time was "right," or some other ethereal causation. Rather, he knew that movements, like successful political campaigns, were the result of people doing hard, often repetitive, and sometimes mundane work. When Ralph Yarbrough campaigned in small Texas towns in the 1950s, Larry was one of Yarbrough's staffers who would stand behind the candidate, with a pencil and pad of paper in hand, writing down the name of every person Yarborough met. Those names would then be added to the campaign's mailing and phone lists, and, in time, there would be follow-up letters and calls. In the campaigns of Larry's youth, votes didn't simply appear. They were earned, by hard work, one at a time.

Texas gave Larry the impetus to go against the grain. For as much as the dominant forces in Lone Star State politics tilted toward unabashed conservatism, the folk culture has always celebrated rugged individualism—from the genre-mixing Western Swing music of Bob Wills to the boom-or-bust exploits of oil field wildcatters.

Other forces shaped him as well.

As the son of a career army officer, he had an unceasing work ethic, a belief in the concept of the loyal opposition, and an innate sense of purpose. He was fine with both the Beat Generation and the counterculture, but signed up for neither one. And despite the fact that he's considered by many to be a radical theorist, he was never estranged from mainstream American culture. Indeed, it often empowered his writing, giving it a riveting common touch, particularly in *Democratic Promise*, but never more potently than in "Wonder and Glory in Another Century," a personal essay that he wrote about Texas football for *Southern Exposure*. Late in his career, his writings—especially his essays—were largely aimed at social theorists, political activists, and other intellectuals, but he could always connect with regular folks as well. And nowhere, perhaps, did he do so better than in the spring of 1981.

The issue was Richard Nixon.

Earlier that year, the administration at Duke had announced plans to bring the Richard M. Nixon Presidential Library and Museum to Duke. Nixon had graduated from the Duke law school in 1937, and the university president argued that Nixon's papers would provide an unprecedented treasure trove of material. Larry didn't buy it. Nor did a handful of other historians and political scientists on campus, who launched a countercampaign against having the Nixon library come to campus. Larry was a master strategist and the campaign's most effective spokesman.

In front of the Watergate Hotel in Washington, DC, later that year at a portable podium hastily set up in front of the scene of the Nixon Administration's most infamous crime, with the wind blowing in his hair and a handful of his former students—me included—Larry spoke eloquently and powerfully while Associated Press and UPI cameramen shot roll after roll of film. It was an inspiring performance, a true shining moment. The next day, Larry's photo appeared in newspapers from coast to coast.

It was also the tipping point. A few weeks later it was announced that the Nixon library wouldn't be coming to Duke.

In the long run, Larry will no doubt be remembered best for his writings. That is how it should be. But he sure shone in the classroom as well. His classes, to say the least, were oftentimes exercises in organized chaos. Course syllabi, often abandoned entirely, were merely helpful hints at best. Larry had a casual relationship to when his classes were actually scheduled to begin and end. During my first year at Duke, one of Larry's recitations was suddenly interrupted by an undergraduate named John Gallalee, who noisily shoved his chair away from the conference table, stood up, and started to collect his belongings. Everyone, including Larry, stopped dead in our tracks and looked at the student.

"I've heard it all before," he said. Then he walked out of class.

Sixteen years later when my wife, Betsy, enrolled in the graduate history program at Duke, there was a repeat performance. Only this time, a group of students from the Oral History Seminar, tired of hearing Larry repeat the same lessons, began holding their own alternative class sessions, held at the same time as the regular class. Larry, to his credit, loved it.

What kept all of us, John Gallalee included, coming back for more were the classes themselves, which, more often than not, were nothing short of dazzling examinations of American culture, politics, power, and race. When Larry was on, which was most of the time, the class discussions felt as if the very future of the nation depended on their outcome. Shibboleths fell, consciousness expanded, and new insights suddenly popped up like desert wildflowers after a sudden rain. Larry was a brilliant interpreter of the American experience, one who was both unfettered by tradition and unafraid to reach for the stars.

Not surprisingly, Larry's classes eventually got so popular that they would immediately fill to capacity as soon as registration opened. Nonetheless, every semester, determined undergraduates kept trying and trying to get in, only to be turned away—usually by Larry himself. A sophomore named Jane Vessels, not so easily swayed, caught Larry in his office. Late one afternoon in the early 1970s, she forcefully made her case. She was extremely interested in Reconstruction, she said, and really, *really* wanted to take his class.

Only Larry didn't say anything.

Plus, she added, like Larry, she too was a journalist—for the Duke *Chronicle*.

Still no response.

Finally she played her trump card. Only last year, she added, she had taken a Latin American literature course, one that used fiction to help explain and illustrate history.

Nada, zip, nothing. She was beat and she knew it.

Then Larry suddenly piped up.

"Did you say your last name was Vessels?" he asked.

"Yes."

"Are you related to Billy Dale Vessels?"

"Um, yes."

"The Billy Dale Vessels who won the Heisman Trophy at OU in 1952?"

"Yes," she said. "He's my dad."

But by then Larry was gazing up at the ceiling, lost in the world of University of Texas football more than two decades earlier. "At the Cotton Bowl in Dallas in 1950," he said, "he absolutely killed us. With three minutes to go in the fourth quarter, he pulled off one of the most breathtaking eleven-yard touchdown runs that I have ever seen. It was pure poetry in motion. The Longhorns lost, fourteen to thirteen."

Vessels stood there for a minute or two, uncertain what to say or do.

Then Larry finally looked up. "See you in class on Thursday."

Part of Larry's appeal as a teacher was his energy and his unpredictability, but being unafraid to tackle big issues head on was also important. A master of the grand statement and the sweeping gesture, he loved to lob verbal bombshells at the beginning of class. "The Democratic Party is a totally owned subsidiary of corporate America." "The United States is the most democratic nation on earth." "The problem with Black nationalism is that it doesn't work." "All whites are white supremacists." Whether the statement was true or not was immaterial.

As a reader of student essays, dissertations, and book manuscripts, he was both a hard taskmaster and an exceeding insightful critic, with a finely tuned nose for sniffing out cant, pomposity, and "weak-kneed" arguments. He was an even better editor, one who would x-out whole paragraphs or even entire pages. Larry marked up some of the pages of the draft of my first book, *Death in a Promised Land*, so much that they looked like sketches by Jackson Pollock.

But at the core of his interactions with students was the fact that Larry genuinely *liked* young people. He wanted to know what they were into, he cared about what they felt, and he had a knack for knowing how to connect with them on a basic human level. "Illegal fun," I heard him once read aloud from a document some of his students were looking at in class. "Now, that sounds pretty good." The classroom erupted in laughter. For those of us who were lucky enough to know him, Larry was one of the greatest experiences of our lives.

He also had one heck of a partner.

For Nell did not simply feed fifty years' worth of students, lend a friendly ear to their wants and woes, and share cigarettes and ice tea with them out on the back deck, she also took them into her heart. When one of the first African American PhD students in history at Duke arrived in Durham shortly after Larry and Nell did, he ran into more than his fair share of racism. One professor even told the student that the B he got on a paper was "about as good as a colored student could get." Finally, sitting at Larry and Nell's kitchen table one night, the student decided that he had had enough. Burying his head in his hands, he said he was going to leave Duke.

Then Nell came over and wrapped her arms around his shoulders.

"No," she said, "we'll get through this."

It was just what the doctor ordered. The young man stayed.

If you are young, and very, very lucky, you may find a mentor.

Not just a teacher, but a predecessor of sorts, someone who understands the struggles you are facing because he or she has faced them as well. Part intellectual journeymate, part adopted family member, such a person is someone who can not only help keep you on task, and guide you through the challenges that lie ahead, but can empathize with the emotional costs, and share in the true joys, that serious work demands.

Someone, in other words, to ride the river with.

For those who knew him best, Larry will always be in our ears, challenging our preconceptions, opening our eyes to other possibilities, and pushing us ever onward. As he used to say, "I'll buy, and you fly!"

# 17

## A History-Changing Partnership

WILLIAM H. CHAFE

When I arrived at Duke in the fall of 1971, the most exciting thing to happen was the new partnership that quickly developed with my colleague Larry Goodwyn. Like me, Larry was a recently minted PhD who had spent many formative years as an activist in politics. Larry had written his dissertation on Texas Populism, the most radical democratic movement in the post–Civil War South. And he had focused specifically on the way white and Black Populists interacted in seeking to create a biracial democratic revolution.

That, of course, became the juncture around which we met. I knew of Larry's article on Blacks and Populism in East Texas. He, in turn, had read my article on Blacks and Kansas Populism. Both our shared history of political involvement and our common focus on issues of race and social movements led us to a common, if unusual, conclusion for historians in the early 1970s: the only way to get an accurate multiracial source base for writing about civil rights was through doing oral histories.

The result was a superb partnership. I had already decided that my next "big" project would be a community study of the civil rights movement, where oral histories would play a key role in uncovering the roots of Black insurgency. When I was in Montgomery with the Northern Student Movement in 1965 at the time of the Selma-to-Montgomery march, James Forman, then leader of SNCC, had already convinced me that I needed to write about history from the bottom up, including a focus on previous biracial movements such as that between whites and Blacks in Populism. The next year, I started graduate school, and my first published article was on Blacks and whites in the Populist movement in Kansas.

I knew that social movements were not epiphanies that appeared, like a Virgin Birth, out of nowhere. They had generations of precursors, role models, traditions of resistance. I believed that the only way to get inside that reality was through doing a study of one community over multiple generations. I had just about decided that the ideal place to conduct that study was Greensboro, North Carolina, fifty miles away. Greensboro was the city that promised to integrate its schools the day after the Supreme Court decision on *Brown,* then took seventeen years to do so. It was the place the sit-in movement started on February 1, 1960, when four Black college freshmen went to the downtown five-and-dime, purchased toothpaste and notebooks at different counters, then went with their receipts to the lunch counter to demand a cup of coffee. When they were rebuffed, they opened their books to study. The next day the four became 23, the day after that the 23 became 66, the following day the 66 became a hundred, and on day five the hundred became a thousand. Within eight weeks, sit-ins had spread to fifty-four cities in nine different states, and a new phase of the civil rights movement had begun.

Larry, meanwhile, had been brought to Duke at the initiative of Terry Sanford, the new Duke president. Sanford had been governor of North Carolina during the early 1960s. His was the strongest political voice in support of civil rights in the state's history. He had taken over as president at Duke after racial turmoil consumed the campus in 1968–69. Terry knew Larry because of his own involvement in southern politics and civil rights. Sanford asked the history department to hire him, and the department was happy to do so. All of a sudden there were two of us, committed to the same focus, methodology and political agenda.

Larry had already initiated contact with the Rockefeller Foundation. He sought support for bringing eight to ten graduate students to Duke over the next few years, with the intention that most would be African American. The initial ask was $250,000, to create the Duke Oral History Program, pay for an administrative assistant, and cover the tuition and stipend for the graduate recruits. Sanford was completely supportive. Even more impressive, the history department weighed in enthusiastically on our side. The result was that after one year, the university and the department had committed to a program that by its very nature promised to transform the historiography of the civil rights movement and race in America.

Soon the Oral History Program was operating on its own head of steam, with Larry and me as codirectors. In Thelma Kithcart we had a terrific administrative assistant who worked beautifully to mentor the new students coming into the program. We had our own section of offices in a building called Old Chemistry. The offices themselves were old and run down. But they had a charm of their own. It was *our* social space, and everyone wandered in and out with total freedom.

Soon our program generated a culture of its own. More and more, our classes attracted a cohort of students interested in social movements, political reform/rebellion, and the intersection of grassroots insurgency and the response of the political elite. Amazingly, we continued to move forward with what seemed like total support from our departmental leaders and colleagues.

Probably the most important events in this entire process were two national conferences we held in the summers of 1974 and 1976. In the first conference, we invited graduate students throughout the country to come to Duke for a two-week summer workshop to explore the origins and evolution of the civil rights movement in Chapel Hill during 1962–63. In effect, this was to be a test case of the validity of our claim that using oral histories and Black sources would produce a radically different understanding of the civil rights struggle than was then current. A white person had already written a widely praised book on the Chapel Hill movement. We sent that book, plus a slew of newspaper stories from the time, to those attending the conference. The participants were equal parts Black and white, female and male. They read all the written sources. Then on day one we sent the students out in pairs, one white, one Black, to talk to Black people who had been active in the movement. The students came back and reported: "The civil rights movement in Chapel Hill didn't start in 1963. It started in 1953 when the NAACP became active in the move for desegregating the schools." "No," a second group said, "it started in 1947 when the kids from all-Black Lincoln High School got together one day after school and said, 'We've got to fight back against all this prejudice.'" By the end of the day we heard countless stories about a history of racial activism in Chapel Hill ranging from Black ministers preaching a gospel of social justice at the local Black Baptist church, to store clerks protesting their unjust treatment by employers.

Those oral histories told a dramatically different story about the origins of the 1963 Chapel Hill demonstrations. They were not started by white UNC students, as the book and the newspaper articles claimed. They emerged from the local Black community. They also reflected the prior activism of Black students at the North Carolina College for Negroes (now North Carolina Central University) in Durham. Their protests in Durham had carried over to Chapel Hill. Only then did the white students get involved. The contrast between the two stories was like night and day. And the material exposing that contrast came directly from using oral histories co-created with Black people as sources for understanding how history had been made.

The second conference proved even more important. Using grant money, we invited a range of scholars and activists from across the country to come to Durham for four days. Among the thirty-to-thirty-five people present were well-known scholars like Paul Gaston from the University of Virginia, Clayborne Carson from Stanford, and Dan Carter from Emory. But the key players were SNCC activists like Joyce Ladner, Worth Long, and Annette Windhorn; Charles Sherrod, who shaped the civil rights effort in southwest Georgia; and Vincent Harding, a Mennonite activist close to both Dr. King and leaders of SNCC like James Forman and John Lewis.

The conference focused on our new program, its emphasis on oral history, and what we hoped to accomplish. Almost immediately it became clear that the key question in the room was why Duke—a historically white racist institution—was initiating this effort. Duke had just admitted Black students for the first time twelve years earlier. How could it be trusted to do *anything* credible with civil rights studies? More specifically, how could these two white guys, Goodwyn and Chafe, lead this effort when there were so many Black people, some of them in the room, who should have been heading it up? Fundamental issues, searing, justifiable questions. The tension was thick. As we were meeting, Alex Haley's *Roots* was premiering on national TV, creating even more controversy about who held the truth and how it should be presented. It was literally touch and go whether the conference would implode, leaving only the wreckage of Black-white cooperation on civil rights history in its wake, or whether, somehow, we could find a common ground to stand on and at least begin the process of collaboration.

At this juncture Vincent Harding stood up. Quiet-spoken, gentle, deeply religious, as much a Quaker as a Mennonite, Harding possessed an authority almost impossible to describe. Despite his gentleness, he was also radical, uncompromising, and deeply committed. Everyone in the movement respected him. Now he took a risk that he alone could carry forward. Harding pointed to the things that we had already done, to our recruitment of Black students, our focus on grassroots insurgency, the work that Larry and I had done on Blacks and Populism, and above all on our desire to center Black sources to get at the roots of civil rights activism. Simply and straightforwardly, but with an explicit recognition of the stakes involved, Harding asked that the people gathered together give us a chance. Let the verdict rest with the product of our efforts. Yes, our affiliation with an elite, historically racist institution gave ample reason for skepticism; but let's give them a chance. For us it was a moment of grace.

With the conference as a foundation, the program building that we had begun in 1972 continued unabated. As we recruited more and more stellar graduate students, people in positions of academic power began to pay more attention. We already had terrific support from Rockefeller. Now the National Endowment for the Humanities (NEH) became involved as well, agreeing to create a Center for the Study of Civil Rights and Race Relations at Duke. NEH said yes to the tune of more than $750,000 over five years. Soon we were recruiting "scholars and activists in residence" to come to Duke, interact with our students, and write their books. Vincent Harding came to Duke for two years, during which time he produced his multivolume history of the movement, *There Is a River*. Paul Gaston of the University of Virginia joined us, as did Worth Long, a venerated SNCC activist, and Bill Strickland, head of the Northern Student Movement.

The Duke Center for the Study of Civil Rights and Race Relations forged a unique connection between graduate students on the one hand and activist-scholars on the other. The interaction created a dynamic synergy where young students could learn from older activists, and the activist-scholars could benefit from the experience of students carving out new areas of grassroots research.

All of this was taking place against a background of amazing political developments. Richard Nixon had been elected president in 1968, although Hubert Humphrey barely missed catching up with him and winning when he came out against the Vietnam War about four days prior to the election. Now the candidate with the "Southern strategy" was in charge. Nixon dismantled the war on poverty, opposed busing to desegregate schools, tried to appoint reactionary white southerners to the Supreme Court, and in general used the tactics of polarization to demonize liberals while making his positions on race the basis for building a solid white South.

In that context, Terry Sanford—and Duke—stood out as exceptions to what was taking place more generally. Our programs started graduating a new generation of young African American historians writing about the civil rights movement from the bottom up, with a focus on deep-rooted local Black activism. Sanford himself ran for the Democratic nomination for president in 1972, pushing for a bold platform of measures to create racial justice. Larry and I both worked for him, writing speeches on busing to create school integration, and working with local communities in North

Carolina. Unfortunately, Governor George Wallace won the primary in North Carolina, but Terry never wavered in his commitment to racial and economic reform. In short, all during this period, the partnership Larry and I had created, with Terry's enthusiastic support, continued unabated. As many as half of the incoming graduate students in history came to Duke to work on issues of race and oral history. Through appearances at national conventions and at other gatherings, our program was achieving significant recognition.

One consequence of our success was that Larry and I became primary players in Terry's efforts to raise Duke's international stature. Boldly, Terry decided to launch an initiative to establish an academic connection to China's professorial elite. Well before other American universities reached out to China, Terry sent our dean of the Faculty of Arts and Sciences, and Larry and myself, to visit Chinese academicians and hopefully establish the kind of partnership that would enable oral history of the sort we were practicing to become a central part of China's effort to recover its own story of mounting a revolution. Just as we were focusing on how grassroots activists in the Black community led the struggle for racial equality, perhaps Chinese academics could be persuaded to use the same oral history approach to do a series of community studies to trace the grassroots origins of the Communist Revolution in China.

The next three weeks were among the most exhilarating of my life. It was just before the 1980 presidential election in America, and the night we left, polls showed Jimmy Carter in a dead heat with Ronald Reagan. We landed in Beijing amazed at the traffic that consisted primarily of bicycles and old cars made in India, yet even more struck by the fact that in this city of millions, there were only two hotels. We were staying at the less expensive and less commodious Friendship Hotel on the outskirts of the city, as opposed to the elite Peking Hotel in the center of downtown. Our tour leader was a business associate of Terry's, but he had hired the daughter of an elite Chinese family to accompany us.

Soon we learned just how much that would mean. Because this woman knew all of the cultural leaders of Beijing—former cabinet leaders who had been furloughed to the countryside during the Cultural Revolution of 1966–76, forced to give up their prestigious positions to work alongside the poorest farmers. She took us each night to meet one of these families, where we listened to extraordinary, intimate conversations about where China had been and where it was going, told by those who had led the Communist Revolution thirty-odd years before. During the day, meanwhile, we met with the current elite of the Chinese academy, exploring how Duke and Chinese academicians could arrange for a new partnership. "Amazing" is the only word to describe these intense interactions.

After a week we journeyed to Nanjing and then to Shanghai, where we met with another set of university leaders and had the chance to interact with ordinary people in the public parks or in large restaurants where Larry and I engaged in intense one-on-one discussions about factory life, the future of Chinese communism, and the possibility of generating a new relationship between Duke and the Chinese people. I had never known a three-week period so full of wholly new experiences and possibilities.

When we came back to the United States, we discovered to our amazement that Ronald Reagan was now to be our president. We tried repeatedly to pursue the possibilities of long-term cooperation with our academic colleagues in China, but there were just too many obstacles. This was all such a new venture. Notwithstanding his creativity and talents, Sanford was not able to bring to fruition his dream of making Duke a partner of one of the most important countries in the world.

*　*　*

That meant, unfortunately, that in order to make the kind of signal contribution that would link his name forever to Duke's preeminence, Terry Sanford would have to come up with a new, equally bold plan. What action could call the attention of the nation and the world to Duke University? Terry's answer was to make Duke the home of the Richard M. Nixon Presidential Library. His decision created a huge uproar, divided the campus, and ended once and for all the partnership that Larry and I had forged with Terry. In effect we discovered a new definition of a roller-coaster ride at Duke: how quickly a relationship with someone in power can plummet downhill into an all-out fight, with both sides adamantly convinced they are in the right.

Where to begin? Sometime before the summer recess, Sanford journeyed to Nixon's home to learn the terms under which the former president would choose Duke as the resting place for his papers. It's hard to know whether the response surprised him, but it amounted to an extraordinary package. Nixon needed 30,000 square feet for the papers of his administration, yet he asked for a 150,000-square-foot library. Why five times larger than the space needed to archive his papers? He imagined a museum celebrating his life and career. This would be a monument to a great president at a premier university, with ample space for conferences, exhibits, paraphernalia, and a cadre of scholars and experts dedicated to elaborating, and affirming, the brilliance of his career.

As often happens with pivotal decisions at a university, Terry's commitment to advance the Nixon library plan was made after school had recessed. There were few faculty on campus. Many department chairs were on summer break. Only a few administrators were pursuing the business of the university. When the decision was announced publicly in early August, it was accepted as a "done deal" by most people at Duke, including faculty.

Not the history department. One of the leaders of our department over a more than thirty-year period had been Richard Watson, a Yale PhD widely respected for his scholarship on early twentieth-century Progressivism in the United States. Dick's most famous moment at Duke to date had come in 1954 when he was a leader of the faculty senate. At that time the president of Duke recommended that the university award Richard Nixon, then vice president of the United States, an honorary degree. Nixon had gone to Duke's law school in the mid-1930s, graduating in 1937. He was an excellent student, but he constantly worried that he might not measure up on exams, in which case he might lose his financial aid. Succumbing to these anxieties, Nixon broke into the office of the law school dean to examine his grades. Only, he was caught in the act. While not expelled, he was suspended and completed his law degree with a cloud over his head. This was someone who would commit a burglary to preserve and protect his own self-interest.

Nixon's subsequent political career also did not sit well with some people. His tenure on the House Un-American Activities Committee made him one of the more prominent "red-baiters" in the country, known for his skill at suggesting disloyalty on the part of left-of-center individuals who served in the federal government. Nixon's own campaigns in California increased distaste for his political ethics. He had been elected in 1946 largely on the basis of attacking his liberal Democratic opponent as being a Communist sympathizer. He then won election to the United States Senate in 1950 by smearing his opponent Helen Gahagan Douglas as "the pink lady," someone who was not quite a "red" but "pink" through and through. In that race too he triumphed, but hardly with a reputation for fairness and aboveboard dealing with his political enemies. Dwight Eisenhower had chosen Nixon as his vice-presidential nominee in 1952 largely to appease the right wing of the Republican Party, and because Nixon's aggressive anticommunism would resonate with that part of the Republican base not comfortable with Ike's internationalism and moderation.

For Richard Watson, that kind of record did not merit the kudos associated with an honorary degree. So when Nixon's name was presented to the Academic Council as a nominee for an honorary doctorate in 1954, Dick stood up and opposed it. By the end of the debate, a majority took his side. Nixon never got an honorary degree from Duke.

Now Dick Watson once again asked probing questions. What was the purpose of this library? To enrich Duke's archives or to glorify a former president who resigned in disgrace? What impact would the library have on the institution of Duke? How would it affect Duke's reputation, its signature in the world of higher education? The questions were important enough that Sanford decided to meet with the history department as a whole at his home. The discussion was brisk, invigorating, challenging. When the meeting ended, Terry believed the contretemps had been set aside. Soon, he believed, the library would be sealed and delivered, his pinnacle achievement.

How wrong he was! As we walked down the driveway from Terry's house, we were already planning our next meeting, the beginning of a campaign to show that in a university, the faculty must have the final say on a matter at the heart of what the university stands for. There were four of us who took the lead. Larry and I were joined by Sydney Nathans, the young instructor who had first recruited me to Duke and who had just completed a biography of Daniel Webster, and Peter Wood, the dynamic colonial historian of America who had been the Rockefeller Foundation humanities officer who gave our oral history program its first breath of life and who, subsequently, had published a pathbreaking book on Black communities in colonial South Carolina.

Interestingly, we were all confident both in the integrity of our cause and in our ability to prevail, no matter how powerful Terry was or how much a friend to us he had been. Soon we became known as the Gang of Four, a fitting allusion to the four people who had transformed Chinese Communism, and a profoundly ironic commentary on the degree to which Larry and I had been central to Sanford's initial plans for a new international program with China. We met on a regular basis, sometimes two or three times a week. Both Larry and I were well acquainted with the world of political journalism. We knew how to call a reporter, plant a question, raise an issue meriting further investigation. We had been doing this throughout the 1960s, Larry with the *Texas Observer* in Austin and in the campaigns of Senator Ralph Yarborough, me in New York City's Reform Democratic movement, the congressional campaigns of Ted Weiss, the mayoral campaign of Herman Badillo, and the US Senate campaign of Richard Ottinger.

Soon a reporter from the *St. Louis Post-Dispatch* came to town to write a story about opposition to the Nixon Library. He was quickly followed by journalists from the *Washington Post*, the *New York Times*, and national magazines.

Still, we were smart enough not to blast the whole idea of bringing a Nixon presidential library to Duke. No, our reasoning—and objectives— were more subtle than that. The issue was not the presidential papers, we insisted; rather, it was the idea of building a *monument* to celebrate the presidency of Richard Nixon. By hammering solely on the issue of celebrating the Nixon presidency, we changed the contours of the argument. We were not opposed to becoming an archive for valuable historical documents. Rather, we stood against Duke becoming part of an effort to promote Nixon as a great president. Did Duke really want to be known for building a gigantic memorial to a president forced to resign in disgrace?

On that question, it was difficult to argue the other side. The first defeat Sanford received, therefore, was a vote by the Academic Council (Duke's faculty senate) that the university should *not* build a monument celebrating the presidency of Richard Nixon. The Council then voted to create a "select committee" on the Richard Nixon library to decide how to proceed. Chaired by a distinguished scientist whose integrity no one dared challenge, the committee proceeded to examine carefully the different issues. We looked at exactly how much space was required for library staff, the papers, the offices and facilities that would be used by scholars coming to do research on the archives: about 30,000 square feet. We then took account of the need for exhibit rooms, auditoriums that would host academic conferences, film and documentary facilities, compared to those provided in other presidential libraries: another 30,000 square feet. The Academic Council's select committee then voted unanimously to support construction of a 60,000-square-foot library to house the Nixon papers and promote research on his administration. By a majority vote, the faculty endorsed our recommendations and sent them forward to President Sanford.

Obviously, most of us knew that however reasonable a proposal this was, it would never be acceptable to Richard Nixon or his followers, because a monument was exactly what they had aspired to and set out to achieve— and this was no monument!

Terry Sanford was angry, disgruntled, and humiliated. After all he had done for us and with us, how could we betray him like this? Yet from our perspective it was Sanford who was betraying the values that had always so much endeared him to us. We were being consistent, we believed, with who we were. It was he who had turned against what we believed he stood for.

Soon it became clear that the Nixon people wanted nothing to do with our select committee's recommendation. They would look elsewhere. Within weeks our group received communiques from Stanford, the University of California at Irvine, and other institutions that had been approached by the Nixon library people as possible sites. The faculty at those institutions asked us for information on how we had responded and for the arguments we had mobilized, and they subsequently responded as we had done. They were willing to house the papers, but not to memorialize a disgraced president.

*   *   *

Now with the drama of the possible Chinese partnership and the Nixon presidential library behind us, the time had come to return to our fundamental mission: to transform the way we conducted research on social justice movements. Specifically, our focus centered on how issues of race and gender constituted both a source of pervasive inequality and the rallying point for organizing movements for justice. Much of the earliest work of our students doing oral histories of civil rights battles had focused on women. During the 1980s we held conferences for high school and college teachers, and we brought in outside scholars to write books about the interaction of sex and race. Eventually the work of our Duke-UNC Center led to the decision to relocate the headquarters of *Signs*, the feminist journal of the women's movement, to Duke University.

At the same time, we persisted in fostering research on grassroots activism in Black communities. We recruited a generation of graduate students in history from many racial and ethnic backgrounds to do work on issues such as Black and white cooperation in tobacco worker unions during World War II, the ways white and Black women reformers worked together, and sometimes clashed, in cities like Durham. Through the National Endowment for the Humanities, we secured funding for our graduate students to conduct interviews with 1,260 African Americans from twenty-two communities in eleven states during the Jim Crow period. Relying on W.E.B. DuBois's quote in *The Souls of Black Folk* (1903), we called this the "Behind the Veil" project, showing how different industrial and racial situations in these communities led to multiple forms of resistance.

Most important, during the late 1980s we experimented with growing our scholarly enterprise in an entirely new and more ambitious direction. With scholars and artists from multiple institutions in North Carolina, we worked to create the Center for Documentary Studies (CDS), a multidisciplinary entity that would use video, radio, oral history interviews, and case studies of local protest movements to create a research base, available on the Web, for scholars seeking to understand movements for social change. Formally instituted in 1989, Duke's Center for Documentary Studies soon became a leader in the nation among those seeking to understand movements for social justice. We secured an endowment of more than $30 million which helped support multiple documentary projects by artists, videographers, graduate students, journalists, and professors. Intentionally, the Center was located on the edge of campus, with direct access to downtown Durham. We wished to be a bridge to the community, not an academic bastion.

By 2005, Duke had granted PhD degrees to forty-five students in oral history. Twenty-eight of these published their dissertations, helping to reshape the historiography of the civil rights movement. And eighteen of these publications won national book awards. In the end, the roller-coaster ride that Larry and I had been on recovered its momentum. Duke was able to continue in the direction that Terry Sanford had helped make possible in the first place. Embracing the values of diversity, of human rights, and of progressive scholarship, the partnership Larry and I had formed in the first months of our time together at Duke played a major role in shaping the new directions that Duke helped pioneer in social history, civil rights scholarship, and women's studies. Sometimes people can come together to make change happen.

# 18

## Ask Unsanctioned Questions

### Interviewing Activists

WESLEY C. HOGAN

It's hard to teach oral history in a classroom setting. It's a craft learned best by apprenticeship. I signed up for Larry Goodwyn's oral history seminar in the early 1990s. Intrigued by my own brief experiences in campus anti-apartheid and Take Back the Night movements, I planned to interview the people who had organized social movements in the 1960s. I wanted to ask them, "How did you make so much positive change in such a short period of time?" Larry's oral history class wasn't where most of my learning happened. Instead I picked things up in conversation with him, sifting through the experiences I had interviewing people after I finished graduate course work. The routine we settled into lasted more than a decade, between the early 1990s and early 2000s. It looked like this: I offered him background information on the interviewee I had lined up. This could include particularly rich and telling experiences the interviewee had that no one had been able to plumb. I gave Larry some questions I'd developed. We discussed potential obstacles: What might be the interview-ending questions? What if I got into territory that I didn't understand? What if I didn't have enough money left over to find a meal or bed for the night? What if I couldn't find child care for the entire length of the interview? What if the tape or battery ran out?[1]

He learned to trust my skill and drive as an interviewer, and taught me all he could. I learned to trust him to hear my underdeveloped questions, my self-doubts, my stumbling around a question, so we could develop a fresh language of asking better questions. In the fall of 1995, all these little dialogues built up to a breakthrough. I had an interview with a person he referred to as a "movement heavy." She hadn't been interviewed much, and was reluctant. I had access through a mutual friend. Yet I felt like I didn't know enough. I scraped my graduate-school-budget pennies together. "I don't want to blow this," I confessed to Larry and Nell on their back deck, over lemonade. "And I'm not sure I have the chops to do this the way it needs to be done." I knew this interviewee to be a major thinker who actually tried to live her philosophy about the nation's democratic potential. She simply acted as if every person *was* "created equal." It meant she'd been a misfit most of her life: a white southerner in the sit-ins, a woman who called out men for being sexist, and an environmentalist who pushed that white-dominated movement to address Indigenous and Black perspectives. "I'm a grad student," I realized. "What the hell do I know?"

Larry fixed me with a gaze of solid reassurance. It was a look I'd rarely seen anyone else pull off: he tilted his chin to the right and looked up at you from it, making it seem that one eye sparkled while the other glinted with rock-hard confidence. "Sit here for a minute with Nell, would you?" he asked. And off he marched to the study, still using a typewriter, and pounded out a six-page memo.

It took some time. I remember Nell and I ate dinner alone. She put a sandwich next to the desk while he furiously typed, thought, typed some more. After a while he shouted, "Ah-hah!" and tore the final sheet out of the typewriter. Carefully stapling the six pages together, he passed them over. "This is what I know about interviewing," he said solemnly. It felt like receiving a set of magnificent tools, master to apprentice, well preserved and developed scrupulously over a lifetime, each embedded with lived memories. "I might have some questions after I read it," I responded, teasing him.

Back home, I began to read. The title already struck me as odd. "Memo for Hogan." Why just me? Wasn't this a broader set of tools available to any of us? In the twenty years since, I've realized it was both—aimed at my particular strengths and weaknesses as an interviewer, and a universal guide.[2] The mix makes it hard to include as a stand-alone document in this collection. Yet to my knowledge, Larry never wrote about interviewing or oral history, despite his bedrock belief in its importance as a methodology for a people's history, and despite the decade he spent developing a pioneering oral history program. So it seems important to share some of what he taught, as well as how he taught it. His unique approaches to both inflected the Duke Oral History Program and its graduates. It also left a trail for those journalists and scholars searching to formulate what writer Rebecca Solnit called for in 2016—better questions about things that really matter.[3]

The memo focused on three key features of oral history: the interview, prior research, and the search for a workable vocabulary. I argued a lot with the memo, but I liked the short part II on prior research: graduate school had equipped me well to do archival research that allowed me "to ask concrete questions," like "What were the reasons you left Jackson in 1964?" or "Who else was with you when you drove from Atlanta to Selma in February?" Larry talked about archival work as essential to create a "'working' sequence of events" for how social movements evolved over time. I also liked its focus on origins. He noted that often we "pick up movements too late." This drew my attention to the fact that the written record contained huge gaps that don't allow scholars to trace how people and groups came together and sometimes created new democratic habits and forms to work within. It gave me permission to look for those early experiences that often put movement people on a fresh path. They no longer were headed to be lawyers, foremen, nurses, farmers, or engineers. Instead they left the beaten path, to "make the road by walking."[4] Part II I understood well from the beginning.

For years the part of the memo that I spent the most time rereading—because I knew the least—was section 1: interviewing. First he taught interviewers how to get someone to the table. "The point is to win a psychological war," Larry noted. "You're not imposing on them by asking for an interview, you're honoring them."

"Drive for concreteness," he wrote. "The value of an interview stands or falls on its concreteness." Most of us will explain our experiences in generalities, he observed. "That was the best night of my life," or "She was simply the most important person to me growing up." Those kinds of statements, littering oral histories of all kinds, are useless as evidence. Completely useless. The experience meant something important to the speaker, but the "average outsider" can't possibly know what, specifically, that "something" was. It wasn't tangible. "If someone was going to parachute in from Mars, would they be able to understand it?" he'd ask. "If I plopped you down in a different country, could you explain to those people what your interviewee meant?"

He recommended that I always start by asking who influenced the interviewee when they were young. Whatever the interviewee answered, "Pause with it. Turn the answer over in your hand," he wrote. "Ask her to look at it and talk about it until you have an answer that (1) means something to you as an 'average outsider' and (2) also means something to the interviewee." In an interview, "never settle for a platitude, even if it is a heartfelt and sincere platitude, like, 'He gave us a kind of moral authority' or 'He gave us hope.'" You have to ask the interviewee to help you understand what that meant, he urged, so that you can, in turn, help your readers understand what people inside the movement experienced.

These movement veterans were crossing terrain that most of us had never walked. After exploring their early influences, and the origins of their movement involvement, an interviewer needed to understand something basic: movement vets' experiences often took them well beyond the day-to-day realities of most people's lives, into a new "democratic social relations plateau." The way the researcher got to that plateau herself, without having experienced it directly, was to drive for concreteness: the context surrounding the moment, and the experience the interviewee had within that context. Both context and experience shift over time, and part of the historian's job is to nail down these shifts. "Where were you when this happened? What time of year? Do you remember what the house looked like? Who else was there? Time of day? Can you reconstruct any of the conversation? What did you do after? What was the name of the restaurant/church/bar/highway? Who did you leave with?" And so on. People grow and change, sometimes extremely rapidly, within social movements. Oral historians have to chart this evolution as well and carefully as possible, to make this "evolving context historically comprehensible." To make it understandable, one has to get the interviewee to give example after specific example. So if I asked someone, "Which church?" or "Who else was in the bar?" I was able to elicit a story or two that helped me to understand how people experienced these evolutions in their own lives within the social movement.

After trying this with a few interviews, though, I learned that I had to lay the groundwork for people as I asked these "concrete" questions. "Nothing is too basic or mundane," I began to tell interviewees early in each interview. "I have as much time as you need. It will help a great deal if you can lay out what this room/church/downtown square looked like, and what was happening inside it." Unless I told people to take their time, they often rushed over the details. It was essential to say: "The details are among the most important part, and here's why."

I frequently liked the people I was interviewing; oftentimes I deeply respected them. I saw them as movement elders, people who had carved out a meaningful life on their own terms.[5] Larry gently took this reality and held it up for me to inspect without mercy. "A good interview is not one you 'enjoy' or good because you admire the person," he wrote. "The value of an interview stands or falls on its concreteness." After reading this sentence many times, I looked back and realized that most of my questions up to that point had not aimed at evidence-collection about a movement, per se. Instead, they had a subtext I didn't see: I wanted to know how these organizers had moved through the world, since I was looking for my place within it. It meant that too often my interview questions were geared toward exploring something for myself, or trying to prove something to my interviewees, like how smart I was or how much I knew. How good my politics were. How worthy I was of being in their world. This was all a massive detour. It kept me away from getting to the research details I needed—to understand the dynamics among those who made up the base of the social movement. When I focused on the interviewee's concrete experiences, all that ego-based questioning fell away. It immediately moved the interview beyond the shallows.

This approach—centered on the interviewee's specific experiences, evolving over time—also kept me grounded and focused when I interviewed someone I did not particularly admire. Several movement vets struggled with arrogance and resentments. In hindsight, I can see such responses as all too understandable in light of the backlash politics dominating the 1980s and 1990s. At the time, I simply found their responses ugly. Often the gap between what they professed to value and what they practiced in their lives was too wide for me to pass over. When one person's life presented contradictions of a very deep nature, I gathered as much loose change as the floor of the car allowed and phoned Larry from a pay phone in Seattle. "What the f*** do I do with this? This person tried to blow up multiple buildings, and claims it was all a quest for justice in response to that napalmed photo of Phan Thi Kim Phuc at nine years old, running down the road. How can I unpack that for the reader? We start again at ten tomorrow morning." He responded, "Darlin', that's no problem. You just start up, and you be yourself—warm, open. Then say, 'Some people's lives kick up contradictions. You, sir, have lived such a life, and I'd like you to run some of them through your mind again and tell me what you come up with.'"

Another time I called, frustrated after an interviewee had straight-up lied, and he said: "Oh. You can handle that one pretty simply." Then he explained, "You just say, 'I'm not complaining, but this doesn't square with the evidence I've seen so far.' And then provide the document or other interview that contradicts the person. Let them explain their perspective, upfront, and openly." This taught me how to break people out of the pat narratives they had told themselves over the years, which were routinely self-serving and sometimes untrue.[6] I learned that if I interviewed movement people and drove insistently toward how their experiences pushed them to new concrete moments of understanding, I could trace their initial reasons for joining the movement. For example, one interviewee left a promising academic career when she realized she was learning more in the civil rights movement about the nature of political power than in her graduate school political science classes. Another young man left seminary because the kindness and justice he witnessed daily in the movement so far surpassed the social relations he observed at Union Theological Seminary that he felt the latter no longer made much sense. By asking the interviewees to illuminate such pivotal moments with a story, I could follow their humane and understandable evolution within the movement. It helped me understand better their disillusion, heartbreak, and burnout.

Over the years, I called the Goodwyn house many, many times from a pay phone a few blocks from an interview I had just completed, voice holding back emotion, trying to make sense of the routinely cruel realities so many movement people experienced, both inside and outside the movement. The man whose stress from surviving nonviolent direct actions while being shot at and beaten led him to isolate himself and sleep only four hours a night. The movement veteran whose post-movement life included four marriages and unparented children. I found that when I centered the interview on gathering tangible detail, even with people whose journeys remained unclear to me, I ended up making a sustained human connection. I learned the details of what had led to their heartbreak, the disintegration of their hope. I could understand why they now resided in cynicism, sourness, or anger. Having absorbed part of their story, I rode heavy. It was often these calls to Larry where I could off-load some of that burden. He too understood the weight of the attempt these activists had made to make the country live up to its promise.

Interviewing movement veterans meant my first job was to "pin down their perceived grievances." Initially, all movement participants could easily tell an interviewer what brought them into the movement. End Jim Crow. Stop the furnishing merchants from ripping off farmers. Equal pay for equal work. That was the first piece: get a handle on what led them off the path of "ordinary life" and into "movement activity." One had to spend some time on that, and get the specifics right.

Yet if people spent any length of time within a social movement, the list of grievances they each had would grow. For example, within the civil rights movement, people realized that ending Jim Crow didn't touch the larger problem of American white supremacy. Life inside the movement involved a process that people experienced as they lived through trying to bat down one tyrannical thing after another. The tyranny could be a habit, a person, or an institution. Larry took the example further. It wasn't just white supremacy they were battling, civil rights veterans often realized, but "the economic dimensions of white supremacy and segregation." And there was more. Movement organizers realized they themselves were "not free of one or more of the cultural inheritances that constitute a barrier to the good society." They too were conditioned to see themselves and one another—Black people, women, workers—as less-than. One example could be seen in the Mississippi freedom struggle. By the time white Yale students came down to help register black voters in 1963, Black Mississippian Curtis (Hayes) Muhammad had been working doggedly for two long years to register his fellow citizens to vote. Arguably he knew more about the inner life of recruiting and the barriers to it in Mississippi than anyone else under thirty on the planet. Yet he realized that despite this expertise, and his demonstrable ingenuity in getting people into the movement, for many years he "always felt inferior to the northern students. . . . I thought they were smarter than we were." On one level he knew it wasn't true, and he experienced how naïve, ignorant, and often disruptive they were as he trained them. Still, he found the belief "they're smarter" hard to shake.

These barnacles of what Larry called "the received culture" glommed on to people's thinking, unsettling and intrusive. Often such barnacles, adhering to all movement participants in some way or other, prompted debates, Larry warned. The debates had happened in the populist movement, in the Polish Solidarity movement, in the US civil rights movement—and in fact in all great movements for democracy. These debates were "about which acts are forthright" and which seemed to be forthright but were in fact products of white supremacy, male supremacy, classism, heterosexism, and so forth. Yet when certain movement people then created a "litmus test," asserting who was "more radical than thou" on any given issue, it created simply a new way to run over one another. Such debates could drive people out of the movement. People lost their ability to explore, much less to be present for a little-*d* democratic conversation.

These evolutions in movement people's perceptions, grounded in experience, were important to chart, Larry noted. A warning to me followed: "Among self-selected radical elites, the easiest experience to have is debate among themselves." Don't get hung up on just what people write about, he wanted me to know. Focus as well on what they do. While I had to recover people's evolution within these movements, including their thinking, he advised that I stay focused on *action* or "activity growing out of perception." If someone wrote something in a position paper, pamphlet, or newspaper article, he warned, that did not mean it changed law, or policy.

"The king has withstood a hundred thousand broadside pamphlets," he'd note. "So has American white supremacy. You have to look for people who through their *actions* bring the king to his knees." Self-proclaimed radicals who gave long speeches or wrote in big-name journals about what "we" should do rarely contributed very much. They weren't going to be down at the barricades. Some use the term "speechifiers" to note this unhelpful but widely noticeable tendency among those who populated the leadership across many movements, and many eras.

This was not to say that oratory had no value. I agreed that speeches by MLK, or SNCC's Prathia Hall or Kwame Ture (Stokely Carmichael), had moved hundreds, sometimes thousands of people into their first steps toward movement participation. A great speech could inspire, and explain, and recruit.[7] But in the history of movements for democracy, speeches had to consistently be yoked to action—deliberate, thoughtful, experiments in what might work. Action and reflection-about-action then became a mutually reinforcing school of sorts. People acted, thought about what worked and what did not, refined their thinking, and acted again. For this reason, historians had to trace both evolving action and movement participants' evolving *thinking* about what they were doing.

An essential part of movement oral history, I learned, was pinning down people's evolving experiential realities, their actions, and the way those experiences changed their perception of themselves, their allies, their movement, and their society. It had to be painstakingly researched. "The actual social relations within" each part of the movement needed to be uncovered. This included (1) organizers' relationships with one another, (2) organizers' relationships with local people, and (3) organizers' relationships with people in the movement who were not organizers. I needed to prod movement vets to explain their thinking at each evolution. For example, when civil rights organizers returned from Mississippi to Ann Arbor or Madison or Berkeley, "What precisely did they bring back home?" Was it a "Sense of self? First steps toward sense of self? What do we mean by sense of self?" Ask these movement organizers to tell you a story illustrating what it meant to have a stronger sense of self, Larry urged. "Tell me a story which illustrates this concept you just talked about."

Asking a person to illustrate a vague or abstract idea with a story became an essential tool. Once an interviewee finished the story, "Tell it back to them," he advised. "Confirm it by repeating to [the movement vet] your understanding of her story." Ask why it sticks in her mind. The "interviewee will almost always provide extra and often central detail to add to the (already finished) story," he wrote. "What you learn AFTER you have received the complete story is usually four or five times more valuable than the original finished story." The reason is simple: the interviewer's summary of what the interviewee has related will "NEVER be as full, as subtly nuanced as it is in the mind of the interviewee. Now that you have made the gap clear, interviewees will move with zeal to close the gap with a raft of necessary detail that had not been previously communicated but (they thought) implied."

By sharing this tool with me, it feels like he saved me from a thousand heartfelt but ultimately useless statements from interviewees. At this point, twenty-plus years later, the most important evidence from oral interviews that I have been able to collect has come from this seemingly simple set of tools: Ask the person to illustrate "hope" or "despair" or "informed agony" with a story. Repeat the story back, asking if you've understood correctly. Encourage the person to move in to add the pieces you've left out. Do it throughout the interview. Always tell interviewees you have the time if they have the time. Be patient with yourself, and with them.

Here is an example from an interview with a SNCC veteran in 1996:

Q: How it felt to be in that kind of pain—can you illustrate that pain with a story, and how you made it through.

A: Well, it went on such a long time. You know, I don't really think I can, to tell you the truth.

Q: Okay.

A: And it goes back to my own childhood. It's almost mythological for me. See, I grew up in my grandparents' house, and my mom remarried when I was ten. And we moved out of my grandmother's house. So I see my whole life as trying to get back to my grandmother's house, where I was safe. So the movement was just another—it was a replay. And then the collapse of being with the guy I had my kids with, another replay. And after that I just really bottomed out. . . . Everybody has had to do recovery work. Everybody.

This SNCC activist continued for another ninety minutes, helping me to understand, in concrete detail, what happened to cause her exit from the southern freedom movement.

Emotional terrain is inescapable in oral history, yet many interviewers try. When the interviewee starts to cry, or yell, or gets agitated, it's a normal human response. All the interviewer has to do is retreat to less explosive territory. The first time a movement vet began to get emotional, my impulse was to ask, "Would you like to take a break? We can come back to this after you've had some time to gather yourself." Larry gave me a very different path forward. "Cash in on the intimate ones," he said. "Stay overnight, spend money you do not have, make a note that you will have to rob a bank next week, but wring them out before leaving town." It was a crucial juncture. "You must do this to get the essential evidence that will make your study different from all the others," he wrote. He knew that my cultural habits as a young female worked against me here, training me to back away out of good manners. And so, in interview after interview that seemed promising, I held my seat.

The guidance he gave here opened up new vistas. There comes a time in each interview where "you need to intervene," he shared. Create a new context for the interviewee. "Tell the person, 'Thanks so far.'" Sit back in your chair, ask the person to take a break, to "'listen for a minute' while you talk a bit." One had to sidle up to a recalcitrant interviewee. "You're being extremely polite, telling me the answers that will make my readers nod as if they understand already the situation. But I came with some high expectations, perhaps they were naïve, perhaps I am disappointed in myself, but I don't want to go away quietly," I learned to say. "Historians know better than most how shaky the written record is, and there are moments when I'm in the presence of someone like you, with a unique angle of vision. So I'd like to invite you to share that unique angle of vision with me. There's a certain way we're trained to see things as historians, but that doesn't mean we understand all of it. We come to these movements, we don't have all the answers. We come to you for answers." Tell them you're going to open up some different kinds of questions, "about candor and intimacy as something that surfaces as an historical reality in all great social movements, a kind of interior glue of collective action." He encouraged me to share with them that movement work often encompassed a reality "full of pain as well as glory and self-discovery that only rarely gets into history books." To move into that reality, we would have to explore "interior life—as it evolved and maybe even was transformed" during the tumult of social experimentation.

It was intimate territory, and I should assure interviewees that I was not trying to pry "in an unseemly way." But I also respected the work they had done. I needed to invite them to go forward onto this terrain that I did not know the outlines of: "I want to hear whatever it is you can tell me." At that point, he recommended, I might lean back myself, and "let them go, without interruption."

I could make notes, he said, of things I wanted to bring up later. In general, though, I should let them go. For a good while. Then, once they begin to wind down, "do NOT rejoice that they are giving you SO MUCH," he wrote. They are "giving you only the tip of the iceberg." Do not end the interview, he continued. Ask your questions. Keep going into that new territory. Stay. Ask the *unsanctioned* questions: Who were they mad at? How did it feel to be lost? Could they illustrate despair with a story? Who did they turn to in that desperate moment, and how did that person respond?

Almost no one had ever asked them those questions: friends, family, colleagues, or interviewers. We either couldn't figure out how to open up the space to ask, or they didn't want to go into what might become unsteady ground. These were questions that had to be asked, however, if the story of this movement was to be made understandable to those outside it. And if the interviewees were willing to answer those questions, it was at that point that they would "supply the detail that makes their 'feeling' concrete." This was the evidence "upon which you can hang your interpretation."

An example of how this began to unfold is here, in an interview with SNCC activist Judy Richardson in August 2000 by telephone:

WH: What I've noticed, and it comes from some work that I did before I got into graduate school. In the movement itself, in trying to figure out how social movements work or don't work, one of the things that is crucial is the quality of the relationships inside between people, and the three qualities that seem to stick out time and again are the degree to which they're able to, one, trust one another, two, be candid, and three, maybe even be kind. The quality of those relationships on the inside [of the movement] is a kind of glue.

JR: Yes.

WH: And that's what, to some degree, allows people to stay in these movements and continue in these areas, rather than just have a movement come together and then dissipate, not really gel or come together at all.

JR: Yes. I'm glad you picked up on this. That's right.

WH: But the problem is that the relationships are filled with pain and difficulty as well as self-discovery, joy, and sharing. That kind of stuff really rarely gets into the history. Yet it seems to me that it has a huge effect on the movement itself, and how it moves forward or doesn't. So, if that brings forward anything from you, where you think, "Yes, I relate to that," I'd like to ask you to talk about whether you think that that thesis is useful or not. Again, what I'm driving for is to figure out what makes movements work, what contributes to their coming apart. This interior quality needs a lot more exploration, so my questions aren't very good, because—

JR: No, they're perfect.

WH: I'm walking in areas where I don't have many guideposts—

JR: Yes, it was absolutely crucial. The reason that my closest friends now are the ones that I got in SNCC all these years later is because there was—and either SNCC or people who came out of a SNCC environment . . . Ivanhoe [Donaldson], Courtland [Cox], Ruth [Howard]. There was a way that we dealt with each other that made it safe. We felt safe with each other. That meant [for example, when] I was shy, I was in awe of everybody. Even if I couldn't do it in the larger meetings, I felt safe enough in, say, the Freedom Houses, to have far ranging discussions, to say stuff. I felt that people had my back. I always felt that I could depend on people. It wasn't just [a trust fall, the kind of exercise] where somebody stands up, you fall over, and everyone has to catch you. It was more. I thought they had my interests at heart. That's what it was. From the smallest little thing. For example, toward the end [of my time in SNCC,] I ended up taking over a mailing from Julian [Bond] when he had to take the [state legislature] seat. I could only do it because everything was so systematic that I didn't even really have to do anything. We were in the new building on Stewart Street [in Atlanta]. There were a bunch of us—I remember Fay Bellamy, Stanley Wise, five or six of us. One of those midnight mailings, lots and lots of envelopes. We had sealed them. And I suddenly remembered, "Oh my God, I forgot, there was another piece of paper that we had to put into it." And I took Stanley aside, and I said, "Look, Stanley, what am I going to do?" I knew everyone was tired, and I was the one coordinating the mailing. He said, "Don't worry." And we go back, and he said, "All right, we're going to have to undo them, we're going to have to tape them shut again, we have this other piece that we have to fold and put in here." And we start singing, because that was the only [way through]—doing freedom songs and stuff. He so matter-of-factly [went about it]. *Nobody* said to me, "Oh, Judy, why didn't you think about this?"

Nobody got on my back about it. They just did it. That was it—Nobody made me feel stupid.

For Richardson, it was a "small detail." For those of us not in the organization, it gave a concrete sense of why they were able to stay—to do the difficult, dangerous, mundane work in the day-to-day life of the freedom movement.

The last third of this interview, Richardson continued to describe the intense interior dynamics of the movement. I learned how to set the stage for this kind of exploration by trying out suggestions from Larry's memo, talking with him about how interviews went, and keeping a journal that included phrases I'd experimented with that worked and, at his suggestion, a Blooper File of things that did not. For example, in the interview above, I thought I had stumbled when I said to Richardson, "My questions aren't very good." Yet this prompted her to close the gap to help me understand. I moved it from the Blooper File to the Experiments That Worked column.

Larry taught me how to handle a situation where I didn't know enough yet. It helped, he said, to end an interview with this last thought: "It's been my experience that at the end of an interview, I'm sometimes disappointed, I'm left with questions I didn't know enough to ask yet. I'd like to ask you if I can follow up, let it sit, and think through the implications of some of what you've told me today." It meant they would be much more likely to respond by phone or email to my follow-up questions.

It wasn't all sunshine and light in this oral history apprenticeship. Yet the disagreements and raucous debates we had over his advice were often great fun and taught me just as much as the parts of the memo that I committed to memory and still use as a central part of my own oral history practice. Sometimes these were minor. He thought women were better interviewers, and better organizers. As a young whippersnapper who knew quite a few authoritarian non-listening women, I enjoyed hoisting him on his own petard: "Houston, we might have a bit of a problem, this thing where you state that 'sweeping generalities are empty of content and therefore meaningless,' and then make a sweeping general observation authoritatively without evidence." There was the playful bantering sustained for fifteen minutes about whether we needed to follow common sense and move our tête-a-tête outside, since I was pregnant and he insisted on smoking in his office. We also had more substantive disagreements:

"What the hell is this thing at the beginning of each interview that you're doing?" he'd growl.

"Those are release forms. People need to see—"

He cut me off: "Those just get in the way of candor," he said. "You're throwing all that legal verbiage in their face before they even know you."

"Yeah, and I'd rather that, than have them feel later like they don't have control over their own story. It's important to make sure they have a sense of the intellectual property situation . . ."

He tuned out. I kept working to refine and make my release forms more democratic (helped greatly in the Internet era by Creative Commons), but I never did convince him they were necessary.[8] Nor did he win me over on the biggest disagreement we sustained after my first book was published. He thought the phase of the movement from "beloved community" to "Black Power" diminished the movement's democratic innovations. For me, the push toward what the Combahee River Collective first called identity politics created the necessary free space to work as full human beings, and the step after that was building democratic coalitions. My evolving research and interviews reflected this, and it caused us some tumult, times when we both hung up the phone and shook our heads in disbelief—and pity for the other person being so hardheaded.

The undeniable impact of the interviewee's and interviewer's gender, race, class, and other identities served as another focal point of debate. We engaged wholeheartedly and sometimes with ferocity. For years! Yet his points served as flint against which to sharpen my own thoughts. He'd also note with tremendous grace when I'd taken one of his tools and improved it. "This section here, that's lovely. I do not know enough to ask those questions you did. How did you figure out . . ." In asking me to talk through how I'd come to new insights or approaches, he also drew my attention toward the fact that I was innovating. I no longer was a student. This model of pedagogical generosity stays in the forefront of my mind as I teach now.

I did not spend much time on Larry's part III, the "search for a workable vocabulary," until I finished my first round of interviews and began to carefully piece the story together. As he predicted, I had a lot of evidence I could not "conveniently characterize." You might discover, he warned, "that we don't have the words for, say, step three and step eight" of the movement's evolution. "You will have to invent these words. People do not join because they're conscripted," he noted. Movements take time away from people's regular lives of paying bills and raising children. So how the hell do people recruit others? It is particularly hard and important to understand why people join movements that risk the very things they value: their jobs, their homes, even the lives of their loved ones and themselves. It isn't magic, it isn't a Hollywood fantasy of "Build it and they will come." Movement organizers have to forge a relationship with someone, and invite them to join, and then, only maybe, they will come. "Recruitment," a term for this process, was not something common among or even well understood by political scientists, sociologists, historians, or others who studied movements. Even some of the organizers at the time did not have the notion of "recruitment" in their heads—that is, the one thing that most determined the fate of the movement. So I'd have to invent terms to lay out the sequential process of how people built movements of hundreds, then thousands, and eventually hundreds of thousands, of people.

At the end of the memo he told me to ask myself, "What are you studying?" Was it an ethos? Wherever I wanted to head, he urged me to make "sure you ask yourself the question before you finish shaping your initial research design." Over that decade, I learned that what I was studying was simple: Some people wanted to move from the "idea" of democracy to actually living it.[9] How did they do that? Could people at the base of society invent political forms that included everyday people in the big decisions that most impacted their lives? They'd experimented with it in the 1770s and 1780s. What about in the twentieth and twenty-first centuries?

So I studied recruitment. That is, how does a movement pull people into its orbit and give them a sense of meaning and belonging, a sense of the value of what they are doing, both for the world and for their own lives. And if people are to belong, to what are they going to belong? Goodwyn called that process of building a movement the creation of a "movement culture." And how do movement people then experiment to find "democratic forms" that could be adopted more widely in the political world? For example, the American revolutionaries created "committees of correspondence" to talk to one another about the new world they hoped to build. In the 1960s, the freedom movement created the Mississippi Freedom Democratic Party (MFDP) to bring their ideas into the nation's public forum. What other "democratic forms" had people created? I wanted to uncover as many as I could.

Then into the toughest part of movement development: how does the movement recruit and organize a large enough mass of people to force established power to accommodate those more democratic forms? If that happened, and it rarely did, I wanted to understand how the movement's ways of operating could then be incorporated into the whole nation's political framework. Recovering such democratic forms allowed me to think in practical terms of other paths the nation could be on. This research invigorated me. These democratic forms could be made much more re-coverable if I asked the right questions of people who'd been there, on the ground, experimenting with them.

Reflecting back on the memo, after years of introducing oral history to others in the classroom, I realize that new interviewers routinely have trouble coming up with good questions because we don't always know how to create the space to try to understand other people's perspectives. We have a set of questions, and we want the others to answer. The gap between language and understanding can be considerable. We think they are an-swering our questions, and they think they are answering our questions, but they don't necessarily know what we are asking and we don't necessarily know what their answers mean.

Yet that gap of understanding means that we probably started out and perhaps even ended up with questions that couldn't reach the interviewees where they are. Larry gave me approaches to try something new, to create a different kind of space between myself and the person I was interview-ing. He taught me how to pose questions that matter to people who'd lived inside movements, who had walked their talk and tried to live on an egali-tarian basis together. And if they didn't respond to my questions, I would ask them again, trying harder to go where the interviewees were taking me.

In recent years, the poet Mark Nepo and other contemplatives have be-gun to lay out a new field: how to make space to listen. It's increasingly hard to do in the evolving culture of the selfie, of endless distraction, of branding and self-promotion. "We must honor that listening is a personal pilgrim-age that takes time and a willingness to circle back," Nepo writes. Listening requires patience, and a lot of time. "With each trouble that stalls us and each wonder that lifts us, we are asked to put down our conclusions and feel and think anew," he realized. "Unpredictable as life itself, the practice of listening is one of the most mysterious, luminous, and challenging art forms on Earth. Each of us is by turns a novice and a master, until the next difficulty or joy undoes us."[10] I learned to listen better by reflecting in this way, and by doing so in the company of *compañeros* like Larry.

Over the years, Larry's memo grew tattered. It became a document with a life of its own, spattered with coffee stains, toddler hand smudges, and notes in the margin from multiple stages of research. I lost it several times, through cross-country moves and file misplacing. I finally made it into a PDF in 2010 and sent it back to Larry. "Damn, I gave you the goods!" he told me over the phone. "We need to go back over that the next time you're down. I need to hear what you think about. . . ." And off he'd go. We'd talk about the particular challenge of driving for specificity, or the need to develop a better set of words to pinpoint the striving of everyday people to have a say in their own lives.

In 2013 I moved back to Durham. During the last few weeks of his life, with the shortness of breath, Larry couldn't talk as much as usual. It felt wrong somehow: if there was an essence to Larry, it rode on the vitality of his conversation. I wanted him to experience his full self in those last days. So I went home and printed out the PDF of "Memo for Hogan" and brought it back. Larry's daughter Lauren was there. She, Nell, Larry, and I sat at the little white kitchen table. We went over the memo. I would read a line, tell him how I'd used it over the years to inform my own investigation of social movements, and pause. Lauren or Nell might make a comment, then Larry would share a bit of a story, and we'd build on it. We went on like that through the end of the evening. As usual, he was not short on superlatives. "This is the best thing on interviewing I ever put together," he said right before I left.

Then he posed his last question to me: "Can you find a way to get it into the world?"

*   *   *

Memo for Hogan
Some relationships between research, interpretation and writing on social movements.
Key areas of inquiry:
**Part I.**
(1) First it is necessary to begin the process of pinning down the perceived grievances that animated the participants. Initially, these are quite broad and easily suggested: (a) ending the American caste system of segregation and (b) making the country more democratic. Soon, the list begins to lengthen. Under (a) it is perceived that segregation is merely a structural artefact within the larger problem of American white supremacy that exists throughout the country whether or not rigid standards of segregation are locally being defended. Still later, the economic dimensions of white supremacy and segregation are perceived. Somewhere in this sequential process of what we may call "increasingly focused perception," it becomes possible to conceptualize that the instruments of "change," the dissenters themselves, are not free of one or more of the cultural inheritances that constitute a barrier to the good society. Says the young black

radical, "We have to get the n*ggerdom out of our heads." There is a debate about what acts are forthright, and what acts seem to be forthright but are in fact products of n*ggerdom (a debate, obviously, that can be bruising for the participants). Alternately, a debate surfaces about what "participatory democracy" does and does not mean. Is the N. O. "elitist" in its behavior? Etc. "Manly" elitism. Etc. Unconscious white supremacy among the "manly elitists," among the radical feminists, etc. Class biases, the emergence of "socialism" as a litmus test, valorization on the basis of who is more socialist than thou. Socialism feminism. Unconscious white supremacy among the socialist feminists, etc.

Perceptions, grounded in some kind of experience. (These are finite experiences that are historically recoverable through a careful research design. Recognize that, among self-selected radical elites, the easiest experience to have is debate among themselves. Discovery that this produces rhetorical display, which is seen, gradually over time, to have steadily decreasing value. "We need to act, not just talk."

(2) Activity beyond perception, or activity growing out of perception. Obviously many dimensions here too. Unpack them and treat them separately as a research task.

(a) First how SCLC happened (*Stride Toward Freedom* is a primary source and *Parting the Waters* is one of many secondary sources.) Second, how SNCC grew out of the Greensboro sit-ins. The Shaw U. meeting and role of Ella Baker and the religious types from Fisk. Charles Sherrod to Albany and the lessons of Albany (looking for a dumb sheriff, the conceptual road that lead to Birmingham and Selma); the Atlanta Office, Moses and the Delta, the coming of COFO, SNCC-SCLC tensions, Freedom Summer as the first major operational conjunction of the C.R. movement and the Student movement.

(b) backtrack to student left. Port Huron, including prior roots of people who went to Huron, down to the emergence of ERAP as an attempt to act on the basis of prior analysis. The experience of ERAP has to be researched—that is, the actual social relations within ERAP have to be uncovered: (1) activists with each other and (2) activists with local people. (3) ERAP activists with non-ERAP SDS people. Talk about evolving perceptions!!

Meanwhile, student movement grows latterly on campuses. Separate experiential world from eraps. The Deep South as site of radicalization of student movement: early impact on people who wrote Huron; later impact on young people who came, particularly the (relatively) large number who participated in freedom summer. Mario Savio et al. Bringing "the spirit of the movement" (dangerous phrase because it is so beguiling and above all empty of content) back home to Berkeley, Ann Arbor, Madison, Austin, etc. What precisely is brought back home? Sense of self? First steps toward sense of self? What do we mean by sense of self?

Cultural Greek Chorus, offstage but everpresent: why do the people of movement sing so goddam much? Why are they so emotionally affected by singing? Ain't Gonna Let Nobody Turn Me Round, Turn me Round, Turn Me Round. (Why Won't I Let Them? Because I'm so strong, so full of love, so full of self-congratulatory illusion? Perhaps because I (now) know that I am not alone, and it is absolutely transforming to discover how alive I can be. Look at us!) The people who populate the preceding parenthesis do not think in terms of how much "energy" they are exuding, but we historians, if we are paying close attention, can see it and document it. It is in their words, their songs, their letters home, their manifestos, and their actions on the streets, schoolyards and courthouses of the South and, later, on the campuses. All is recoverable in oral interviews if you ask the right questions. (Look at us here at UM, OT, UC, Uanywhere! But also look at us in the NO, at conventions of ourselves, on Forsyth St in Atlanta. Boy, can we theorize! And I do mean "boy." For the latter insight, we can thank Casey Hayden (mostly) and Mary King and some prior tensions and conversations between black and white women; and white women and black men. It turns out that experiential learning is not always synonymous with loving.

Sample interview with, say, Casey Hayden. The premovement Casey, in Victoria Texas grade school thru high school. Casey at UT, Casey at Christian Faith and Life community. Is Ronnie Dugger an influence? Concretely, why? Whatever she says, pause with it, turn the answer over in your hand, look at it, ask her to look at it and talk about it til you have an answer that (1) means something to you as "average outsider" and also means something to Casey. In short, in interview, do not settle for a platitude, even if it is a heartfelt and sincere platitude like "He gave us a kind of moral authority," or "he gave us hope." What do those words mean, Casey, help me out, help me understand so I am equipped to help my readers to understand.

Your whole purpose here is to FIX Sandra Cason in time, BEFORE she goes to the deep South. Stop the camera and ask her to fix herself at that time: what she thought about Negroes; about the South, about America, about herself. Take time here. Give her the sense that you have the time if she has the time.

(Let's take the time, here, Casey, to try to get this moment of time pretty well fixed.) She is going to grow so much in the next decade, far beyond the growth that Dugger experiences (he did not join any movements) but she does not know this, because she was not in Texas during these years of change so she does not know Ronnie fixed himself in an experiential vacuum. This is no loss for you, in any case, as you are not relying on Casey for a fix on Ronnie, but rather for a fix on herself.

Now, then, (to continue with the mock Hayden interview,) her first six months in SNCC. You're looking for moments. CONCRETE MOMENTS. Her sense of the importance of each moment is a product of the surrounding context which she understands but may not communicate in her story. So you have to ask for the context. Interviewees will willingly provide context, even eagerly provide it, but they do not intuitively or uniformly supply it by themselves. You must be SURE you understand each story. Confirm it by repeating to her your understanding of her story. Is this why it sticks in your mind, Casey? Interviewees will almost always provide extra and often central detail to add to the (already finished) story. What I am saying here, Wesley, is that what you learn AFTER you have received the complete story, is usually four/five times more valuable than the original finished story. Reason is, your summary of what you think you have heard will NEVER be as fully, as subtly nuanced as it is in the mind of the interviewee and now that you have made the gap clear, interviewees will move with zeal to close the gap with a raft of necessary detail that had not been previously communicated but (they thought) implied.

Then next six months, etc. etc. Follow her out of movement and into her angst. To NY, to wherever in the hell she, in her informed agony, went. Was she mad? In despair? Lost? Who was she mad at? Or what was the precise nature of her despair. Can she illustrate despair with a story?

At certain junctures in all promising interviews, you want to intervene, tell person thanks so far, take a break, lean back in chair, and listen for a minute while you talk a bit, with aim of creating a

new context for the moment, one in which you can ask some different kinds of questions. Talk about candor and intimacy as something
that surfaces as an historical reality in all great social movements,
a kind of interior glue of collective action, one full of pain as well
as glory and self-discovery, and one that only very rarely gets into
history books. All of which (Casey, or whoever) brings us to your
interior life as it evolved and maybe even was transformed, maybe
even a roller coaster, during these tumultuous days. Interior life, of
course, is also very intimate and I don't want to pry in an unseemly
way, but I do respect your life a great deal and I want to hear whatever
it is you can tell me. When they begin talking, let them go, without
interruption, but make occasional one or two word notes of things
you want to bring up when it is appropriate. Her feeling about so and
so person, so and so event, so and so national political happening.
The point here is that these questions, which you will probably ask
anyway, need to be asked when the interview has reached a stage of
intimacy. Many interviews, unfortunately, never reach that stage because of the inherent guardedness of the interviewee: (think of all the
boys in high school, all the men you did not marry, all the teachers
who bored you). But with the others, the Casey Haydens, Greg Cal-
verts, Cynthia Washingtons and Wretha Riley Hansons of this world,
you do not let them go, you do NOT rejoice that they are giving you
SO MUCH, they are (unless wrung out by you, gracefully wrung out,
but wrung out nevertheless) giving you only the tip of the iceberg.
Cash in on the intimate ones. Stay overnight, spend money you do
not have, make a note that you will have to rob a bank next week, but
wring them out before leaving town. You must do this to get the essential evidence that will make your study different from every other
study ever done on the sixties. You are very well equipped to do this
sort of thing, Wesley; you need only give yourself the assignment to
do it.

ALWAYS, THE PURPOSE OF AN INTERVIEW IS TO GENER-
ATE CONCRETE EVIDENCE UPON WHICH YOU CAN HANG
YOUR INTERPRETATION. Drive for concreteness. As distinct from
mood. Help people to supply the detail that makes their "feeling"
concrete. A good interview is not one you "enjoy" or good because
it makes you admire the person: the value of an interview stands or
falls on its concreteness; and the overriding value of any piece of concrete evidence is the surrounding context into which it fits. So you are

driving for two kinds of concreteness: the specifics of context; and the specifics of detailed experience within that (necessarily shifting) context. I say "necessarily" shifting because the encounter of movements with received traditions always yields a constantly altering context of thrust and parry, introspection, counterthrust etc. The element that makes this evolving context historically comprehensible is concrete evidence concerning each stage of the evolution. I absolutely cannot emphasize this enough.

**Part II.**

Prior research. In secondary sources, originally. Your initial drive is for origins. Scholars pick up movements too late. So start at the start, then consciously construct a "working" sequence of events. "Working" because you will be augmenting it as you go along. Do anything you can to help you formalize, i.e. make sense of, this "sequence." Try to fashion a time line for example. Even if you discover that you cannot, you will learn, more concretely than you had previously learned, what it is that you do not have, and even perhaps why you do not have it.

This "research" in written sources has the specific purpose of creating a concretized overview of the movements over time. Not yet the people over time, but the movements over time. Contextual scaffolding. This constitutes the structural framework in your mind that you carry with you to interviews. It helps you formulate specific questions. Remember: you do not get answers to questions you do not ask. It is your prior research that equips you to ask concrete questions.

**Part III.**

The search for a workable vocabulary. If you[r] research is good enough, you will end up with more evidence than you can conveniently characterize. You discover we don't have the words for, say, step three and step eight, of your sequence. You will have to invent these words.

Remember, these are voluntary social formations. People have to be recruited to them. How is this done? It is not magic: "Build it and they will come." Only in the movies of fantasy. You have to get in touch with them, then ask them to come and then, maybe, they will come. It is called recruitment, a word that is not an organic or sanctioned term of description in the lexicon of political science.

What are you studying? You do not have to have, at this point, an absolutely well-defined answer to this question, but you will need one before the end of the year. Are you studying two social movements? Mass movements? The activists of two movements? Some selected activists? What governs the selection process? Are you studying people activated by two movements which includes people who actually participated in one or both, plus others who became independently active? Like Cortés. Like Wretha Riley Hanson and Cynthia Washington—two of the most astonishing people of the era. Washington intersected with SNCC, probably something before SNCC. Same with Hanson. John Richards of the Center for Responsive Politics in Washington probably can tell you where to find Washington and Washington can tell you where to find Hanson. Use my name with Richards.

It is my personal understanding and also my historical understanding that the civil rights movement was the galvanizing force for everything we call "the sixties." But certain elements of "the black revolution" have roots deep in the black experience in America and, accordingly, go back a long way. You will probably have to deal with this at least to some extent, four-to-ten pages, early in your book.

But, in any event, are you studying an "ethos" or what? The question I am posing here is an innocent and straightforward one, ie. not loaded. I will be content with your answer. I just want to be sure you ask yourself the question before you finish shaping your initial research design. I say "initial" because it will be augmented as you learn more.

## Notes

1. I'd like to thank Dirk Philipsen, Emilye Crosby, Tim Tyson, Hasan Kwame Jeffries, Paul Ortiz, Peter Wood, Nishani Frazier, and Faulkner Fox for giving me candid, superb feedback on this piece. It was hard to move an essay into useful territory when it centered on someone I'd been close to for a long time, and not have it be simply a praise song. Larry would hate that: he always said "you can't honor people by romanticizing them." Thus my significant gratitude to those listed above for pulling out questions and sharpening my points.

2. This dynamic was a problematic of Larry's teaching, an example of something mentioned in the book's introduction. Larry wrote up this incredibly helpful memo—just for me. He did the same for others at times, one by one. It's strange that only toward the end of his life did he realize that the world should have access to this private information. But why couldn't Larry, someone who valued democracy so much, spread his wisdom more broadly—in his classes? Picking favorites and sharing information just with them

created and exacerbated the "I knew Larry better" dynamic. I lived with the contradiction, and didn't challenge him on it. I wish I had given him a chance to respond. Thanks to Faulkner Fox for helping me develop this point.

3. Rebecca Solnit reflected that she was on the search for better metaphors, better stories. "I want more openness," she noted. "I want better questions." Questions and stories were tools to contend with "the amazing possibilities and the terrible realities that we face." Too often, we have "clumsy, inadequate tools that failed to open our eyes or shed light. "They don't lead us to interesting places. They don't let us know how powerful we can be. They don't help us ask the questions that really matter." Rebecca Solnit, interview by Krista Tippett, "Falling Together," *On Being* podcast, May 26, 2016, https://onbeing. org/programs/rebecca-solnit-falling-together/.

4. This phrase is taken from Myles Horton and Paolo Freire, *We Make the Road by Walking: Conversations on Education and Social Change* (Philadelphia: Temple University Press, 1990).

5. As one interviewee once said, "It was like you went to the end of the known world, and just jumped off." The experiences people had within these social movements often meant they no longer shared the common guideposts of "a good life" with the rest of society. Signs of success were no longer a stable job, a warm family life, or external indicators of accomplishment. Instead, their markers of what constituted a good life included things like "Did we win a healthier environment for workers at the chicken factory?" and "Are people who were previously denied access to the vote, or health care, or higher education now able to enter those doors?" It made it hard for people outside those movement experiences to understand their work or sometimes even see it as valuable. They felt "illegible" to most of their fellow citizens who were not in the movement.

6. It also provided a better model for thinking about "lying" in general. In truth, how could I know whether the person was lying or misremembering? Enough research has emerged in the intervening twenty years about the neuroscience of memory to beguile and confuse even the most experienced oral historian on such a question. (An important academic site for this discussion is the interdisciplinary British journal *Memory Studies*, which began publishing in 2008; books aimed at a general audience include Joshua Foer's *Moonwalking with Einstein* (2011) and Douwe Draaisma's *Why Life Speeds Up As You Get Older* (2004).) We can't possibly know how each person we interview has constructed their memories. My approach is to create a careful research design, unearth as much of the available archival research as possible, and continually improve my capacity to listen and ask questions.

7. Tim Tyson pointed out that powerful oratory "can also bolster the movement's morale and hold it together at difficult moments and feed people spiritually." It therefore helps people recruit and organize others into the movement, even if sometimes people can "depend upon that drug too much." And speechifying wasn't just limited to orators, but "movement word merchants who write the manifestoes and theorize everything and high-hat people with clouds of language that are not useful for movement building." All true.

8. Several people in this volume have noted Goodwyn's maverick qualities. This held true in terms of oral history orthodoxies as well, as loose as they are and were. In ad-

dition to scorning release forms, and perhaps due to his background as a journalist, he rejected participation in IRB procedures. In the classroom, we didn't use an oral history text. He had us examine our own experiences as interviewers, as well as jointly watch clips from masters in the wider field such as Bill Greider interviewing Bob Woodward in *Who Will Tell the People*. Larry sometimes showed the class examples of interviewers who could not swim in the deep end of the pool, and asked us how we would have moved the interview forward if we were sitting in the interviewer's chair. He consistently had us interview, reflect, and interview again. That formed the basis of his classroom pedagogy. I learned a great deal, but I simply did not have time with three other classes to do that many interviews. It was after I finished my graduate course work, when I did have that research time, that continuing the conversation with Goodwyn proved so invaluable to my own learning as an oral historian.

9. Emilye Crosby raises an important point here. In my first book I made a study of SNCC and Students for a Democratic Society (SDS) because, to my mind, they made significant contributions to democratic practice in the nation's history and had not received significant historical attention for those efforts. However, what if particular SNCC and SDSers did not see themselves in those terms? In other words, what if they were not driven to act by a desire for more democracy but, instead, were striving toward another goal? How to grapple with what they might understand for themselves, compared to what I saw in their activity? Again, the key is to trace, carefully, their understanding of their own activity, as well as illuminate the meaning I see it might have for democratic practice. Some in SNCC saw themselves as democratic innovators, but that didn't mobilize or motivate everyone, or even most. How to tell that complex truth is something I found almost impossible in my collective biography of SNCC.

10. Mark Nepo, *Seven Thousand Ways to Listen: Staying Close to What Is Sacred* (New York: Free Press, 2012,) Kindle location 60.

# PART III

★　★　★　★　★　★　★　★

## Challenge the Smug Orthodoxy

### Democratic Money and Writing History

★　★　★　★　★　★　★　★

Arguably the most important tool Goodwyn resuscitated from the dustbin of history was the Populists' Sub-Treasury Plan. As Connie Lester expertly explains, its goal was simple: put money at the service of farmers, take power away from the banks. The Populists envisioned a plan to democratize the nation's monetary system. In terms of Texas politics, the Sub-Treasury Plan reflected the tag line of Yarborough's 1950s campaign, "Put the jam on the bottom shelf where the little man can reach it." As a challenge to the power of banks to create money and control credit, of course, financial elites totally dismissed the plan, in the 1880s as much as in the late 1970s when Goodwyn brought the Sub-Treasury Plan back to people's attention with the publication of *Democratic Promise*.

Just trying to make sure, and not an economist by training himself, Goodwyn showed up outside the office door of Bill Yohe, a well-regarded economist at Duke who specialized in monetary policy, and asked him simply: "This is the Sub-Treasury Plan that the Populists floated. Can you run the numbers, and see if it would have worked, either then or now?" Yohe agreed. After studying the plan, his answer was clear: it was a sound idea. It "constituted a workable basis for the monetary system" and would have achieved "real income redistribution in favor of 'the producing classes.'" Yohe thought it would have worked in the 1800s, except that it threatened the banks.[1] Giving government direct authority to provide loans to the producing classes, helping small farmers escape the often usurious and crippling credit conditions of private banks—it was a simple, revolutionary idea, then and now.

Its revolutionary potential, in the end, was precisely the reason why elites fought so hard to kill the proposal. Democratizing credit might well have ended the rule of private finance, more pronounced in the twenty-first century than at any previous point in US history.

The original populism constituted a moment in US history in which ordinary people challenged a core feature of the established order—the creation and control of credit—from below. These farmers at the base were, in the eyes of elites then and now, essentially invisible; they were people who worked with their hands, too unsophisticated to question the established order. And yet, as Goodwyn showed, they not only generated the largest working-class movement in US history, they also mounted one of the most promising challenges to the established order.

For later generations, the problem became one of seeing, or not seeing. As so often in US history, the victors told the tale. Stories were reduced to the deeds of leaders. Populism largely vanished from widespread view the same way as the Regulators, the Readjuster Party, or many other nonelite actors before them. Goodwyn's face always purpled when academics, big-city newspaper editors, or talking heads on television attached the term "populist" to any insurgency that questioned the wisdom of the (supposedly) meritocratic elite. The preeminent question for generations of Goodwyn's students—and the question animating this book—has been how to bring the insights, experiences, and lessons of people's movements back to life and demonstrate their importance in informing struggles for justice in the present; how to make them part of what teachers teach and students learn about the richly embattled tapestry that is US history; how to process the lessons from Populism, both in success and in eventual defeat, for new generations of small-*d* democratic activists.

Making everyday people's innovations visible to the wider public remains Goodwyn's largest gift to the pursuit of justice. In this section Bill Greider, Tim Tyson, and George Waldrep reflect on the ways they learned to see and then share their own pathbreaking forms of everyday people making history. "He gave me the language and the nerve to write seriously about the idea of democracy," recalled Greider, "to reject the dominant culture's cynicism and self-congratulations, to tune out the mass-market propaganda that passes for political speech." Greider also expounds on Goodwyn's repeated admonition that "the facts do not speak for themselves." No. For Goodwyn, facts always required context and perspective. Without giving facts meaning, they were literally meaningless.

Clarity, imagination, storytelling. To give a person permission to think and imagine outside inherited patterns of thinking was the great promise of self-organized political community, as Waldrep notes. Tyson's hilarious story of Larry joining his graduate students' Saturday night ring dance provides a rare glimpse into Goodwyn's unstoppable personal drive to build community. Larry often told of his father saying, "Southerners act the way they do because they don't know any better." Yet he and several of his students set out, vividly and successfully, to share tales of southerners who actually did find a better way to live.

Lane Windham and Marsha Darling use the lenses Goodwyn helped them develop to show these tools in action. We see through Windham's oral histories a portrait of movement and institution building—and how they reinforce one another. Movement culture, or "collective self-confidence," served as a powerful battering ram against the idea that "this is just the way it is and is always going to be." Darling's call to arms at the beginning of the new decade and the dawn of the Biden-Harris administration reminds us of the organizing work we must do in order to bring a new generation of people power together.

Sadly, as this book was making its way to light, William Greider passed on to the ancestors. Greider's towering achievements as a journalist have been registered elsewhere.[2] We asked Bill to contribute to this volume because of the clarity and depth of his work, long before other people could see, on ideas that have now become truisms: the corporate takeover of democracy, the financialization of political power, the globalization of capitalism with borders opened for goods but not people. Greider was above all else someone who measured politics against the promise of America. In the last three decades, he chronicled betrayal everywhere. "Pessimism and resignation are in the saddle," Greider reflected. But "faith in the democratic idea requires the long view of history. Even in adversity, it is an accomplishment to keep the idea alive for the next generation."

## Notes

1. William P. Yohe, "An Economic Appraisal of the Sub-Treasury Plan," Appendix B to *Democratic Promise: The Populist Moment in America*, by Lawrence Goodwyn (New York: Oxford University Press, 1976), 580.

2. See in particular Jessica Corbett, "A Stark Loss for American Journalism," *Common Dreams*, December 27, 2019, https://www.commondreams.org/news/2019/12/27/stark-loss-american-journalism-reporter-and-author-william-greider-dies-age-83; Katrina vanden Heuvel, "Remembering Bill Greider," *Nation*, December 27, 2019, https://www.thenation.com/article/william-greider-obituary/.

# 19

## To Break the Hold of the Money Class
### The Sub-Treasury Plan

CONNIE L. LESTER

The most innovative ideas on the role of government in the economy emerged from the so-called agrarian revolution of the late nineteenth century. Alliancemen and Populists described their actions as a fight against the "money class" of industrialists and a rising class of "middlemen." In his 1891 inaugural address, Tennessee governor John P. Buchanan, former president of the state's Farmers' Alliance, articulated the fundamental difference between the emerging industrial capitalism and republican visions of a more egalitarian political economy: "Progress does not mean a mushroom growth of 'booms' and wild speculation in which a few are enriched to the detriment of the many." Unprecedented levels of inequality marked the transformation of the American economy from that of an agrarian–small manufacturing nation to an urban, industrial society whose innovation in processing, construction, and transportation expanded wealth, improved health, and created consumerism. The negative consequences of the new economy were experienced most by small farmers and agricultural labor, small manufacturers, and factory workers. In ways that parallel our own recent movement to post-industrialization, the working people of the late nineteenth century struggled with displacement geographically, politically, and economically.[1]

Even as the events that constituted the agrarian uprising unfolded, they were being documented and interpreted by scholars. W. Scott Morgan saw the rural unrest as an "impending revolution." N. A. Dunning was less inflammatory in his rhetoric, but he described an insurgency that was no less transformative. In the 1930s as the nation grappled with the Great Depression, John D. Hicks interpreted the rise of the Farmers' Alliance and Populism within the context of economic upheaval and the closing of the frontier to argue that farmers reacted in a practical manner to the barriers that industrialization placed before them. In *The Age of Reform* (1955), Richard Hofstadter analyzed the Populist revolt within the context of recent world experiences with European populism and concluded that the farmers suffered from "status anxiety" as they confronted the social and political repercussions of industrial capitalism. Their responses placed them on the margins of American history. Writing in the aftermath of the successes of grassroots organizing in the civil rights era, historians of the 1970s sympathized with the farmers of the late nineteenth century. Robert C. McMath Jr. focused on the social connections that supported the growth of farmer organizations such as the Agricultural Wheel and the Farmers' Alliance. Lawrence Goodwyn found the origins of the People's Party in the cooperative movement of the Farmers' Alliance and argued that these grassroots organizations represented the democratic promise that had long remained unfulfilled.

In 1976 with his pathbreaking history of the Farmers' Alliance, *Democratic Promise: The Populist Moment in America*, Goodwyn fundamentally changed historians' understanding of the Populists for the next half century. He arguably shifted many historians' understanding of social movements more broadly, and of economic theories, and perhaps even shifted some economists' thinking as well. Certainly his work reset the framework for understanding the populists' economic theories more generally.[2]

The central problem farmers in the 1870s and 1880s faced was an economic one. As the nation became an industrial power and farmers moved from sustainable, family-oriented, diverse production to market-oriented agriculture, they assumed higher costs as they purchased additional land, new labor-saving equipment, improved seed, and fertilizer. The costs of meeting new market standards and transporting crops to distant cities added to their economic burdens. The expected payoff for engaging in market production proved elusive. In an age of monetary deflation, which benefited industrialists, the return to farmers remained perilously low, sometimes falling below the costs of production. Whereas farmers once sold locally to men they knew, they now dealt with elevator and warehouse operators, railroads whose policies and prices originated in corporate offices, and so-called middlemen who profited from big-city commodity markets and futures markets. In the end, farmers earned the least of all the lengthening line of men who profited from their hard, sweaty work. The specifics of the imbalance varied slightly from region to region, but the results were the same. Whereas farming once provided a competency for rural families across generations, by the second half of the nineteenth century it too often led to impoverishment and bankruptcy.[3]

The Homestead Act of 1892 and the United States' military campaigns of aggression against Native Americans opened land in the middle of the continent for settlement. The ability to acquire 160 acres for the cost of a filing fee attracted many young men and their families, who saw an opportunity to establish a farm and build wealth for themselves and their children. Although the plains states experienced a number of years of adequate rain and good weather in the 1880s, the so-called American desert was a harsh environment—hot in the summer, with deep cold in the winter, and plagues of insects, tornadoes, and grass fires of biblical proportion. In addition, the deep-rooted prairie grass, limited rainfall, treeless landscape, and the necessity of expensive technology to provide water meant the challenges for living west of the 100th meridian were not for the faint of heart.

Although the land was free, the US Department of Agriculture (USDA) estimated that the cost of turning the land, digging a well and building a windmill to bring the water to the surface, and putting in the first crop was $1,000 or more, at a time when the average farm income was $250–$300. Farmers did not move to the plains to practice self-sufficiency or safety-first agriculture. They produced for the market, and many found that 160 acres was not enough. As they expanded their acreage, they invested in additional technology, mortgaging land to pay for harvesters, balers, and eventually powered tractors. When the good weather ended and the plains states once again returned to dry summers, insect infestations, and crop failures, many farmers recognized their own situation in the sign attached to a wagon loaded with family heading east: *In God we trusted, in Kansas we busted.* Selling their corn and wheat on global markets, American farmers competed with settlers on newly opened lands in western Canada, in Australia, and in Eastern Europe. A crop failure in Kansas or Nebraska did not raise prices—there were too many producers in other areas of the world selling their abundance on the global market.[4]

In the South, farmers faced similar challenges in regard to world markets, but under somewhat different circumstances. In his seminal book *The Mind of the South*, W. J. Cash described the region in the aftermath of the Civil War as a return to the frontier.[5] Intentional and incidental destruction caused by the movement of armies of unprecedented size left orchards destroyed, fences burned, fields trampled, and livestock killed or scattered. Fields that had gone unworked for years now grew brambles and weeds.

Seed rotted, wells filled in, tools were lost or were now essentially useless. Men returned from the fighting without limbs, addicted to morphine, reduced in strength by endless bouts of diarrhea, and shattered in mind and spirit. Starting over was a feat in human determination.

If the barriers to rebuilding the farms were significant for whites, they were almost insurmountable for freed people. Without land, tools, livestock, and money, many African American farmers initially sought to live off the land until whites instituted Black Codes that punished unemployment and vagrancy with court-imposed sentences that required work on white-owned farms and plantations. As freedmen sought work in agriculture, they did so on terms they hoped would lead to future land ownership. They refused to work under the regimen of gang labor that had characterized slavery and insisted on working individual plots of land. They moved cabins formerly used by enslaved people away from the plantation house and entered a system of sharecropping that provided them with tools, seeds, a mule, a cabin, a basic food supply, and a share of the crop they produced. The expectations of Black farmers that they would move up the agricultural ladder from tenancy to land ownership were largely foiled as the strictures imposed by annual contracts left most farmers in perpetual debt to plantation stores or to local crossroads merchants. Unable to pay off the loan after the sale of the crop, sharecroppers signed a contract for another year of work.[6]

White farmers needed cash to rebuild. But cash, never in abundance in the South, was extremely limited in the 1870s. Dependent on rural merchants for store credit to obtain seed and tools, farmers who had previously practiced subsistence agriculture to provide for their needs and avoid risk quickly found themselves in debt. With no assets except their future crops, the farmers who worked marginal lands were pushed into production for commercial markets and found themselves locked in an endless cycle of debt and hard work. Like the farmers on the plains, southern producers competed in a global market. The need for new seeds, tools, and fertilizers was met with a crop lien whereby the merchant charged excessive rates for credit and collected his loan when the farmer sold his crop at market.

In a highly competitive market, cotton and tobacco prices dropped; by the mid-1890s, cotton sold at 5 cents per pound, although the USDA reported that the cost of producing a pound of cotton was 10 cents. Farm leaders counseled small farmers to abandon cotton and "live at home," producing for their basic needs and marketing the excess, as they had done before the war. Their debts to merchants dictated otherwise. Inevitably they signed for another year of credit, and the merchant demanded the planting of cotton as a marketable crop that he could sell. For many the store debt finally became unsustainable, and the merchant took control of the debtor's land; farmers in many parts of the South were working land as tenants that they had once owned.[7]

The Farmers' Alliance, which organized and spread throughout the South and the plains states, operated to remedy the impoverishment of American farmers. Its economic agenda initially focused on the development of farmer-owned cooperatives that would sell farm seeds, tools, and fertilizers to members at wholesale prices, thus reducing the input costs for producing commercial crops. Farmer-owned marketing cooperatives hoped to raise commodity prices by marketing the production of hundreds, or even thousands, of farms. With lower input costs and higher market prices, farmers would emerge from debt, return to competency, and protect their land assets for future generations. Cooperatives depended on self-financing by farmer-members. Purchasing through the cooperative stores required cash. Alliance cooperatives were successful for limited periods in some areas, but overall the farm community could not sustain the cooperative model.[8]

At the 1890 meeting of the Southern Farmers' Alliance in conjunction with the Colored Farmers' Alliance and the Farmers Mutual Benefit Association, a multilayered plan was devised to address the related political and social struggles farmers faced. Labeled the Ocala Demands, the document articulated seven major points. Banking and money demands were designed to create a modest inflation to address the problems of debt. Farmers wanted the abolition of national banks, a change that was designed to prevent the exit of money from the agricultural regions to higher-interest investment in the northeastern cities. They demanded an increase in circulating capital to $50 per capita in order to reduce dependency on credit and promote investment in rural areas. In another nod to the need for "soft money" policies, they demanded the free and unlimited coinage of silver. In language that had its origins in antebellum democratic politics, they pronounced their adherence to the "doctrine of equal rights to all and special privileges to none," a position that they interpreted to mean that national legislation would not privilege one segment of the economy over another, would remove extraordinary tariffs, and would reduce government expenditures to the necessities. In order to pay for government, they demanded a graduated income tax. They demanded regulation of transportation and communication systems, and if regulation did not produce the desired results, they wanted government ownership of these public necessities. They demanded the abolition of the futures market. They wanted laws prohibiting alien ownership of land, to reduce the amount of land held by syndicates. They also wanted ownership of land by railroads and corporations reduced to what was needed for use. Finally, in order to ensure that their influence in Congress equaled that of industries and corporations, they demanded the popular election of US senators.

The most controversial demand appeared near the beginning of the document. Called the Sub-Treasury Plan, it relied on federal support for its administration and stability. As Lawrence Goodwyn noted, "the sub-treasury was the one issue that addressed the enduring realities in the lives of most Southern farmers, the furnishing merchant and his crop lien." Historian Charles Postel called it "one of the most innovative proposals for federal intervention in the economy ever to enter American politics."[9]

Simply put, the Sub-Treasury Plan (STP) offered loans for small farmers with either their land or their crops as collateral. If farmers used their land as collateral, they paid 1 percent interest for a fifty-year loan; if farmers used crops as collateral, they paid 2 percent interest for a one-year loan. The STP proposed that a "subtreasury" office of the US Treasury Department run the STP, produce the cash, and administer the mortgages. The Plan aimed to increase the overall amount of money in proportion to the number of people because, as activist Harry Tracy noted, "the history of mankind furnishes no instance wherein the people in any civilized nation were contented, prosperous or happy while money was scarce or while it was concentrated in just a few hands."[10]

First articulated at Ocala and later incorporated into the platform of the People's Party, the Sub-Treasury Plan marked a radical departure from citizens' understanding of the role of government in securing and sustaining wealth. From the outset of the republic, the federal government had provided a means of wealth development by making public lands available for settlement. The structured scheme for land distribution encapsulated in the Northwest Ordinances first enacted under the Articles of Confederation continued in the early republic and found renewed vigor with the Homestead Act of 1862. Although the best land seldom went to the poorest men, settlers colonized the land stolen by the US government from Indigenous people, following their violent displacement and genocide. White men had reason to believe they might use this land to secure a comfortable living for themselves and pass down the opportunity to profit from the land to their heirs. Such promise was inherent in their understanding of the American dream.

The Sub-Treasury Plan would have added a new layer of federal support for agricultural prosperity and the ability of ordinary farmers to secure their claims of personal wealth and prosperity. The plan required the construction of government-supported warehouses in every county that produced staple crops: corn, wheat, cotton, and tobacco. Farmers could deposit their crops in the warehouse and obtain negotiable warehouse receipts. They could sell their crops throughout the year. (Farmers understood that one reason for low prices was the necessity of selling all the crop immediately after harvesting, dumping large amounts on the market and driving down prices.) At the end of the crop year, any crop remaining in the warehouse would be sold at market price. Farmers paid a small fee for storage and 2 percent interest on the money advanced through warehouse receipts. The subtreasury provided a mechanism for southern farmers to bypass the crop lien, get out of debt, purchase their farm inputs with cash, and manage the marketing of their crops. In other words, small farmers could enter the market with less risk and engage in wealth-producing strategies rather than simply servicing debt.

As might be imagined, push-back against the plan was formidable. Bankers feared losing their ability to charge farmers 8 percent and more on loans. Agricultural commodity speculators feared that farmers, given the ability to store their harvest and stagger their sales, could be their *own* speculators. Large planters would lose their profits from exploitative crop-lien financing of their tenants.[11] Southern Democrats used advocacy for the subtreasury as a yardstick for measuring loyalty to the party; they pushed men who supported it into the newly established People's (Populist) Party. Both Democratic and Republican Party stalwarts denounced the plan as unworkable and a product of the ramblings of uneducated "rubes." Plains-states and western farmers had their doubts as well, and many insisted that land be added to the list of agricultural assets that could be used to secure cash for farm families. In the end, the Sub-Treasury Plan died with the defeat of the Populists in the 1892 and 1896 elections. For the foreseeable future, fair and easy access to credit for farmers was dead.

And yet, the idea of government intervention in agriculture and in protecting access to wealth development remained. We see its resurrection in the New Deal with the Agricultural Adjustment Act, the Farm Credit Bill, and other efforts to support agricultural prices and provide farmers with the means to engage competitively in global markets and live comfortably in the emerging consumer society. When Duke economist Bill Yohe, who specialized in monetary policy, ran the numbers in the 1970s for Goodwyn on the eve of publication of *Democratic Promise*, Yohe concluded that not only would the STP have worked but its "mechanism for making land and commodity loans was a very subtle one." After extensive testing, Yohe found that the STP "simultaneously would have contended with the problems of financing cooperatives, the seasonal volatility of basic commodity prices, the scarcity of banking offices in rural areas, the lack of a 'lender of last resort' for agriculture, inefficient storage and cross-shipping, the downward stickiness of prices paid by farmers vis-à-vis prices received for crops, and the efforts of the secular deflation on farmers' debt burdens." It was a single mechanism to address every one of these problems, Yohe concluded, "all of which, in a far less comprehensive fashion, were the objects of legislation in the next five decades."[12] In short, it would have worked, and provided a clear solution to give the small farmer access to fair credit.

Today, although independent small-scale farmers continue to struggle in the markets and remain vulnerable to incremental changes in commodity prices, the range of people involved in agriculture—from farm laborers to independent farmers to employees of corporate agriculture—constitute less than 1 percent of the workforce. The repeating pattern from the past, however, is a clear through-line: the inability to build and transfer wealth for working-class and middle-class Americans.

In place of crop liens, high transportation costs, and futures markets, Americans now face rising debt from health care costs, student loans, and the price of housing. Working Americans receiving the lowest wages cannot open and maintain bank accounts and are dependent on payday loans at exorbitant rates to meet demands their earnings will not cover. Too many working Americans are homeless or near-homeless. Hard work and frugal living does not protect working people. They are vulnerable to the descent into poverty that prevents the accumulation of wealth to address personal disasters, plan for comfortable aging, or provide a reasonable inheritance for the next generation.[13] At this point in the postindustrial/information economy, no popular movements have put forward an equivalent plan that allows working people fair and accessible credit. Nonetheless, the Sub-Treasury Plan remains, visible if not well known, as an idea on which present and future citizens might build.

# Notes

1. Robert H. White, ed., *Messages of the Governors of Tennessee* (Nashville: Tennessee Historical Commission, 1952–90), 7: 370; Connie L. Lester, *Up from the Mudsills of Hell: The Farmers' Alliance, Populism, and Progressive Agriculture in Tennessee, 1870–1915* (Athens: University of Georgia Press, 2006), 96.

2. By the early twenty-first century, scholars questioned the view of earlier scholars that populism and the agrarian insurgency ended with the 1896 election. Charles Postel examined "protest thought in a time of technological transformation, incorporation, and globalization" and found that the populist vision was one of remarkable modernity in its intellectual foundations, its public mobilization, and its commitment to progress. Using roll call votes, Elizabeth Sanders demonstrated the ways in which Populist ideas were transformed into Progressive laws in the early decades of the twentieth century. Connie Lester followed the Alliance and Populist leaders in Tennessee as they continued their advocacy post-1896, not as political candidates, but embedded in the new state and federal agricultural bureaucracies. W. Scott Morgan, *History of the Wheel and Alliance and the Impending Revolution* (Hardy, Ark., 1889); N. A. Dunning, *The Farmers' Alliance History and Agricultural Digest* (Washington, DC: Farmers' Alliance, 1889); John D. Hicks, *The Populist Revolt: The Farmers' Alliance and the People's Party* (1931; repr., Minneapolis: University of Minnesota Press, 1955); Richard Hofstadter, *The Age of Reform: From Bryan to FDR* (New York: Knopf, 1955); Robert C. McMath Jr., *American Populism: A Social History, 1877–1898* (New York: Hill & Wang, 1978); Lawrence Goodwyn, *Democratic Promise: The Populist Moment in America* (New York: Oxford University Press, 1976); Charles Postel, *The Populist Vision* (New York: Oxford University Press, 2007), 4; Elizabeth Sanders, *Roots of Reform: Farmers, Workers, and the American State, 1877–1917* (Chicago: University of Chicago Press, 1999); Lester, *Up from the Mudsills of Hell.*

3. William Cronon, *Nature's Metropolis: Chicago and the Great West* (New York: Norton, 1991), 97–147; Roger L. Ransom and Richard Sutch, "Debt Peonage in the Cotton South after the Civil War," *Journal of Economic History* 32.3 (1972): 641–99; David Silkenat, "'Hard Times Is the Cry': Debt in Populist Thought in North Carolina," in *Populism in the South Revisited: New Interpretations and New Departures,* ed. James M. Beeby (Jackson: University Press of Mississippi, 2012), 101–27.

4. Julie Courtwright, "The Great Plains," in *The Routledge History of Rural America,* ed. Pamela Riney-Kehrberg (New York: Routledge, 2016), 70–85.

5. W. J. Cash, *The Mind of the South* (New York: Knopf, 1941).

6. Roger L. Ransom and Richard Sutch, *One Kind of Freedom: The Economic Consequences of Emancipation* (Cambridge: Cambridge University Press, 1977); Gerald H. Gaither, *Blacks and the Populist Movement: Ballots and Bigotry in the New South* (Tuscaloosa: University of Alabama Press, 1977); Omar H. Ali, *In the Lion's Mouth: Black Populism in the New South, 1886–1900* (Jackson: University Press of Mississippi, 2010); Steven Hahn, *A Nation under Our Feet: Black Political Struggles in the Rural South from Slavery to the Great Migration* (Cambridge, MA: Belknap Press of Harvard University Press, 2003).

7. Ransom and Sutch, *One Kind of Freedom*; Robert Tracy McKenzie, *One South or Many? Plantation Belt and Upcountry in Civil War–Era Tennessee* (New York: Cambridge University Press, 1994).

8. Goodwyn, *Democratic Promise*, conclusion; Postel, *The Populist Vision*, 116–24; Donna A. Barnes, *Farmers in Rebellion: The Rise and Fall of the Southern Farmers Alliance and People's Party in Texas* (Austin: University of Texas Press, 1984), 54–65.

9. Goodwyn, *Democratic Promise*, 222; Postel, *The Populist Vision*, 153. As Postel notes on page 319, several versions of the Sub-Treasury Plan circulated in the 1890s. The best known was Charles Macune's, but William Peffer and Tom Watson circulated similar plans. In 1894 the Honorable Harry Tracy of Dallas, publisher of the *Southern Mercury*, contributed a summary titled "A Valuable Appendix, Treating of the Sub-Treasury Plan" to *A Political Revelation*, by James H. Davis. It is available as a PDF: https://babel.hathitrust.org/cgi/pt?id=nyp.33433084768633&view=1up&seq=7.

10. See Tracy, "A Valuable Appendix," 295; Barnes, *Farmers in Rebellion*, 112.

11. Barnes, *Farmers in Rebellion*, 121–22; Lawrence Goodwyn, *The Populist Moment: A Short History of the Agrarian Revolt in America* (New York: Oxford University Press, 1978), 98–115.

12. William P. Yohe, "An Economic Appraisal of the Sub-Treasury Plan," Appendix B in Goodwyn, *Democratic Promise*, 580.

13. David Graeber, *Debt: The First 5,000 Years* (Brooklyn, NY: Melville House, 2014), 374–77, 388–89.

# 20

## Unfulfilled Thirst

WILLIAM GREIDER

With his usual directness, Professor Lawrence Goodwyn told his doctor to tell the truth. How long did he have? Weeks, months, the doctor said. My old friend and Nell Goodwyn, his wife, shared the news. A great historian was dying, I realized, the teacher who has been my lodestar for more than a generation. I told Larry I needed to say some things, in case we didn't get another chance. Glad that I did. He died a month later on September 29, 2013; soon thereafter Duke held a memorial celebration on campus where he taught for thirty-one years.

Earlier that year, in August 2013, I was swimming in warm memories and I reminded him of some of our best moments. I didn't go to Duke myself. I met Larry through his classic history of the agrarian revolt, *Democratic Promise: The Populist Moment in America*, published in 1976. I was then a young reporter at the *Washington Post*, and it was a liberating encounter for me. His book reordered American political history as it is conventionally taught, actually turned it upside down. What I learned from Larry and his books is reflected in every book I wrote myself.[1]

The Professor, as I liked to call him, gave me an empowering way of thinking about our country—both critical and loving, sternly unsentimental on the facts but sustained by what I call Goodwyn's radical optimism. He believed democracy is possible, not more than that, and only if people learn how to organize themselves and demand it from the powerful forces that dominate their lives. Larry liked to say this idea of democracy is "unsanctioned" by the established authorities who run things. That sounded like solid ground to me, given the deformed and decayed condition of the American governing system.

We began a long-running conversation that stretched over thirty years in which we frequently exchanged ideas and understandings and he sometimes gently upbraided woolly digressions (sometimes not so gently). He gave me the language and the nerve to write seriously about the idea of democracy, to reject the dominant culture's cynicism and self-congratulations, to tune out the mass-market propaganda that passes for political speech. What a wonderful gift.

Goodwyn pushed students to recognize that by his measure Americans have never realized authentic democracy, not even close. Yet their unfulfilled thirst for voice and power endures despite the hostile circumstances. Democracy is hard to do, always has been. Genuine social movements are rare, he taught, and frequently fail. But if people persist over years, even generations, their activated consciousness can become the core force driving progress and justice, not the machinations of political parties or powerful leaders.

I think Goodwyn's singular accomplishment was to rescue this idea of democracy from the indifference of worn-out elites. At least he convinced me. I happen to know he convinced a lot of the young people who had taken his course on social movements. Some of them are organizers now, having learned what Goodwyn himself experienced about democracy and power in his younger years as a civil rights organizer in the South and campaigning for liberal candidates in Texas.

Larry's teaching style was insistent and uncompromising but also generous. I experienced it personally a couple of times and was taken aback by his intensity, also his artful method. I sent him the unedited text of my 1992 book *Who Will Tell the People: The Betrayal of American Democracy*, hoping for his endorsement. Instead, the Professor showed up at my door. He plopped the manuscript on my desk, picked up chapter 1, and demanded to know, "What is this chapter about?"

I thought it was obvious. But I fumbled around for an answer and didn't come up with a good one. I mumbled something vague. "Show me where in this chapter you say that." I thumbed through the pages, searching for a sentence that might get me off the hook. Couldn't find one. Larry scribbled a one-sentence critique on a PostIt and pasted it at the top of my computer screen. "The facts do not speak for themselves."

Then he picked up chapter 2 and went at me again. "What is this chapter about?" I scanned the pages, he repeated his mantra "The facts do not speak for themselves." That got us to the real question. "What do you want this book to say? Why don't you just say it?" We went through the drill for every chapter. After two days we were both exhausted, but I had a stack of fresh notes and a clear understanding of what the book needed.

On another occasion I went to Duke to deliver a lecture, and Larry lined up drop-by discussions for me at numerous departments. The most important was his own course on the history of social movements. When I arrived at the classroom, however, the discontent was palpable. The Professor announced that students must put aside their scheduled reading assignment and listen instead to his pal Greider.

The students exploded in rage and rebellion. One after another, they rose to rebuke Goodwyn for imposing his friend on the class without ever consulting them. They agreed the class would discuss instead the imperious professor who teaches "democracy" but damn sure does not practice it. The teaching assistant, Dirk Philipsen, tried to mediate but sided with the students. I was aghast and embarrassed. I never did get to talk.

Goodwyn, meanwhile, seemed oddly pleased with himself. He didn't yield, didn't apologize. Afterward, he explained. Goodwyn believed the principal asset for ordinary people trying to gain voice and influence in politics is their common experience—the knowledge they acquire from everyday life or inherit from family and values, even folk wisdom. Elites may acquire their knowledge from books and learned professors, but most folks get theirs from life itself.

While the Professor taught the concrete history of social movements, theory and principles, he wanted his students to experience the anger and frustration of being ignored and abused by implacable power, someone who refuses to respond to just demands. Larry evidently played the role of autocratic leader convincingly. Usually, he told me, it took five or six weeks of his irascible arrogance to provoke an uprising by the students, sometimes sooner if he was especially arrogant.

It's always about power—who has it, who doesn't—and power is almost never yielded without a fight. Larry knew this from experience. But that was not the radical element of his democratic faith. I once asked him, "When you talk about democracy, what do you mean?" "This is an unsanctioned idea," he said, "but this is the democratic idea. That the people will participate in the process by which their lives are organized."

Ask yourself: Do they? Most Americans are now used to saying, no, not really. They are either ignored or marginalized or easily manipulated by powerful interests. But Larry insisted that is not the end of the story. He never promised happy endings, but his radical optimism did assert that ordinary people are capable of changing outcomes, and far more ready and willing than elites will acknowledge. The system reduces people to infantile status, then dismisses them as babies.

The Goodwyn club for democratic promise is clearly a minority faction for now. Pessimism and resignation are in the saddle. But Larry always said that faith in the democratic idea requires the long view of history. Even in adversity, it is an accomplishment to keep the idea alive for the next generation. Larry did that surely. For a vivid sample of Goodwyn's thinking, check out "Democratic Money," a forum we staged in St. Louis in 1989 to illuminate the antidemocratic nature of the Federal Reserve.[2]

Larry documented a basis for sustaining our radical optimism. His other seminal book—*Breaking the Barrier: The Rise of Solidarity in Poland* (1991)—tells the extraordinary tale of how Polish shipyard workers kept alive their struggle to create an independent trade union for two generations. After the Communists crushed them in the 1950s, these insurgents went underground for years until the moment in 1980 when they resurfaced and their great strike foreshadowed the demise of Soviet domination.

My last conversation with Larry, strange as it sounds, was exuberant. It was two weeks before he died. I was explaining how the handful of progressive Senate Democrats managed to roll President Obama on his desire to appoint Larry Summers as Federal Reserve chair. This is a potential opening for more progressive upheavals ahead, I told the Professor, maybe even a change in direction at the Fed. Because the president will have the opportunity to name four or five new Fed governors in the months ahead and—if he has the nerve—Barack Obama could change a central bank, maybe even mount a joint campaign to revive the economy.

Larry grilled me for more political details and picked up on my enthusiasm. I ran down the names of governors and described their policy inclinations and party affiliations. He asked how to spell one of the names, which I did. "What's his first name?" For the moment, I couldn't remember. Later on, he asked again. It dawned on me. Larry must be taking notes, rigorous to the end.

## Notes

1. William Greider, The Education of David Stockman and Other Americans (New York: Dutton 1982); Secrets of the Temple: How the Federal Reserve Runs the Country (New York: Simon & Schuster, 1987); The Trouble with Money: A Prescription for America's Financial Fever (Knoxville, TN: Whittle Direct Books, 1989); Who Will Tell the People?: The Betrayal of American Democracy (New York: Simon & Schuster, 1992); One World, Ready or Not: The Manic Logic of Global Capitalism (New York: Simon & Schuster, 1997); Fortress America: The American Military and the Consequences of

Peace (New York: Public Affairs, 1998); The Soul of Capitalism: Opening Paths to a Moral Economy (New York: Simon & Schuster, 2003).

2. Lawrence Goodwyn and William Greider, "Democratic Money: A Populist Perspective," remarks delivered in St. Louis, MO, December 9, 1989, on the 100th anniversary of the Populist Sub-Treasury Plan, https://www.populist.com/Goodwyn.Greider.html.

# 21

## How Lawrence Goodwyn Gave Me My Life

TIM TYSON

Goodwyn ranks as one of the handful of US historians who have had something timeless to say. He frequently used to note that ordinary citizens, under every government ever known, harbor a deep sense of grievance. Around kitchen tables and in barroom booths, people vent their sense that their government exercises an unaccountable dominion over their lives and offers them little in return. And yet, Professor Goodwyn would continue, popular uprisings are rare and successful revolutions virtually unknown.

In 1988 Larry shared his office in the basement of West Duke with me, an act of breathtaking generosity from a professor to a graduate student. He was working on *Breaking the Barrier* and other writings that sought to nail down what he knew about popular movements. Perhaps he was inspired to this generosity by my tireless capacity to drink with the stream of Polish intellectuals and organizers who visited in those days, accompanied by their weary, indifferent Communist handlers. We'd crowd and sometimes pound the tables at Val's Upstairs, talking about movements and democracy. My boxes of papers are still littered with ink-stained cocktail napkins, blotted upon them phrases like "democracy is an unsanctioned idea everywhere" and "thoughts about lack of power are themselves silenced as inadmissible" and "popular skepticism recoups dignity but remains largely a terminology of resignation."

Goodwyn's meditations on democracy became increasingly useful as I grew into a historian of the postwar civil rights movement in the South. Larry never wrote about the civil rights movement as a historian, but his insights about social movements partook of his experiences in it. At a party in Madison, Wisconsin, I once met a man who had been in jail with Larry after a sit-in demonstration in a remote Texas border town, though Larry had never spoken of it. His intimate knowledge of the movement helped to ground my historical understanding.

Larry understood what an obstacle being a white southerner could be to someone writing African American history. By its very nature, he taught me, the subject makes you a dissident from your own culture, a culture that has a lot invested in forgetting much of that history. I was pretty comfortable being a dissident, but Goodwyn called my attention to the power of received culture.

Although people commonly live in a quiet posture of resentful resignation toward their governments, many things keep them from protesting, Goodwyn thought. Sure, there are reprisals and coercions of many kinds for open dissidents. But stronger still are received cultures that render protest as some kind of betrayal. It is humiliating not to have an effective voice, but human beings say cynical things like "you can't fight City Hall" or "it's not what you know, it's who you know," and myriad explanations for why the world is unjust and resistance is pointless.

These private complaints save our dignity—at least we know we're being shortchanged, and sometimes we even cite real injustice—but offer us only a language of resignation. We render unto Caesar those things that Caesar claims belong to him; more often than not, organized religion strikes a deal with entrenched power, too, and only rarely compares our highest values with our government's actions. In the South, white Protestant ministers in the civil rights era usually preached from the assumption that the church's mission was to help sinners toward personal salvation, not to use the teachings of Jesus to examine the world around us.

Social movements break through this torpor when people get organized, Goodwyn believed. It doesn't happen because of some spontaneous uprising; it doesn't happen when times get hard enough; and most of the ways we have learned to talk about social movements disguise their actual history and future promise. Where social movements are concerned, tides don't rise, floodwaters don't sweep the land, and nothing spreads like a prairie fire. When we use the metaphors of meteorology to describe a social movement, it usually means we don't really know what occurred or how.

Goodwyn called these ways of talking about movements "the view from afar." That is, only someone very distant from the process can see the movement as a wind, a tide, a flood, or a fire. Activists make movements happen, usually working in a tradition of struggle, most often using networks and resources gathered over many years to spur uprisings that distant admirers will soon romanticize as "spontaneous." Sometimes the organizers are able to recruit and mobilize enough people, and those people are able to educate themselves enough through their own experiences, to build a movement that changes things for the better, for a time, in a place—and these are the moments, as the poet Seamus Heaney writes, when "justice can rise up / And hope and history rhyme." But social revolution is not the weather, and the best weather means nothing if people don't manage to raise a sail.

The movement always begins at some kitchen table, Goodwyn liked to say, where a handful of citizens with an unusual sense of their own self-worth and a well-grounded set of grievances start to realize that they are not alone in their predicaments. When they begin to recruit others, the movement begins. For that, they have to figure out how to get beyond their own kitchen tables. A recruitment strategy develops: come join us and do X, and you won't suffer unduly and it might even help matters. If the proposal is persuasive, the movement grows. As it does, it sees itself as a democratic insurgency in action. It starts to develop a movement culture; this creates a sense of belonging that strengthens all and attracts others. In time, there will be a response from the authorities, and this will be instructive: suddenly the barriers become visible, and the movement learns much about the limits of the society it is trying to change, and often so do any number of onlookers, many of whom are recruited to the movement by their newfound knowledge. The movement's outlook becomes steadily more radical: that is, it cuts to the roots of what must change.

With each successive experience, the movement learns more about the larger society and goes to school on its own experience. More epiphanies occur as the society responds to its growing dissident insurgency. And if the movement is able to grow enough, and if it manages to foster enough hope in the hearts of its adherents, it will eventually become powerful enough to change the existing social order. But this sequential development is usually interrupted somewhere along the way, or the movement loses sight of its mission and eventually peters out.

Everything depends upon the movement drawing the right lessons from its experience, and ultimately it comes down to recruitment: if a movement continues to recruit, it will ultimately be able to create a new regime more in line with its values. Solidarity in Poland grew until virtually all of the adults in the country belonged to the same union, and then that union became the government. The Populists prospered until they nearly took power, but they lost sight of their hard-won analysis and got co-opted by a presidential election that they lost. The civil rights movement grew large and powerful enough to effect some important changes, but fractured internally and wasn't able to recruit enough adherents to address its higher ambitions, particularly in the realm of economics.

I can't begin to capture Goodwyn's lifetime of hard-won wisdom in a few paragraphs, but these are some of the ways that we talked about democratic social movements. Sometimes we'd gather a few friends at Val's Upstairs, a local taproom that in Durham, North Carolina, was one of the "unsteepled" places of worship that E. P. Thompson wrote about in *The Making of the English Working Class*, free spaces where people could talk freely about their society and engage in democratic experimentation. We'd gather at a table in the back and hash out ideas and tell stories about democratic social movements, with Larry holding court, really. If he did more than his share of the talking, most of us didn't mind, because we were learning what we wanted to know most: how ordinary people have tried to change history and sometimes succeeded.

More often we drank coffee at our desks in the musty basement of West Duke, writing more than we talked. As he honed his sentences, Larry might read me a passage that he thought worked pretty well. His yardstick was a radical historian twenty years his senior, C. Vann Woodward, with whom he shared a distinctly southern and steely irony and a Faulknerian sense of tragedy, whether Larry was writing about East Texas or Eastern Europe.

Perhaps my favorite passage, however, is about a hillside in Pennsylvania where Confederate general Robert E. Lee decided, defying fundamental logic, to launch Pickett's Charge. It is a passage, I think, that achieves its clarity through Larry's love for his father, who told him, as Larry told me many times, "Southerners do what they do because they don't know any better."

Larry wrote: "The army of the South, and the society it represented, impaled itself on the guns of Cemetery Ridge, on a present it could not understand, on a future it could not contemplate, because it had renounced the . . . capacity for critical reflection. It was one of those tragic junctures in history when people died because they could not think. . . . A fearful dynamic was set loose on the younger generation and on the unborn generations. . . . From this moment, the South was to be defended, not appraised. . . . [Henceforth] the cause required the defense of hierarchy itself. . . . One defended one's captains."

On rare occasions when he thought he'd hit one that well, Larry would say, almost to himself, "The old man would have liked that." He meant Woodward. But I believe he meant his father, too.

I will offer one tale that few remember. Our crew in the doctoral program survived by an acute sense of community that Larry understood instinctively and admired unreservedly. He was perhaps the only one who saw no contradiction when Colonel Dave Johnson, one of the most accomplished soldiers of his generation, and I, an inveterate antiwar protestor, became such close friends. He knew intuitively that we were developing our own movement culture, and he recognized its rituals when he saw them unfold. Community itself was an act of resistance to being diminished by the thoughtless hierarchies and many-sided idiocies of the academy. Larry taught us to understand not only history but our own lives.

To that end, and perhaps others, we had parties. Yes, we did. Quite possibly they were at my house. Occasionally Larry dropped by and talked politics at the kitchen table for hours.

But Larry happened never to have witnessed one of our group rituals, an almost tribal dance performed to songs like Grace Jones's "Bullshit." At some point in the evening, we would crank up the music and move into a circle, clapping in polyrhythmic defiance, chanting, "I'm sick and tired of all this bullshit." We all danced together and then, in turn, each of us would shuffle into the center, perform our own unique step, and then yield to the next member of the circle. This ritual seemed a little like the ring shout in the early Black church. And I know now that we were, in fact, a church of sorts.

Larry arrived one night just as this wholly unfamiliar dance ritual began. He stepped right into our circle. Dancing was clearly not his habit, but he refused to be the one to break community. Shifting from one foot to the next awkwardly, he made himself as comfortable as he could. But then we started our dancing one by one into the center and I saw Larry's face struck by mild terror. He hadn't expected a public solo.

But when his turn came, Larry strode to the center. And there he performed what I can only call an interpretive dance. It was not, strictly speaking, dancing in any conventional sense. But Larry used his hands, feet, and face, acting out in jazz rhythm his uneasy age, his awkward professional position, his fear of making a fool of himself, his adoration for our community, and his decision to dive into its dance with all of his being. The astonishing performance art of Larry's dance-drama could not have been exceeded by an artiste with a grant from the National Endowment for the Humanities and an off-Broadway stage.

Larry saw the best in us, and he rose to meet it. One day, as we sat quietly in the office, he looked up at me and smiled. "You know the problem with you, Tyson?" He gave me a moment to be bewildered. "You want to lead the Revolution. And then you want to get a nice thank-you note from the king." He went back to his work, muttering, "Damned if you might not pull it off."

# 22

## Collective Self-Confidence

### African American Women's Organizing in Tobacco Leaf Houses

LANE WINDHAM

When I was considering going back to history graduate school after having worked in the labor movement for nearly twenty years, I called Larry Goodwyn to talk it over. "Well, Windham," he growled in that tobacco-roughened voice. "Politically, it's not as good. You won't have as much of an impact. But there is the teaching. The whole point of the entire thing, all the academics, is the teaching."

Teaching what, exactly? I know Goodwyn taught me about the Populists when I was his undergraduate student at Duke, but I remembered precious little of it by the time I prepared for my graduate school exams. We discussed books as he stood smoking by the window—but texts were never the point of the thing. What mattered was learning that social progress is never inevitable; it grows from collective efforts, and those collective efforts rarely succeed without mindful and careful organizing. Larry's great lesson to me was his deep respect for organizers, and his absolute confidence that I could be one of them.

The essay that follows features three interviews with African American women of different generations who worked and organized in North Carolina's seasonal tobacco processing industry, over a cumulative span of nearly ninety years. I started this project when I interviewed Annie Little for my undergraduate thesis in 1990, a project that Larry Goodwyn helped advise. Little was part of the wave of 10,000 tobacco leaf stemmers who formed Local 10 of the Food, Tobacco, Agricultural and Allied Workers (FTA) union in 1946, a successful bright spot in the Congress of Industrial Organizations' (CIO) Operation Dixie, but Local 10 quickly folded in the face of red-baiting and employer resistance.[1] Was there more to this story? It took me decades to find out. I went on to organize unions throughout the South with the clothing and textile workers union, and then did media work for the national AFL-CIO. By 2011 I found myself back in tobacco leaf stemmers' living rooms, researching how and why these workers remained active in unions well into the 1970s and beyond. It turns out that for these women, a labor union offered economic and workplace power within a racially stratified capitalism, even when their labor organizations were less radical than the CIO of the 1940s. Yet those unions had to be fought for and reinforced, over and over, through constant struggle. Annie Little, Mable Harrison, and Dorothy Bunch thus each served as a leader in her own unique historical moment, challenging her coworkers to action and often reaching beyond what seemed possible.

## Annie Little: The 1920s to the 1940s

Annie Little hired on as a tobacco stemmer at Export Tobacco in Greenville, North Carolina, in 1924 when she was fifteen years old. "It's like anybody cooking collards . . . Pull that stem, break it, and strip it out." She illustrated, her strong hands flying as we talked in her shotgun-style white house on a quiet Greenville street. "Sometimes we sat at tables like the one where we eat . . . some places they had little tables and everybody back to back, just like schoolchildren, and a belt go by you and strips go by you."[2] Like Little, in the 1940s three-quarters of North Carolina leaf house workers were African American women. White foremen stood over the groups of women and governed their most basic movements, like whether to talk or how long to take a bathroom break. Black men worked in the sheds, too, often receiving the tobacco and feeding it into machines. The season lasted from August to December, and the companies pushed the workers to the physical limit. "They had those women beating and shaking that tobacco and some of them would fall out. We had an old nail keg filled up with water and an old pork and bean can hanging from a piece of wire and everybody drank out of that can," remembered Cornelius Simmons, who worked alongside Little at Export.[3]

North Carolina's 26,000 leaf house workers struggled at a subsistence level, frequently making less than the minimum wage of forty cents an hour.[4] They worked twelve-hour shifts, six days a week at the height of the season. As part of Operation Dixie, the CIO's post–World War II effort to organize the South, the FTA set out to organize the leaf house workers in eastern North Carolina in 1946. In contrast to the Tobacco Workers International Union (TWIU) with its historic practice of having segregated locals, the CIO's FTA brought Black and white workers together after winning a historic victory at R. J. Reynolds in Winston-Salem in 1943. FTA hoped to use this egalitarianism to win members.[5]

"Two men came to Greenville looking for someone that could try to start the Local 10 labor union," Annie Little wrote in a four-page, handwritten letter that she presented to me as soon as I stepped past her screen door. "We starter [sic] to talk to our people in the plants we was working with. Although most of them did not believe what we were saying . . . we kept trying to convince them."[6] The men were FTA rank-and-file organizers from Winston-Salem, and they worked with Little to quickly sign up her coworkers on union cards in order to trigger a National Labor Relations Board (NLRB) election. For many workers it would be the first time they had voted in any federal election, because Jim Crow robbed them of their electoral rights.

The FTA's rival was the American Federation of Labor's TWIU. The TWIU had only halfheartedly tried to organize leaf house workers over the preceding decades. William Banks, an African American tobacco worker from Richmond who later became a high-ranking official in the union, remembered that the TWIU "wouldn't bother with those other workers like our seasonal workers until the CIO came in."[7] The TWIU used the threat of the FTA to induce the companies to sign sweetheart deals in closed door meetings. Liggett and Myers, for example, signed an agreement with the TWIU on August 19, 1946, when barely half the workers were even at work yet and only two of five departments were in operation.[8]

Little recounted one foreman's discovery of the CIO organizing drive, transforming her voice to enliven each character in her story. "He said, 'Annie. Go in that scrap room . . . where Mammy and Maquelyn and Joe Adams is working.'

"I thought, 'What in the devil?' . . . And I went right down into storage. And when I go there, there was a place where they back the truck in between the two buildings . . . if you close the door you wouldn't know what was going on in there.

"He said, 'Annie, one thing I want to talk about.'

"I said, 'What is it?'

"'Oh, uh, I just want to tell you we got a message this morning about this labor union, this CIO you all are trying to get in here. I thought I'd get you in here and get you to go out and tell your people . . . tell them not to vote for no union. . . . If the CIO come in here, they're going to close the plant down. But if they vote for the AF of L or no union, they can still work.'

"I said, 'I'm not going to tell them anything. They know what they're doing themselves.'"[9]

Little was right. The CIO drive swept the state with success after success, and leaf house workers won 25 of 27 elections, enrolling 10,000 workers by the end of the season.[10] In preparation for negotiations, they chose 175 workers to represent them in a leaf house conference, including Little. Unlike the TWIU, the FTA brought rank-and-file workers to the table, and the companies suddenly found themselves having to negotiate with people with whom they would never eat or share a bus seat. Little recalls one manager who was particularly slow to accept the situation: "I don't know what it was he said to me, but I gave him a smart answer. . . . He said, 'Well, if you all are going to act like that we'll close the whole plant down.'"[11] When the company dragged its feet in negotiations, Local 10 members began walking out for ten minutes at a time. This tactic particularly alarmed company officials, because tobacco could catch on fire if left in the re-drying oven for fifteen or twenty minutes. FTA won seventeen signed agreements that first year, though many of them were weak—the contracts did not include much of what workers had won in Winston-Salem, such as the right to overtime pay after eight hours.[12]

The FTA, however, saw its role as larger than swelling meager paychecks. "Our main job was to organize the tobacco workers," asserted Robert Black, a Local 22 member and organizer. "Our second task . . . was to bring the local leadership and the masses of the people to a point where they would develop enough militancy to take care of themselves . . . such as registering to vote and electing people to the city council and state."[13] Local voter registration offices often asked African Americans first to read the preamble to the Constitution and then asked them to write it down from memory. The FTA Local 10's Education Committee had postcards printed with the preamble and helped people to register, years before the voter registration drives of the 1960s. A sympathetic white law student from Duke University, Laurent Franz, allowed the union activists to introduce him to the registrar as a bona fide attorney. Little remembers the difference this tactic made: "This old man (registrar) had been the devil with the people but when we got there he was standing there, 'Y'all come on in so you can get registered.' . . . Everybody that wanted to get on the books loaded up the places and they got on the books."[14] Local 10 worked to desegregate a local pool and movie theater, and in 1949 stood up for two teenage boys, Bennie and Lloyd Ray Daniels, who the community felt were falsely accused of brutally murdering a white taxi driver and who were beaten in jail and later executed.[15]

After the momentous 1946 drive, however, Local 10's struggles mounted. Top FTA leaders refused to take the new anticommunist pledge required by the 1947 Taft-Hartley Act, and the CIO expelled the union. The FTA quickly lost members, as other unions raided their ranks and companies no longer had to legally honor their contracts. The FTA shrunk rapidly, moving from the seventh largest CIO union to a shadow of itself when it merged with the Distributive, Processing and Office Workers of America (DPOWA) in 1950.[16] The FTA's new parent unions officially picked up Local 10 but essentially ignored many of its needs. Local 10 continued as a weak presence in some plants, but without legal and staff support, so the companies were able to resist signing contracts. Mechanization in the stemmeries meant fewer jobs and fewer members. By 1960, Local 10 was forced to close even its small office in Rocky Mount, though it continued to negotiate a few weak contracts until about 1980.[17]

## The Value of Institutions in Movements

The tobacco stemmers' organizing effort seemed to have just petered out, and the archival trail went cold. But I wasn't headed to the archives, anyway. After college graduation, I was proud to accept my first job as a union organizer on a campaign in Monroe, Louisiana. Within a week, I was stunned when one of my first recruits was fired. She'd gone into the plant energized about the union and felt newly empowered to speak her mind. We were both twenty-three years old and she had a chubby baby. It was a painful lesson that became central to the next stage of my education about social change and movements: the stakes and consequences of challenging power structures are achingly real. People need organizations and, preferably, potent laws that can effectively support them in making social change. Building those organizations and social policies is a slow and deliberate process. Throughout the early 1990s, at door after door, in small town after small town, I had conversations with working people about what it means to form a union. I learned to be very clear about just how weak US labor law had become, and what the stakes for unionizing could be. Many signed up anyway.

According to *The Populist Moment*, step one of democratic movement building is establishing an autonomous institution. Then there is recruiting and educating, and finally politicization. [18] Along those rural routes I traveled as a southern organizer, I learned that movement building and institution building are deeply intertwined. The first is romantic and fun; the second is decidedly neither. Yet the slow recruitment and teaching (there it is again) are crucial building blocks for organizational success. People must have viable organizations through which they can effect change, even if those organizations are flawed and contradictory—making those institutions, in fact, rather like most humans.

Nearly twenty years later, I finally did go back to the archives, and I was determined to find out what happened to the tobacco stemmers. My broader and more patient understanding of movement and institutions served me well. I could now see that though Local 10's story ended, the workers' story did not. Rather, the women who stemmed tobacco continued to exercise their labor rights through the union that survived the red-baiting era: the TWIU. On the surface, this union looked like the antithesis of the CIO's "civil rights unionism."[19] It had segregated locals until the 1960s and never had the larger community agenda of the CIO. However, the TWIU was the union that continued to soldier on into the 1950s and 1960s. In Wilson and Rocky Mount, for example, leaf house workers—some of whom had won their unions through those AFL sweetheart deals—continued to have a seniority procedure and other basic contract protections with the TWIU long after many of the former Local 10 members lost these rights.[20] TWIU organizers continued to help leaf house workers form unions, securing increased workplace democracy even within the racism and inequities of midcentury North Carolina.

## Mable Harrison: The 1950s and 1960s

Mable Harrison started work in 1955 at a seasonal stemmery, J. P. Taylor, in Henderson, North Carolina. Her mother, Addie Alston, had worked at the very same factory in 1946 when the workers won an election as part of the CIO's Operation Dixie. That year, CIO organizer Frank Green remembered walking with a Henderson union supporter "down the street together and she just calls out as we pass every house, 'Come on, we're going to the union meeting.' And by the time we got to the church, there were a hundred people walking down the street."[21]

Yet that heady moment was brief. By the 1950s and 1960s, there was no longer a union in the plant where Harrison worked alongside her mother. "It was the only place that Black people had to work here in this little town. . . . Before the union come in there . . . they would hire us like we was a pack of wolves out on the field. . . . We all had to stand in a bunch and they would come and pick over you. Just pick over you." Harrison and her coworkers turned to Reverend L. B. Russell, the leader of the local NAACP, to help them gain leverage with their employer. Russell and J. P. Green, the town's only Black doctor, met with the company to complain on the workers' behalf, and the company promised they would fix twenty-one of the workers' grievances. [22]

By 1965, when the company had not kept its word, the workers started a union organizing drive with the TWIU. Harrison was not sure about the union at first, but she remembers that management refused to rehire her aging mother for the season. "I went in, I asked the man why they didn't hire her. So he told me that when she leave the belt and go to the bathroom she kind of stagger. . . . You know if you are on that belt and that belt was running, he would stagger too. . . . So when that union came in and asked me would I stand up, I said yes."[23]

Management fought their efforts: "Our foreman, he would take us in there two at a time and was telling us about the unions and the disadvantage it was. . . . They didn't know at that time that I was standing up for it." But the company soon found out where Harrison stood on the union when she served as an official observer for the NLRB election. "And of course we won," with nearly four hundred voting for the union.[24]

One of the most important victories the workers secured with their TWIU union concerned seniority. As the leaf houses mechanized, white workers became more interested in the jobs. The year before the workers organized, J. P. Taylor began hiring whites for work always done by Black workers. "When the union came in, and became official and seniority took over [it] knocked them out. . . . They would have taken over that plant hadn't that union come in." Harrison and her coworkers won the right to be recalled first each season. Gone were the days when they were picked out "like a pack of wolves." Now they'd receive a card in the mail telling them when to return to their job for the season. Building the union was slow going at first. They could not even win a dues checkoff agreement from the company in the first contract, but then they slowly won wage increases, holidays, and improved conditions over the next five years.[25]

## Collective Self-Confidence

Goodwyn's history of the populists makes clear the mechanisms through which people overthrow a cultural deference to power; through a movement-building process, they see in a fresh way the surrounding hierarchical structures and become willing to challenge them. He calls this building a "collective self-confidence" or a "movement culture."[26] I'm quite sure that Larry did not gain that central understanding in a classroom, but developed it as a firsthand witness and participant in the civil rights movement. There he saw the transformative power of the movement's challenge to the United States' deeply ingrained racial caste system.

Once unleashed, social movements can recast society far beyond their intended target. The Progressives grew, in part, from the Populists. Working people built the New Deal on the Progressives' ideas. In the 1970s, America's working women and men gained tremendous momentum for their labor activism from the civil and women's rights movements. If the long-standing mores surrounding race and gender at work could crumble, then why should working people put up with disrespect, low pay, and shoddy benefits on the job? The new rights consciousness from these movements fed the union fires, especially among young people, women, and people of color, and inspired workers to take a stand on the job.[27] African American women were especially eager to form unions. By 1979, a quarter of Black women working in the private sector were members of a union, nearly double the rate for white women.[28]

The women who worked as tobacco leaf stemmers into the 1960s and 1970s gained a new "collective self-confidence" from the gains of the civil rights movement, and they brought this to their union. The women were upset that while the TWIU represented several thousand leaf house workers like Harrison in North Carolina by the late 1960s, the contracts were far inferior to those in the cigarette manufacturing plants, where the workers were more likely to be white. The average wage in the cigarette industry in North Carolina was $3.59 an hour, yet the leaf house workers' minimum pay was only $1.82 an hour.[29] Unlike the cigarette workers, many of the leaf house workers did not have retirement benefits, and they had very few paid holidays.[30] By early 1970s, the women leaf house workers were fed up and pushed for more equity.

## Dorothy Bunch: The 1970s to the Present

Dorothy Bunch has been around tobacco all her life; she was five when she started working in her father's fields. I met her in 2011, chatting with her and her relatives in a cluster of mobile homes set back off the main highway in a small town near Wilson, North Carolina. "I was born over there, across the woods," she told me, pointing toward a stand of pine trees beyond the kitchen window. "My daddy farmed, he grew tobacco, corn, all his food, hogs, chickens." After he died, "we worked on other people's farms, chopping tobacco, putting in tobacco." Bunch then worked as a domestic worker in her teens, earning twenty dollars a week, and was thrilled to get a sweeping job in 1970 at Export Tobacco in Wilson.[31]

She remembers that intoxicating day in 1971 when she and her sister raised their hands high to vote for a strike, gathering with hundreds of other tobacco workers at the local Holiday Inn. Though the company offered a dime raise, workers wanted a twenty-five-cent increase and better benefits. Five locals voted to strike in what would be the first such strike in the TWIU leaf house union's history.[32] The pickets went up in Wilson on June 28, 1971. Only 100 full-time workers of TWIU Local 259 were officially on strike at this point because the other 1400 seasonal workers would not start work until August.[33] Yet many of the seasonal workers, like Bunch, walked the picket line, singing such song as "We Don't Want Your Lousy Dime."[34]

The company sent out a letter to all workers on July 19 warning them that "the Company will permanently replace striking employees whenever possible."[35] The company then began to run ads in the Wilson paper advertising for strikebreakers, making good use of striker replacements years before Reagan made headlines firing the air traffic controllers.[36]

Bunch and her coworkers appealed to the community to honor their strike, passing out a leaflet to shoppers at local businesses and reading it aloud in Black churches: "We ask the help of all of our people. . . . The company will attempt to break us down. They will try to hire new workers to take our jobs. We ask you, yes, we plead with you, do not cross our picket lines to take these jobs. . . . it's all of our struggles. We shall overcome, we will win, we shall not be moved." The union broadcast a similar message on radio stations on June 25, urging the community not to take the jobs in the plant.[37] Leaf house workers from across the state joined the workers for a march and rally on August 8, 1971. A thousand people marched twelve blocks through town and then met at the old Wilson church for speeches.[38]

Early on, only three workers crossed the line, but as the strike wore on, solidarity lagged. As many as forty or fifty people began to cross the lines each day. "A lot of them went to work," recalls Bunch. "But we wouldn't. We wouldn't go to work. . . . Some people were throwing stuff at people, some were fighting, trying to keep the people from going in and they would go in anyway . . . I was half-way scared. . . . one lady, they tore her collar."[39]

When the Nixon administration instituted a ninety-day wage and price freeze, the national union called off the strike. The company never called a number of the seasonal workers back to work, because the strike replacement workers had landed their jobs, though the union fought for their right to draw unemployment benefits.[40] The workers only won a dime increase in their contract that year, and a nickel the next. The top wage in 1971 was $2.02 an hour. The fact that they had been willing to strike, however, gave them new heft at the bargaining table when it came time to negotiate the contract two years later. Bunch and her coworkers won a thirty-five-cent raise, along with increased vacation pay. They continued negotiating solid wage gains over the next decade, and by 1981, Bunch recalls, their collective bargaining "got us retirement, death days, good insurance."[41]

Meanwhile, Bunch worked her way up the job ladder. Employers nationwide increased their hiring of women into jobs that were sex-typed for males, especially after 1972, when Congress gave the Equal Employment Opportunity Commission the power to sue in federal court. [42] Bunch recalls that in the mid-1970s, leaf house management opened up new jobs to women beyond stemming and sweeping: "They had a training test and they wanted to try out some women. . . . I told my boss man, look, put me in there. . . . I was the second woman working on a forklift." She was eager to please, but the job was far more difficult than she had anticipated. "I cried . . . I wanted to tell them I wasn't going to drive no more." But she stuck with it for decades, and by the twenty-first century she was moving from pallet to pallet the tobacco leaves that began arriving from as far away as China. Bunch remembers that when she first started, "there weren't white people on the factory belts. They were only supervisors and in the office." Over the years, the workforce became far more diverse, growing to include more Latinos and some whites. Meanwhile, the company changed hands several times, yet the workers kept their union contract. Bunch continued to be an activist in the union, serving as a local union officer and attending trainings at the union's headquarters in Maryland. "If I was a young person, you could not get me to not be in the union. . . . I'm a union person." [43]

When Dorothy Bunch and I last spoke in 2012, she still drove a forklift and was deciding when to take the union-backed retirement benefits for which she had worked so hard. Mable Harrison's daughter told me her mother's health was failing fast, and we lost Annie Little in 1998 when she was ninety years old. While the forms of each of these women's activism differed according to the decades in which she lived and the particular configuration of capitalism in which she worked, there was a steady constant: each was determined to improve life for herself and her family, and each chose collective action within an institution as the most forceful tool with which to leverage such power.

These three women's stories remind us that movements need scaffolding in order to succeed in the long term. Democratic institutions, supportive social policy and law, and educational and recruitment mechanisms are all key components of social change; these take decades to build. That scaffolding does not necessarily have to be a union contract. Annie Little and Cornelius Simmons took on the local power structures in Greenville, North Carolina, through community and political organizing, as well as by leveraging the legal system undergirding unions. Little's more radical union in the 1940s then opened space for Mable Harrison to use a less progressive TWIU to fight for her rights in the 1960s. Mable Harrison built a union that would then be available to Dorothy Bunch and her colleagues when, inspired by the civil rights movement, they became willing to demand more from their union and to strike in 1971.

Those "policies and institutions" that "continually shape and reshape the social landscape," in historian Jacquelyn Hall's terms, mattered deeply to these women. Movements are most likely to weather political backlash and have a long-term impact when organizers have helped people build such democratic institutions. Yet to inspire people to build those institutions, organizers first must push the boundaries. They agitate and educate in order to urge people to shed their "inherited assumptions" and work to build what Larry Goodwyn named a "democratic community."[44]

## Notes

1. Lane Windham, "Greenhands: A History of Local 10 of the Food, Tobacco, Agricultural, and Allied Workers of America in Greenville, NC, 1946," Senior Honors thesis, Duke University, 1991. Larry Goodwyn served as a mentor for this honors project, along with Alex Keyssar and Robert Korstad.

2. Annie Little, interview with Lane Windham, Greenville, NC, July 17, 1990, interview E-0136, Southern Oral History Project (SOHP), Center for the Study of the American South, University of North Carolina, Chapel Hill (hereafter SOHP).

3. Cornelius Simmons, interview with Lane Windham, Durham, NC, September 2, 1990, interview E-0158, SOHP.

4. Herbert R. Northrup and Richard L. Rowan, *Negro Employment in Southern Industry: A Study of Racial Policies in Five Industries* (Philadelphia: University of Pennsylvania, 1970); "Hours and Earnings of Employees in Independent Leaf-Tobacco Dealers," *Monthly Labor Review*, July 1941, 216

5. Robert Rodgers Korstad, *Civil Rights Unionism: Tobacco Workers and the Struggle for Democracy in the Mid-Twentieth-Century South* (Chapel Hill: University of North Carolina Press, 2003); Windham, "Greenhands."

6. Annie Little to Lane Windham, July 17, 1990, in the author's possession.

7. Stuart Bruce Kaufman, *Challenge & Change: The History of the Tobacco Workers International Union* (Urbana: University of Illinois Press, 1986), 113.

8. NLRB case No. 5-R-2646, in the matter of Liggett and Myers Tobacco Co and FTA, April 8, 1947, Box 89, Congress of Industrial Organizations Operation Dixie records, David M. Rubenstein Rare Book & Manuscript Library, Duke University, Durham, NC (hereafter Operation Dixie records); B. E. Davis to Liggett and Myers Tobacco Company, September 7, 1946, Box 89, Operation Dixie records.

9. Little interview, July 17, 1990.

10. Compiled from NLRB tallies of each election at each plant, September 5–November 1, 1946, Box 56, Operation Dixie records; membership data compiled from State Directors' Initiation Fees and Membership Records, Box 70, Operation Dixie records.

11. Annie Little interview with Lane Windham, October 15, 1990, interview E-0137, SOHP.

12. Simmons interview; "Leaf Workers List Gains," *FTA News*, January 15, 1947, 11, Operation Dixie records; "Plan 100% Drive in NC," *FTA News*, February 15, 1947, 3, Operation Dixie records; contract from Export Leaf Tobacco Company, Winston-Salem, NC, July 1946, in author's possession; *Report of the General Executive Officers of Food, Tobacco, Agricultural, and Allied Workers Union of America, Sixth National Convention* (Philadelphia: Food, Tobacco, Agricultural, and Allied Workers Union, CIO, 1947), 39; "Leaf Workers Get First Contract in History," *FTA News*, December 1, 1946, 1; "Seasonal Leaf Workers in Reynolds Make Big Gains in New Union Contract," Folder 4, Box 89, Operation Dixie papers.

13. Robert Black, interview with Lane Windham and Karl Korstad, Greensboro, NC, April 29, 1990, interview E-0105, SOHP.

14. Little interview, October 15, 1990; Korstad, *Civil Rights Unionism*, 296.

15. Simmons interview; Little interview, October 15, 1990; Black interview; "Fate of Daniels Cousins Hangs in Balance," *Carolina Times*, February 25, 1950, 3.

16. Vicki L. Ruiz, *Cannery Women, Cannery Lives: Mexican Women, Unionization, and the California Food Processing Industry, 1930–1950* (Albuquerque: University of New Mexico Press, 1987); Korstad, *Civil Rights Unionism*, 351–53; 392–413; Leon Fink and Brian Greenberg, *Upheaval in the Quiet Zone: 1199SEIU and the Politics of Health Care Unionism* (Urbana: University of Illinois Press, 2009), 25.

17. Marjorie Dunn, phone interview with Lane Windham, November 8, 1990.

18. Lawrence Goodwyn, *The Populist Moment: A Short History of the Agrarian Revolt in America* (New York: Oxford University Press, 1978), xviii–xix.

19. Korstad, *Civil Rights Unionism*.

20. "Wage Increases for Locals 259, 283," *Tobacco Worker*, July 1967, 4, Tobacco Worker International Union archive, Hornbake Library, University of Maryland, College Park (hereafter TWIU archive); "Seasonal Pacts Reflect New International Emphasis," *Tobacco Worker*, September 1969, 1.

21. As quoted in Korstad, *Civil Rights Unionism*, 295.

22. Mable Harrison, phone interview with the author, March 17, 2011.

23. Harrison interview.

24. Harrison interview; "TWIU Wins Election in North Carolina," *Tobacco Worker*, November 1965, 1.

25. Harrison interview; "Seasonal Pacts Reflect New International Emphasis," *Tobacco Worker*, September 1969, 1.

26. Goodwyn, *The Populist Moment*, xix.

27. Lane Windham, *Knocking on Labor's Door: Union Organizing in the 1970s and the Roots of a New Economic Divide* (Chapel Hill: University of North Carolina Press, 2017).

28. Jake Rosenfeld, *What Unions No Longer Do* (Cambridge, MA: Harvard University Press, 2014), 100–130, esp. 103.

29. Wage data for cigarette industry in North Carolina from US Department of Labor, Bureau of Labor Statistics, Employment and Earnings, States and Areas, 1939–1971, as detailed in report in "history" folder, Series 1, Box 66, TWIU archive; wage data for Wilson found in Local 270 contract from 1969, unprocessed files, Box 29, TWIU archive.

30. For cigarette locals' agreements on retirement, see, for example, "6 1/2-Week Lorillard Strike Ends as Improved 3-Year Pact Is Accepted," *Tobacco Worker*, May 1971, 1; on holidays, see "Local 270 Pact Wins Increase, *Tobacco Worker*, August 1970, and "New American Tobacco Company Contract Ratified by Local 182, 183, and 192," *Tobacco Worker*, March 1971, 1; Rene Rondou to William Banks, January 1971, Series 2, Box 2, TWIU archive.

31. Dorothy Bunch, interview with Lane Windham, Lacama, NC, March 20, 2011.

32. "The Following Message is Brought to You from Local 259, TWIU, Wilson, NC," memo in Executive Board Meeting, July 26–30, 1971 folder, Series 1, Box 58, TWIU archive; "Leaf Union's 'Strike Support' Rally Here Tomorrow Eyed Closely," *Wilson Daily Times*, August 7, 1971, 1.

33. "Some 100 Export Leaf Workers Are on Strike," *Wilson Daily Times*, June 28, 1971, 2; Employment Security Commission of North Carolina, Decision No. 780-L in the mat-

ter of W. Applewhite and Export Leaf Tobacco Company, September 19, 1971, TWIU archive.

34. Interview with Annie Lewis, March 21, 2011, by Lane Windham, Fremont, NC; Melvin Ward report, July 17, 1971, Series 2, Box 62, TWIU archive.

35. Memo to all Wilson Plant Employees from Wilson Plant, July 14, 1971, Executive Board Meeting folder (see note 32).

36. Ad run by Export on July 20, 1971, in *Wilson Daily Times*, Executive Board Meeting folder (see note 32); Joseph A. McCartin, *Collision Course: Ronald Reagan, the Air Traffic Controllers, and the Strike That Changed America* (New York: Oxford University Press, 2011).

37. "We Are on Strike—Why???," July 19, 1971, leaflet, in Executive Board Meeting folder (see note 32). Employment Security Commission of North Carolina, Decision No. 780-L, September 19, 1971.

38. Harrison interview; "Address by Vice President Wallace A. Mergler to Wilson, NC Meeting," *Tobacco Worker*, August 1971, 1; Craig Deanhardt, "Tobacco Worker Rally Here Attended by More than 1000," *Wilson Daily Times*, August 9, 1971, 1; Bunch interview.

39. Bunch interview; Dugas weekly report, August 7, 1971, Series 2, Box 19, TWIU archives.

40. Telegram to Rene Rondou from Roland Edwards, Local 259 President, and Wallace Mergler, TWIU First Vice President, Series 1, Box 72, TWIU archives; Bunch interview; Dugas report, August 28, Series 2, Box 19, TWIU Archive; Employment Security Commission of North Carolina, Decision No. 780-L.

41. Labor agreement between Export Leaf Tobacco Company, Wilson, and TWIU, Local 259, from August 23, 1971 in unprocessed files, Acc 89–99, Box 29, TWIU archive; "Export Tobacco Co. Employees Win 35-Cent Wage Increase," *Tobacco Worker*, July 1973; see also Notes on 1973 contract in unprocessed files, Acc 89–99, Box 29, TWIU archive; "Local 271 Members Sign New Agreement," *Tobacco Worker*, September 1975; "Local 336 Ratifies Contract with J.P. Taylor Tobacco Co," *Tobacco Worker*, July 1974; Bunch interview.

42. Nancy MacLean, *Freedom Is Not Enough: The Opening of the American Work Place* (New York: R. Sage; Cambridge, MA: Harvard University Press, 2006), 109–10; Toure F. Reed, "Title VII, The Rise of Workplace Fairness, and the Decline of Economic Justice, 1964–2013," *Labor* 11.3 (2014): 33.

43. Bunch interview.

44. Hall, Jacquelyn Dowd. "The Long Civil Rights Movement and the Political Uses of the Past," *Journal of American History* 91.4 (2005): 1263; Goodwyn, *The Populist Moment*, xix, xxiii–xiv.

# 23

# Imagination, Silence, and Movement Life

## G. C. WALDREP

When I matriculated into Duke's PhD program in the fall of 1990, the defining features of the historiographical landscape—for anyone interested in southern labor history—were Larry's *Democratic Promise: The Populist Movement in America* and Jacquelyn Dowd Hall et al.'s *Like a Family: The Making of a Southern Cotton Mill World*. One book understood movement culture, the other, alongside George Lipsitz's *Rainbow at Midnight*, cultures of movement. What neither book explored or explained, to my satisfaction, was silence.

Larry's book honored it while posing in its epilogue a critical longitudinal question: how silence moves forward in historical and social time. *Like a Family* acknowledged the problem of silence without really dissecting its implications, for the union movement or for southern society more generally. I found my time at Duke disconcerting in many ways, not least of which was the extraordinary cultural permissioning that surrounded investigations of the civil rights movement, which could be construed along a positive narrative axis, however embattled: no one doubted the importance, the cultural value, of investigating how the civil rights movement unfolded in even the smallest social venues. It represented a victory, even if that victory was contested, ongoing. This was all very different from what I knew and had experienced in working-class communities across the South. To put it simply: telling the losers' story is hard in America.

Larry's essential contribution to my understanding of social life was that of course there is no real silence. There is only the appearance of silence, the implication of a point of view. "Silence," like "mystification" and "quiescence" and many other words that were then current in the historiographical discourse of working people, was just one more of those terms that, as

Larry never ceased to remind us, obscure the social reality they purport to describe.

My master's thesis, on the Red-led United Furniture Workers' Union in Thomasville, North Carolina, between 1946 and 1954, was an attempt to reconstruct what lay behind decades of silence—a silence that included the principal African American union leader, who was also a Communist Party member, faking his own death. Ultimately it was about my inability to tell that story, in spite of the fact that the local union president was still alive, as was the police chief who had kept a detailed scrapbook of those years, including internal police memos and photographs. Thomasville was the first place I found myself shadowed by police, and where—in an absurd unconscious reference to the original *Invasion of the Body Snatchers*—librarians produced bound volumes of the town newspaper with selected articles razored out.

As it happens, Larry went to see that police chief on my behalf, and he called that erstwhile union president. The practice of history was part of movement practice. But even Larry, speaking as only a southern white man of a certain age might speak to two other southern white men of a certain age, couldn't unpick the knotty sign that silence wove, not in this case. My master's thesis wound up exploring a story I couldn't tell.

My dissertation was planned as a more geographically varied assault on the same problem in Spartanburg, South Carolina; Gadsden, Alabama; and Lake Charles, Louisiana. I hoped that different industries, regional variations, and a comparative approach would perhaps enable me to speak more directly about what Thomasville stubbornly refused to yield. I spent two years conducting four-hundred-plus interviews as well as countless hours in archives. I included Gadsden and Lake Charles because the union stories there were ostensibly successful—unlike Spartanburg, which I presumed (almost but not quite correctly) still lay in the thrall of the General Textile Strike of 1934, the great silence Jacquelyn Hall et al. had illuminated.

The questions I had were not just about silence but also about imagination: how does one *imagine* that which one cannot socially *experience*? I was interested in the union movement, because it fostered one way of training that imagination, that is, of using the imagination to develop a more equitable social and economic setting within twentieth-century American capitalism. I was interested in various forms of Christianity, which might (or might not) foster another way of doing more or less the same thing. And I was keenly interested in the *limitations* of that imagination: for instance, the implacable racism that crippled both the union movement and white working-class Christianity. A limitation is of course a border, and also therefore a possibility. I was interested in moments when the imaginative contents of, say, the union movement, or certain forms of working-class Christianity, were brought to bear on, say, the problem of racism.

These moments of contact, of imbrication or supervention, even of contagion—when the life of the imagination is brought to bear on the social whole, sometimes for the better, sometimes for the worse—were the leitmotifs of my work as a historian in the 1990s. In Gadsden a Goodyear worker confessed to me, with nightmarish glee, his role in the rape of a female union leader. In Lake Charles one of the few white champions of interracial unionism in the early petrochemical industry explained that he had been a teenaged gunman in the 1921 Tulsa race riot, did not know whether he'd killed anyone, and would spend the rest of his life in postures of penance. Less than a mile away I interviewed an African American woman who claimed to be the last surviving participant in a 1914 Wobblyled lumber mill strike. In the tiny sawmill town of Huttig, Arkansas, I interviewed men and women, Black and white, who witnessed (a few of whom were responsible for) the lynching and public gibbeting of another African American woman—whose infant daughter, whisked away to relative safety in Little Rock, would become Daisy Bates, the NAACP representative of desegregation fame.

In Spartanburg one surviving former union leader quietly but firmly asked me to leave his house when I raised the issue of his union past; a second, when confronted with his letters as local union secretary to the National Labor Relations Board in Washington, burst into tears and sobbed uncontrollably until I slipped out on my own. A third opened her door wide to me and said, "I've been waiting sixty years for you to come. Now sit."

I told some of these stories in the book that resulted, *Southern Workers and the Search for Community: Spartanburg County, South Carolina, 1880–1950*. Others I've never told.

When I was done writing my dissertation, in 1996, I stepped away from academia. It is very difficult to write meaningfully about community and the imagination without being part of a community oneself. To deny that exercise would be, I felt, to be complicit in a much greater, more damaging silence. For reasons I've discussed elsewhere, I moved into an intentional religious community that had just been established thirty-odd miles northwest of Durham.

Larry was shocked, but he understood. I think by then he was used to his students putting their bodies where silence was, or seemed to be. This is movement gospel, after all.

*　*　*

The relationship between the practice of poetry, to which I turned after completing my PhD, and the practice of history is a vexed one. The poet and social activist Carolyn Forché tried to articulate a "poetry of witness" in her 1993 anthology *Against Forgetting*, but she was widely criticized for the vagueness of her term as well as the crusading romanticism of the anthology's critical apparatus. For a few years shortly after the turn of the millennium I taught a class called "Poetry and the Uses of History," in which my students explored works of the great twentieth-century modernist poets (T. S. Eliot, William Carlos Williams, Gertrude Stein, Paul Celan, Czeslaw Milosz, Aimé Césaire) within the context of Forché's theory of witness, Adorno's infamous quip concerning the intrinsic barbarity of poetry after Auschwitz, et cetera. When I finally entered the academic job market, in creative writing, in 2005–7, the question I was asked most often—and the one that I had the most difficulty answering—was how my training as a historian had influenced my development as a poet (which had occurred during my time in the Yanceyville Amish community, after leaving Duke and the professional practice of history behind). It was an obvious question; it was even a good question. It stumped me.

The history of poetry in English since the late Middle Ages may be written as one of successive diminishments: the loss of record-keeping and historical functions to prose, and then again the loss of the art of narrative, to that upstart genre the novel. The Renaissance and then Romanticism offered a certain freedom within the all-powerful lyric "I," but the "I"—the relentlessly personal "I"—eventually became its own liability as the lyric became ever more inwardly turned, more symptom than cause. The flowering of confessional verse in America during the 1960s and 1970s played a minor role in the various social movements of those decades (for instance, the Black Arts movement) before devolving into personal anecdote, preferably capped with a stirring existential or metaphysical coda. Anyone interested in this devolution may read almost any recent back issue of the *New Yorker* for samples.

Over time, I crafted a sort of answer to my interlocutors' questions about history and poetry. "Silence," I told them. "Silence (or its appearance) was the provocative backdrop of my work as a historian, and it's also the provocative backdrop of my work as a poet." It was a glib answer, intended to buy off my audience and secure a position. But it was also true, truer than I knew when I first used it: a deep truth that Paul Celan in particular could have taught me. Celan, of course, had an abiding interest in, indeed an obsession with, the relationship between history, the imagination, and silence. He was also terribly, and in the end fatally, alone.

*   *   *

One thing I'm interested in right now, in the context of my historical training, theories of silence, the imagination, and Larry's example of an academic practice that extends beyond the classroom and into other/larger communities, is the scope of possibilities of a documentary poetics: a lyric pursuit (with corresponding innovations in form) that recovers (indeed, insists upon) the qualitative weft of social experience. This interest proceeds from *Southern Workers and the Search for Community*, in particular some reviewers' objection that certain lines of inquiry—for example, the emotional and spiritual lives of the men and women I was writing about— were somehow less valid than others. It was difficult, I found, for those workers to pick apart race, gender, their Marxist class position, religion, sex, neighborhood rivalries, cinema, and whether or not management was going to install a water fountain in the mill. Within the community of labor historians, some of these aspects were clearly more important than others; some were pernicious distractions (that is, examples of "mystification"). But to correct or replace the difficulties faced by the men and women I was writing about with an external hierarchy of gratification, aspiration, and/ or control seemed to me a flattening of human experience. Conveying the texture of their predicament was as important to me as interpreting it.

A documentary poetics, then: a poetics that would respect those difficulties, that would in fact reproduce them—in all their ambivalence, but within the clarifications of poetic form. As Larry would have noted, we do no honor to those whose lives, whose struggles we simplify or falsify for the sake of some notional shapeliness, some external ideal form. I think often of the twentieth-century American poet and leftist organizer George Oppen, who in his famous poem "Route" argued "Clarity, clarity, surely clarity is the most beautiful / thing in the world. . . . I have not and never did have any motive of poetry / But to achieve clarity." Oppen's "clarity," however, embraced context and nuance—indeed, up to and including the fundamental indeterminism of much of our human experience. "All this is reportage," Oppen insisted. He prized "the purity of the materials," which for Oppen meant "to present the circumstances." For Oppen, the layered subjective was an integral, organic dimension of "the circumstances." "Route" instructs: "Imagine a man in the ditch, / The wheels of the over-turned wreck / Still spinning—// I don't mean he despairs, I mean if he does not / He sees in the manner of poetry."

Mark Nowak's *Coal Mountain Elementary* (2006) represents one set of options. *Coal Mountain Elementary* is a collage, in effect a book-length found poem consisting of interspliced text from three sources: excerpted congressional testimony in the wake of the 2006 mine disaster in Sago, West Virginia; contemporary newspaper coverage of other mine disasters in China; and, most vertiginously, the American Coal Foundation's curriculum of coal-mining-related projects for schoolchildren. It's a bravura performance, especially when Nowak breaks up the ACF curriculum's suggested activities beneath headings that come in context to seem sinister: "Time Needed," "Materials," "Procedure," and so on. An "Assessment" fragment following an experiment to grow "coal flowers" in the classroom (sandwiched in between paragraphs of brutal mine disaster testimony) puts it this way: "Either photograph / the crystals / or have the students / draw them and explain / in their own words / how they made / the flowers. / They should describe / the process / as well as the changes / they noticed over time." The power of such a moment in Nowak's presentation is how the aesthetic exercise proposed by the ACF trades in traditional notions of beauty while displacing the social, economic, and (yes) aesthetic contexts. By recasting this sophistry as lyric poetry, Nowak doubles down on both text and context, drawing attention ironically to what in fact the American Coal Foundation is keen to avoid: "the process / as well as the changes" we all notice, over time.

I'm more interested in C. D. Wright's *One with Others* (2010). *One with Others* is in part a tribute to one of Wright's mentors, a housewife living in the Arkansas Delta who happened to be the only local white to participate in a 1969 Black-led March Against Fear; in part it's a kaleidoscopic account of that action and its aftermath in a very small place, in the backwaters of a movement, a region, a history we otherwise think we know. Wright's method is less collage (or juxtaposition) than *constellation*: she constructs an epic-length poem from fragments of newspaper advertisements, oral interview transcripts, a dutiful roster of secondary sources, and her own Arkansas childhood. "This is not a work of history," Wright admonishes in a preface: "It is a report full of holes . . . a welter of associations." "Just *to act*, was the glorious thing," Wright at one point apostrophizes: "And those so grievously harmed, who do the forgiving, do so, that they not be deformed by the lie." Not to be deformed by the lie: this is at the crux of Wright's work as a poet. It's hard work, and it's a constant struggle, for any of us, in any setting. In the end, it may or may not involve forgiveness.

Elsewhere Wright has written, "It is poetry that remarks on the barely perceptible disappearances from our world such as that of the sleeping porch or the root cellar. And poetry that notes the barely perceptible appearances." Furthermore, "Poetry is the language of intensity. Because we are going to die, an expression of intensity is justified." And finally, "It falls on the sweet neck of poetry to keep the rain-pitted face of love from leaving us once and for all."

The demand for a language of intensity, indeed of mortal stakes; a devotion to the perceptible appearances and disappearances that mark our passage through this world; and above all, love—Larry would have admitted these witnesses to his court, any hour, any day, any year.

*   *   *

My life as part of a particular movement culture—the intentional communities associated with Anabaptist Christianity—has not been a smooth one. Amish, conservative Mennonite, and other Anabaptist communities are intrinsically countercultural, and even with going-on-five-hundred years of practice they are, like any worthwhile form of human community, fragile. The Yanceyville community I was part of left the Amish in 2000–2001 and disbanded entirely in 2004. I spent time in Indiana and Iowa before making the decision to return to full-time academic employment (after years working in various carpentry shops and as a baker in my own bakery). The church community in which I currently hold my membership—the Lancaster, Pennsylvania, district of the Old Order River Brethren, a small related group—faces an uncertain future. It's the same old question: *must* institutionalizing the revolution mean betraying the revolution?

In the received cultures of twentieth-century American social movements, the exercise of the individual imagination often represents a turning *inward*, which is to say a turning *away* from the social. This can be construed as an abdication, even treachery (for example, the Soviet Communist Party's insistence on social realism as the only acceptable aesthetic mode, or Jean Toomer vis-à-vis other writers from the Harlem Renaissance). It wasn't always so, as the Dada and Surrealist movements demonstrated: it is possible to pursue an aesthetic vision and a political vision at the same time, indeed to insist they accommodate the same vision. If there is one thing Dada and Surrealism have to teach twenty-first-century Americans, it's how much the near-total decanting of the life of the imagination, on both the Left and the Right, has cost us. The imagination is a faculty, a muscle: when it's not exercised, it atrophies. This exacts an aesthetic cost, but also a social cost.

"Every work is a hymn from the other side of memory to a memory that is spellbound," observed the twentieth-century Francophone poet Edmond Jabès, in exile from his native Egypt. The French poet René Char, in the aftermath of his service in the Resistance, put it this way: "In whatever I trace and undertake, I feel bound neither to a bordering death nor to its rush in a heightened and hazardous freedom, but to the mirrors and harvests of our burning world." I think often of these two assertions, and of what the British poet Peter Larkin, writing in an ecological context, has more recently termed "the counter-abandonment." Silence has a history (or the appearance of a history) stretching backward: but the imagination's history stretches *forward* in time.

One may figure it as a lamp, a hand, a vision, a movement—almost anything, really.

What Larry lent me was a sense of the present as the moving point through which the illusion of silence ends and the figure of the imagination brushes the body. He was not immune to the mirrors and harvests of our burning world; neither did he renounce them. Like Oppen, he insisted on "the purity of the materials." I would like to talk with Larry about Oppen, and about language as itself a sort of exile from the social; about imagination and silence; and about Mark Nowak and C. D. Wright and Edmond Jabès and René Char. But I can't now.

# 24

## Reclaiming Democracy in the Twenty-First Century

### A Challenge

MARSHA J. TYSON DARLING

I want to use this space to stir an essential conversation about the darkness that is threatening our democracy. We face much more than a moral dilemma. We now confront not only a determined effort by dark monied interests to subvert the state's governing apparatus, its democratic electoral processes, but also a shredding of the 14th and 15th Amendments in its defining covenant, the Constitution-as-amended. This essay is a clarion call to movement organizing, civil society advocacy, and personal engagement in order preserve a number of the hard-won gains of the twentieth century that were crucial to expanding participation in our democracy for a very diverse range of stakeholders. As the saying goes, democracy withers in the dark. In the spirit of Larry Goodwyn's lifelong quest for a more democratic nation, this essay offers suggestions for activist organizing and citizen engagement. To be clear, as we proceed into the third decade of what is already a tumultuous century, we must counter the odious economic, political, cultural, and racial backlash that has been unleashed on our institutions and many peoples.

We are at a crossroads, a threshold place in which dark money, white supremacy, the intensification of the carceral state, and a resurgent patriarchy threaten to devour immigrant and refugee human rights, the civil rights of African Americans, Latinos, and other people of color, women's reproductive liberty, and voter participation by low-income people and racial/ethnic minorities. The grave danger of tyranny replacing democracy is too near, as lies, alternative realities, and fake news threaten to blind and conquer us from within. As Larry Goodwyn noted, "More often than not, the triumph of the received culture is so subtle it is not apparent to its victims. Content with what they can see, they have lost the capacity to imagine what they can no longer see. Ideas about freedom get obscured in this way."[1]

## Twentieth-Century Gains

Consider the social development gains that our ancestors fought to attain in the twentieth century. Hard won to be sure and costing more than a small number of persons their lives. Coalition building and rights-based identity movements promoted causes including worker rights, civil rights, women's reproductive liberty, and the exercise of human rights by Black, Indigenous, and People of Color (BIPOC), the poor, the elderly, and the differently abled. Direct action protest, legal battles, intergenerational organizing, and other tactics were used to win civil rights, collective bargaining rights, fairer housing laws, and other progressive social changes that moved society in the direction of greater liberty and equality for all.[2] In the twenty-first century, all of these fragile gains are in grave jeopardy. White supremacy, blame-the-victim radio talk-show hosts, and blatant lying and scaremongering on social media urge us to turn on each other instead of toward each other for solutions to contemporary problems.[3]

In order to promote what Larry Goodwyn called "little-*d* democracy," we must reclaim the democratic high ground and advance freedom and equality for the many and not just the few. That involves our making a personal commitment to delve more deeply for accurate information and missing perspectives as a foundation for making decisions and to act in ways that strategically advance social justice. It requires building on the activist interventions of poor, working-class, and even middle-class people who often have been acting on their interests to not lose what had been attained. Noam Chomsky notes that activism is key: "The activists are the people who have created the rights that we enjoy. They're not only carrying out policies based on information that they're receiving, but also contributing to the understanding. Remember, it's a reciprocal process. You try to do things. You learn. . . . That feeds back to the understanding of how to go on."[4] There is much that is at stake right now, and we are called to exert an intentional and determined degree of agency to affect the course of our future as concerned and progressive Americans.

Looking over our shoulders at the past, social movements ushered in measurable progress in equity and social justice in a society that was mired in inequality and racial terrorism in the decades after the Civil War. In what Mark Twain and Charles Dudley Warner aptly called the Gilded Age of the late nineteenth century, unfettered capitalism had brought rot and corruption to the nation's governing institutions. As Goodwyn observed, "In the first instance, the dynamics of the controlling market that materialized under capitalism inexorably yielded enormous concentrations of economic power that not only narrowed the range of sanctioned political debate but also produced transparent social excesses and systemic human suffering."[5] Workers' movements, especially the Committee for Industrial Organization (CIO), spurred the New Deal, which sought to stabilize the economy while also ameliorating gross social inequities.

It was not easy. In a series of fits and starts, the modern welfare state was created as a way to contain social upheaval, as well as out of the conviction that government could be a vehicle for protecting citizens from the concentration of economic power. At every step of the way, hellraisers and troublemakers like Mother Jones, the Industrial Workers of the World, Eugene Debs, and many others pushed progressive reformers hard in pursuit of the dream of a more just and equitable public good grounded in a balance between economic development, popular democracy, and a more accountable state able and willing to curb corporate excesses.

Fighting for legal reforms was equally critical. A series of disastrous Supreme Court rulings in the wake of Reconstruction undermined the democratizing influence of the 14th and 15th Amendments, and even invoked the former to support of the rights of railroads at the expense of African Americans. Lawrence Goldstone has detailed how the Supreme Court, "On the altar of strict adherence to the law . . . ruled time and again to deny fundamental rights to black Americans."[6] At the outset of World War II, the National Association for the Advancement of Colored People's Legal Defense Fund, anchored by Charles Hamilton Houston, Thurgood Marshall, and Pauli Murray, began creating legal strategies to challenge discrimination in housing, education, the workplace, and other arenas of American life. Direct action protest and organizing in the form of a threatened march on Washington in 1941 by the Brotherhood of Sleeping Car Porters and Maids, under the leadership of A. Philip Randolph, forced Franklin Delano Roosevelt to create the Fair Employment Practice Committee (FEPC), which opened up defense industry employment to African Americans, women, and other minorities. While the FEPC was abolished after the war, its operations set the crucial underpinnings for what became the Civil Rights Act of 1964.

Progressive Era, New Deal, and Great Society policies created an incomplete safety net for poor women and children, orphans, abused children, the unemployed, the homeless, impoverished seniors, the disabled, and the mentally ill. Industrial unionism provided the social momentum needed to create Social Security, unemployment benefits, and a relatively stable regime of collective bargaining that replaced generations of violent labor-management relations in mining, steel, auto, and other basic industries.[7] Yet, as scholars have pointed out, these reforms excluded many including African American and Latina/o farmworkers, southern white textile laborers, and many immigrants. In the wake of World War II, the United States created the GI Bill and other entitlement programs for military veterans including public housing, health care, unemployment insurance, and some measure of wealth redistribution through government-backed mortgages and significant tax relief. Yet again, however, many of these benefits were funneled directly to white middle-class families.[8]

## Elites Pose Challenges That Threaten Democracy

It took a combination of popular insurgencies, legal strategies, and direct action to bring a modicum of equity to social and political life in the United States. Today, however, all of these gains, modest though they were, are under attack. Low voter turnout and despair at the rapid ascendancy of corporate power jeopardize citizen participation in American political life. We turn our attention to economic, political, and social development forces that have assumed dominance in the United States and the world. We have to consider the economic and political forces that have been positioned to usurp control of social development, and the architecture of global power that has emerged to attempt to replace the state with corporate governance and dominance.

In the past several decades, capital and corporations have moved across national and regional boundaries, becoming multinational and, still later, transnational. World capitalism, and its vehicle for building a global infrastructure called economic globalization, is a dominant force at the planetary level.[9] Globalization has been facilitated by the creation and operation of the World Trade Organization.[10] The "monetarists" who created the WTO contend that private enterprise and the private sector must be protected from government infringements and regulations and kept "free" from public interference, including the actions of unions (which monetarists insist interfere with the "liberties" of employers and workers).[11]

The monetarists' mantra that markets should be free of all barriers and impediments encourages the shrinking of corporate taxation, the curtailing of the regulation of businesses, the privatization of public industries, draconian cuts in government spending on social programs, increased funding for the police that are provided with military arms and equipment, increased foreign investment, demolishing of worker protections and collective bargaining, job outsourcing and export-focused growth, strict monetary policies on deficits and balance of payments, and competitive market capitalism, including the privatization of increasing functions, operations, and activities within the public domain. Monetarists propose the "free" operation of the market, unrestrained by state intervention; they insist that business and industry will self-regulate.[12] Is anyone naïve about the takeaway message here?

This development entails shrinking citizen agency, as growing numbers of conservatives in public leadership have begun to enact policies that curtail the state's concern for worker stakeholder interests. Such austere policies include cancelling retirement and pension plans for workers. In some locales conservative mayors are choosing the expediency and political power associated with declaring bankruptcy, which grants them the authority to cancel retirement and pension obligations to workers, many of whom have spent most of the decades of their productive adult lives toiling at civil service jobs, and for businesses that service government.[13] While there are indeed varied factors responsible for a growing number of cities and towns filing for bankruptcy, the collapse of worker pension and retirement funds has often been the most painful casualty in places like Detroit. This abrogation of an obligation to return monies collected and accrued on behalf of workers is a tool of the political right, as aging workers are denied an enabling economic resource due them. The result is deepening economic inequality, even as compensation packages, salaries, and bonuses for executives and senior-level management have climbed steadily upward (the CEO-to-worker pay ratio was 20:1 in the 1950s, and in 2018 had reached 361:1).[14]

In an interesting assessment of our times, Pankaj Mishra has written about deep-seated anger and despair arising from abandonment and betrayal by political leaders: "Their evidently natural rights to life, liberty and security, already challenged by deep-rooted inequality, are threatened by political dysfunction and economic stagnation. . . . An existential resentment of other people's being, caused by an intense mix of envy and sense of humiliation and powerlessness, *ressentiment*, as it lingers and deepens, poisons civil society and undermines political liberty, and is presently making for a global turn to authoritarianism and toxic forms of chauvinism."[15]

Furthering the goal of strengthening corporate agency, the Supreme Court decision in *Citizens United v. Federal Elections Commission* (2010) regarding campaign spending restrained the federal government from restricting speech-related corporate spending. One of the consequences: "dark money" lobbying and donations by those uninterested in affirming the state and its role in negotiating competing market and human security issues. The right-wing Tea Party members, many members of the Republican Party who have been bought by Big Pharma or the insurance companies, and conservative financiers like the Koch brothers, powerful religious fundamentalists, and some secret societies with deep pockets have set their sights on undermining the state's role in social development. Enter billionaire Donald Trump, the prototypical authoritarian leader and a man with a cunning ability to build a coalition of pissed-off white folks who fear economic abandonment as factories close down and relocate to low-resource countries, thereby outsourcing jobs; white supremacists who fear the changing racial demographics in the nation and who do not want to coexist in a multiracial democracy; Christian evangelicals and religious fundamentalists who want to eclipse women's reproductive liberty and LGBTQ+ civil rights; far-right white fascists whose displays of hate have shocked many; and many conservative Republicans. Trump took control of the Republican Party. He chose to make them useful; they did not choose him.[16]

The elites committed to infusing large sums of money into mechanisms that subvert the state into becoming an apparatus for corporations are serious about weakening popular sovereignty and social democratic governance—both arising from worker and voter influence in the creation of laws and political and bureaucratic regulation of many aspects of business conduct (most often toward the goal of extending and protecting social benefits and human security). Furthermore, the dark money that is operating at the state and federal levels within the nation is responsible for the increasing income inequality which is often cited. Dark money monetarists who believe that worker and voter stakeholder behaviors weaken the liberty of employers have been "buying up" the political influence of especially members of the Republican Party in the past few decades.[17]

While decades ago it was the southern Democratic Party, it is now the Republican Party that is again engaging in the undemocratic politics of advancing white supremacy, unabashedly resorting to gerrymandering, voter suppression, and voter purges directed at African Americans, Latinos, Asians, and other people of color. Gerrymandering, voter suppression, and voter purges are old strategies embedded deep in our nation's history of politically partisan, class, racial/ ethnic, and gender advantage. In her best-seller *One Person, No Vote*, historian Carol Anderson notes, "Two distinct types of gerrymandering emerged on the American landscape. One was racial; the other, partisan. Both were lethal. Racial gerrymandering . . . is designed to create an all-white power structure virtually impervious to the rights, claims, and public policy needs of minorities. Partisan gerryman-dering, on the other hand, supposedly eschews race altogether for party affiliation and seeks to ensconce in power, regardless of the vote count, a particular party's candidates while eliminating the competition (and con-stituents) from having any real say." Either way, democracy is the loser.[18]

The extensive level of voter exclusion policies and practices emerging in many states across the country: voter purges, outright voter suppression, requiring documentary proof of citizenship, closing polling stations with-out any advance notice, and outdated voter registration practices, especially as they affect minority communities is a glaring violation of the 14th and 15th Amendments.[19] To the question of why this is happening, one answer is that Section 5 of the Voting Rights Act of 1965 has been neutered by the US Supreme Court's decision in *Shelby County, Alabama v Holder* (2013). Chief Justice Roberts joined the Court's conservatives in striking down the formula used to determine if an election plan will have the effect of creating voter suppression; despite evidence of voter suppression efforts detailed by Congress, Justice Roberts writing for the majority insisted that times have changed and the "preclearance" requirements as defined in the VRA are no longer needed.[20]

## Reclaiming What Matters

So, how are many progressives responding to the challenges that confront those being marginalized among us? How can we send the looming dark threat back to the shadows from which it emerged? To begin with, as it relates to the Trumpocracy, we have to remember that with a tremen-dous amount of effective voting turnout organizing effort, "this too shall pass," not because it is inevitable but because, according to Exit Polls 2020 data published by MSNBC,[21] the current post-electoral tally of voters in the presidential election from across the nation shows that 41 percent of Whites, 87 percent of Blacks, 65 percent of Latinos, and 61 percent of Asians produced an advantage of more than seven million votes and an Electoral

College victory for Democrats Joe Biden and Kamala Harris, thereby affirming that there will be life after Trump.

There is much we can do in the present moment to reinvigorate democracy.[22] Remember that the Voting Rights Act of 1965 is still law and a bipartisan group in both the House of Representatives and the Senate have introduced legislation (H.R. 885) which has been reintroduced a few times but has not been enacted. The Voting Rights Amendment Act would address the challenge posed by the *Shelby* decision by inserting a "rolling trigger" standard into Section 4 and strengthening Section 3. So, we should organize citizen pressure on Congress to enact legislation that restores federal election systems oversight and voting rights.

Also, a number of civil society advocates and individuals directly affected by voter suppression are filing lawsuits opposing voting restrictions. Activists, civil society advocates, and some lawmakers have been advocating for restoration of voting rights for persons with former felony convictions; for instance, in Alabama in 2017 Governor Kay Ivey signed legislation restoring voting rights to as many as 60,000 persons with prior felony convictions. In addition, stay informed and talk with family, friends, neighbors, and coworkers about the issues connected with the 2020 Census, and know which states have sued the Trump administration. Scholars June Gary Hopps and Dorcas Davis Bowles recommend forming or joining Referral Groups, informal networks of activists who work in communities and with powerful institutions like churches to "provide specific information relative to how to register and vote, what ID is needed and what should be done if there is difficulty. The desired goal is to help people become literate regarding the voting process as well as important issues and preferred candidates."[23] And, keep abreast of the efforts under way to expand same-day voter registration, and Automatic Voter Registration (AVR), whereby eligible citizens who interact with government agencies are added to voting rolls unless they opt out; sixteen states and the District of Columbia have approved the measure and legislation is pending in another thirty-nine states.[24] Finally, on voting, add your energy to the "Abolish the Electoral College" initiative that entails states pledging their electoral votes to the winner of the popular vote; currently fifteen states and DC have approved the National Popular Vote Interstate Compact (NPV).[25]

The New Jim and Jane Crow, the expanding carceral state is a serious issue at crisis point for African American and Latinx communities. The long-standing collapse of equal protection and due process rights for especially young African American men (New York City's stop-and-frisk police policy that was terminated only after a judge ruled against it), the militarization of domestic police departments by the Pentagon, the erection and operation of a privatized for-profit prison industrial complex, and draconian practices directed at undocumented persons and immigrants living in the country all require our steadfast and engaged attention and action. We should be in solidarity with communities asserting that Black Lives Matter, as killer cops should be prosecuted for murder.[26]

We, those interested in progressive coalitions that effectively challenge usurpations of shared governance, and in the restoration of seriously eroded democratic processes, should continue to focus on organizing campaigns for legislatures—even in such deep politically red southern states as Georgia, where the recent victories of two new senators, Rev. Raphael Warnock and Jon Ossoff, secured Democratic control of the 117th Congress—and set them to work on repairing access to democratic participation where it has been compromised.

*   *   *

In conclusion, while the issues explored in this essay have differing wellsprings, they all have consequences for human social development and human security, the exercise of human rights, and the survival of participatory democracy in the twenty-first century. There is still much work to be done in this century if the vital human, civil, and social rights achievements of the past and present century are to remain vibrant measures of progressive human social development. With the election of Joe Biden and Kamala Harris there is an opportunity for progressive leadership to engage with the many pressing social issues that are bearing down on the nation and driving intense citizen polarization. It is clear that Americans committed to democracy will have to be very intentional and smart to ensure its survival in the twenty-first century. We do know from nearly a century's experience that participatory political decision-making, protecting access to the franchise, strengthens democracy.

Many people are concerned that the twentieth century's hard-won laws and regulations governing voting, labor, consumer, environmental, racial/ethnic, gender, disability, age, and sexual orientation civil rights and human rights protections are being swept away by a corporate takeover of government. There is little evidence to suggest that transnational corporate governance will further human security and human rights, other than for rich people. Too often executive or corporate excesses against racial and ethnic minorities, women, the poor, worker agency, and consumer protections rend the fabric of societies in ways that would have been unimaginable a few decades ago, with headlines here at home announcing the growing numbers of high government, corporate, and financial executives charged with neglect, malicious intent, or dishonesty.

We must create opportunities to promote democracy as a social development tool. This includes the reaffirmation of the core values of grassroots participation in civil society, the defense of human rights and the building of a new society based on nonviolence, one that jettisons the aggressive militarism of the Cold War. We have an obligation to advance intergenerational justice because we know the errors of the past, as Larry so often wrote, and we know we must move beyond allowing them to happen again. There is everything at stake in an era of various fundamentalisms seeking to erase the present: white supremacy attacks on BIPOC, patriarchy's resurgence, computer algorithms that reinforce racism and misogyny, nuclear weapons, and biotechnologies that will kill as bioweapons.

As stakeholders in planetary matters, we all have an investment in the future. The crisis moment we are living in now requires what Goodwyn repeatedly urged in his writings and activism: citizens undertaking greater organized civic engagement, coalition building, and resistance against those interests that act to exclude the exercise of meaningful democratic participation in the twenty-first century. Acting in the traditions of the great social movements of American history, it is our turn to step up to reclaim democracy.

## Notes

1. Lawrence Goodwyn, *Democratic Promise: The Populist Moment in America* (New York: Oxford University Press, 1976), ix.

2. See Harvard Sitkoff, ed., *Perspectives on Modern America: Making Sense of the Twentieth Century* (New York: Oxford University Press, 2000); Kim E. Nielsen, *A Disability History of the United States* (Boston: Beacon, 2012).

3. See Jane Mayer, *Dark Money: The Hidden History of the Billionaires behind the Rise of the Radical Right* (New York: Doubleday, 2016).

4. Noam Chomsky, *Requiem for the American Dream: The 10 Principles of Concentration of Wealth & Power*, ed. Peter Hutchison, Kelly Nyks, and Jared P. Scott (New York: Seven Stories, 2017), 148.

5. Goodwyn, *Democratic Promise*, 258.

6. Lawrence Goldstone, *Inherently Unequal: The Betrayal of Equal Rights by the Supreme Court, 1865–1903* (New York: Walker, 2011), 196; Sarah Haley, *No Mercy Here: Gender, Punishment, and the Making of Jim Crow Modernity* (Chapel Hill: University of North Carolina Press, 2016); Paul Ortiz, *Emancipation Betrayed: The Hidden History of*

*Black Organizing and White Violence in Florida from Reconstruction to the Bloody Election of 1920* (Berkeley: University of California Press, 2005).

7. See Ira Katznelson, *Fear Itself: The New Deal and the Origins of Our Time* (New York: Liveright, 2013).

8. See Ira Katznelson, *When Affirmative Action Was White: An Untold History of Racial Inequality in Twentieth-Century America* (New York: Norton, 2005); Richard Rothstein, *The Color of Law: A Forgotten History of How Our Government Segregated America* (New York: Liveright, 2017); Tim J. Wise, *Affirmative Action: Racial Preference in Black and White* (New York: Routledge, 2005); Dalton Conley, *Being Black, Living in the Red: Race, Wealth, and Social Policy in America* (Berkeley: University of California Press, 1999).

9. Globalization is a set of processes that exert political impacts that affect nation-states, economic impacts that affect the markets, profits, and wages of global North and South nations and peoples, and social/cultural impacts that affect the human rights and human security of the vast majority of people on the planet. Economic globalization in our contemporary world is propelled by economic liberalization and the utilization of technological innovation. A key US advantage is the accelerating rate of technological innovation, the removal of many trade barriers, corporate-friendly revisions to the tax code, and the pursuit of cheap labor in global markets without restrictions, commonly called outsourcing. Many in government and private industry have sought to liberalize global trade by creating an international trade organization whose authority is unencumbered by political processes within nation-states; enter the World Trade Organization (WTO). Importantly, American citizens have no direct electoral franchise for conferring representative authority on the WTO, which was created in 1995 through a series of talks convened at the Uruguay Round (1986–94). Pursuing the weakening of nation-state governance, the WTO is powerful in its reach, crafting agreements, regulations, and protocols that often conflict with or preempt nation-state laws and homegrown citizen/consumer/environmental protections, thereby weakening citizen engagement with state governance. See Peter Dobkin Hall, "The New Globalism," in *Transnational Civil Society: An Introduction*, ed. Srilatha Batliwala and L. David Brown (Bloomfield, CT: Kumarian, 2006); Michael T. Snarr, "Introducing Globalization and Global Issues," in *Introducing Global Issues*, ed. Michael T. Snarr and D. Neil Snarr, 2nd ed. (Boulder, CO: Lynne Rienner, 2002); Jerry Mander, "Facing the Rising Tide," and Edward Goldsmith, "Global Trade and the Environment," in *The Case Against the Global Economy*, ed. Jerry Mander and Edward Goldsmith (San Francisco: Sierra Club, 1996); Wendy Brown, *Undoing the Demos: Neoliberalism's Stealth Revolution* (Brooklyn, NY: Zone, 2015).

10. The WTO is the new power broker, as many of its agreements, for instance TRIPS (Agreement on Trade Related Aspects of Intellectual Property Rights) and AOA (Agreement on Agriculture), bind the leadership of nation-states to actions that eclipse the protective and social welfare workings of local, state, and federal laws and regulations here in the United States and elsewhere. See Marsha J. Tyson Darling, "Who Really Rules the World," in Batliwala and Brown, *Transnational Civil Society*; Silva Rodriquez Cervantes, "Changing and Combined Strategies to Strengthen Intellectual Property on Life and Knowledge," in *A Patented World? Privatisation of Life and Knowledge*, ed. Ana

Agostino and Glenn Ashton (Johannesburg: Fanele, 2006), available at www.boell.org. za. Arguably, the government leaders and the leadership of transnational corporations are using the WTO to eliminate all barriers to the movement of capital, goods, and services, thereby circumventing the consequences of elected representation as a means to link citizen self-interest and consumer protection with political and economic outcomes. Hence, the WTO now rivals all existing governance mechanisms anywhere in the world, and it is the economic platform for the emergence of a new global world order. See Lori Wallach and Michelle Sforza, *Whose Trade Organization? Corporate Globalization and the Erosion of Democracy: An Assessment of the World Trade Organization* (Washington, DC: Public Citizen, 1999); Anand Giridharadas, *Winners Take All: The Elite Charade of Changing the World* (New York: Knopf, 2018).

11. A monetarist is an adherent to the school of thought founded by Milton Friedman, who emphasized the principal importance of the supply of money in an economy as an indication of that society's overall performance and health. Trade unions, in monetarist thinking, prevent the market from working properly by resisting falling wages, as they press governments to regulate industry standards and working conditions and to subsidize health and social security benefits. Viewed in this manner, monetarists, who seem ever preoccupied with the laws governing individual exchange, see the existence and influence of trade unions and consumer protective measures as impediments to the "liberty" of employers.

12. Events in the past decade reveal the folly of such assertions: for instance, the government's criminal case against General Motors for knowingly ignoring that some GM vehicles had faulty ignition switches, resulting in 169 confirmed deaths; GM is paying $900 million to settle criminal charges and another $575 million to settle civil lawsuits brought on behalf of victims. See Debra Satz, *Why Some Things Should Not Be For Sale: The Moral Limits of Markets* (New York: Oxford University Press, 2010); Tom Hays and Tom Krisher, "General Motors Will Settle Criminal Case over Ignition Switches," *U.S. News & World Report*, September 17, 2015.

13. We are also currently observing the strengthening of a reactionary agenda, driven by elites who provide large sums of campaign dollars to political candidates who promise to further reactionary goals, among them shrinking the state and undermining efforts and protections on behalf of workers, poor men, women, and children, consumers, the environment, and the political, legal, and economic gains of multiple communities of a diverse range of social and political minorities. In different parts of the nation a number of conservative and reactionary mayors, state legislators, and governors have waged a frontal attack on labor unions and weakened or nearly destroyed worker agency based on collective bargaining. Labor unions have been instrumental in helping people learn how to represent their interests. Many union members learned about speaking publicly, doing research, and mobilizing and organizing others in pursuit of collective goals and objectives. Importantly, they learned that their voices were important in the social development of communities and the nation. See Tim Wise, *Dear White America: Letter to a New Minority* (San Francisco: City Lights Books, 2012); Paula S. Rothenberg, *White Privilege: Essential Readings on the Other Side of Racism*, 5th ed. (New York: Worth, 2016); Rep. Earl Blumenauer (D-OR), "Unions Are Not! Destroying America," *Huffing-*

*ton Post: The Blog*, September 15, 2011, updated November 15, 2011. See also the Supreme Court case aimed at destroying labor unions as they have functioned, *Friedrichs v. CTA* (2016).

14. See Katrina vanden Heuvel, "My Stand Opinion: Fix Economic Inequality," *American Civil Liberties Union*, Winter 2015, 10; Nancy MacLean, *Democracy in Chains: The Deep History of the Radical Right's Stealth Plan for America* (New York: Viking, 2017); Diana Hembree, "CEO Pay Skyrockets to 361 Times That of the Average Worker," *Forbes*, May 22, 2019.

15. Pankaj Mishra, *Age of Anger: A History of the Present* (New York: Farrar, Straus and Giroux, 2017), 14. See also Dan Gallin, "Transnational Pioneers: The International Labor Movement," and John D. Clark, "Dot-Causes and Protest: Transnational Economic Justice Movements," and Peggy Antrobus and Gita Sen, "The Personal Is Global: The Project and Politics of the Transnational Women's Movement," in Batliwala and Brown, *Transnational Civil Society*; David Morris, "Communities: Building Authority, Responsibility, and Capacity," in Mander and Goldsmith, *The Case against the Global Economy*; Sunera Thobani, Sherene H. Razack, and Malinda S. Smith, eds., *States of Race: Critical Race Feminism for the 21st Century* (Toronto: Between the Lines, 2010); Carol Gilligan and David A. J. Richards, *Darkness Now Visible: Patriarchy's Resurgence and Feminist Resistance* (New York: Cambridge University Press, 2018).

16. Trump and the Republicans have attacked government's efforts dating back to the Obama administration's measures to insist on providing affordable health care coverage for the staggering numbers of Americans who live without any health insurance. We have watched as a viable social development asset was trashed, trivialized, and essentially neutered. In the wake of more than 250,000 Americans killed by a ravaging COVID pandemic, health insurance is a current example of the weakening of the state's interest and ability to help those who need help. Trump has had a disturbing relationship with authoritarian leaders and aspired to be perhaps the last president of the United States. See David Frum, *Trumpocracy: The Corruption of the American Republic* (New York: HarperCollins, 2018); Malcolm Nance, *The Plot to Destroy Democracy: How Putin and His Spies are Undermining America and Dismantling the West* (New York: Hachette, 2018); Kathleen Belew, *Bring the War Home: The White Power Movement and Paramilitary America* (Cambridge, MA: Harvard University Press, 2018), Jim Marrs, *The Rise of the Fourth Reich: The Secret Societies That Threaten to Take Over America* (New York: William Morrow, 2008); Timothy Snyder, *On Tyranny: Twenty Lessons from the Twentieth Century* (New York: Tim Duggan Books, 2017).

17. Steering economic globalization, advocates of neoliberalism have increasingly sought to restrain the state, particularly its governance and regulatory regimes, trade unions, consumer and environmental protection agencies, development organizations, and civil society institutions, and particularly in the global North while pursuing neocolonial relationships with many global South nations. In this vein, outside of constitutional democracies in the global North, neoliberalism has served as the impetus for the austerity Structural Adjustment Policies (SAPs) and practices of "conditionality" held steadfastly in place by two International Financial Institutions (IFIs) that serve capital's interests—the World Bank (WB), and the International Monetary Fund (IMF).

18. Carol Anderson, *One Person, No Vote: How Voter Suppression Is Destroying Our Democracy* (New York: Bloomsbury, 2018), 98; see also Andy Kroll, "Justice Kagan's Gerrymandering Dissent," *Rolling Stone*, June 27, 2019; David Daley, "The Supreme Court's Shameless—and Shameful—Endorsement of Gerrymandering," *Guardian*, June 28, 2019; Adrian Horton, Tom McCarthy, and Jessica Glenza, "How Gerrymandering Paved the Way for the US Anti-Abortion Movement," *Guardian*, June 18, 2019.

19. See, from the Brennan Center for Justice: Zachary Roth and Wendy R. Weiser, "This Is the Worst Voter Suppression We've Seen in the Modern Era," November 2, 2018, https://www.brennancenter.org/blog/worst-voter-suppression-weve-seen-modern-era; Kevin Morris, Myrna Perez, Jonathan Brater, and Christopher Deluzio, "Purges: A Growing Threat to the Right to Vote," July 20, 2018, https://www.brennancenter.org/our-work/research-reports/purges-growing-threat-right-vote; Kevin Morris, "Voter Purge Rates Remain High, Analysis Finds: New Data Reveal That Counties with a History of Voter Discrimination Have Continued Purging People from the Rolls at Elevated Rates," August 1, 2019, https://www.brennancenter.org/our-work/analysis-opinion/voter-purge-rates-remain-high-analysis-finds/. See also Keith G. Bentele and Erin E. O'Brien, "Jim Crow 2.0? Why States Consider and Adopt Restrictive Voter Access Policies," *Perspectives on Politics* 11.4 (2013): 1088–1116; Ari Berman, *Give Us the Ballot: The Modern Struggle for Voting Rights in America* (New York: Farrar, Straus and Giroux, 2015).

20. The Voting Rights Act (VRA) of 1965 is the most far-reaching civil rights legislation ever enacted, as its Section 5 required "covered jurisdictions" with a known and documented history of voter suppression to submit their election plans to the Department of Justice or a federal court for review and "preclearance." The effect of the VRA's voting rights "enforcement" provision usurped the voter suppression practices of white supremacists especially in the South, thereby permitting African Americans access to long-denied voting rights. So until Congress acts to reauthorize the VRA's voter suppression "test" formula, those vulnerable to having their voting rights denied will be excluded. See William Yeomans, "After 'Shelby County,'" *Human Rights* 40.2 (July 2014): 3–6; Myrna Perez, "After Supreme Court, Congress Must Move on Voting Rights Act," *Christian Science Monitor*, June 25, 2013. See also, from the Brennan Center, searchable at https://www.brennancenter.org, Wendy R. Weiser, "Section 5 Is Still Crucial to Maintaining American's Right to Vote," February 27, 2013; "The Voting Rights Act: Protecting Voters for Nearly Five Decades," February 26, 2013; Wendy R. Weiser and Max Feldman, "Special Report: The State of Voting," June 5, 2013; "*Shelby County v. Holder*: States Covered by Section 5 at the time of the Shelby Decision," August 4, 2018; "The Effects of *Shelby v Holder*," August 6, 2018.

21. NBC News, "Exit Polls 2020," www.nbcnews.com/politics/2020-elections/exit-polls.

22. See E. J. Dionne Jr., Norman J. Ornstein, and Thomas E. Mann, *One Nation after Trump: A Guide for the Perplexed, the Disillusioned, the Desperate, and the Not-Yet Deported* (New York: St. Martin's, 2017); Mary Frances Berry, *History Teaches Us to Resist: How Progressive Movements Have Succeeded in Challenging Times* (Boston: Beacon, 2018); Silvia Federici, *Re-enchanting the World: Feminism and the Politics of the Commons* (Oakland, CA: PM, 2019); Ruha Benjamin, *Race after Technology: Abolitionist Tools for*

the New Jim Code (Medford, MA: Polity, 2019); Safiya Umoja Noble, *Algorithms of Oppression: How Search Engines Reinforce Racism* (New York: New York University Press, 2018); Andrea Flynn, Susan R. Holmberg, Dorian T. Warren, and Felicia J. Wong, *The Hidden Rules of Race: Barriers to an Inclusive Economy* (New York: Cambridge University Press, 2017); Mark Engler and Paul Engler, *This Is an Uprising: How Nonviolent Revolt is Shaping the Twenty-First Century* (New York: Nation Books, 2016).

23. See June Gary Hopps and Dorcas Davis Bowles, "A Response to *Shelby County, Alabama v Holder*: Energizing, Educating and Empowering Voters," *Phylon* 52.2 (Winter 2015): 1–23.

24. Ibid.; from the Brennan Center, searchable at https://www.brennancenter.org, Peter Dunphy, "When It Comes to Voter Suppression, Don't Forget about Alabama," November 5, 2018, 3; Max Feldman and Peter Dunphy, "States with Ongoing Litigation against Voting Restrictions," July 31, 2019; Wendy R. Weiser and Thomas Wolf, "Why the Census Asking about Citizenship Is Such a Problem," March 27, 2018; Michael Li, Thomas Wolf, Annie Lo, "The State of Redistricting Litigation," August 2, 2019; "Litigation about the 2020 Census," August 5, 2019.

25. See Adam Eichen, "The Case against the Electoral College," *New Republic*, August 2, 2019.

26. Despite important civil rights gains made as an outgrowth of the activism of the civil rights movement, the nation's criminal justice system and many of its police departments remain mired in a long tradition of racially disparate policing particularly of Black and brown men. We are challenged to engage and confront the long-standing racist tradition of criminalizing Blackness and in recent decades an expanding new racial caste system: the carceral state. See Khalil Gibran Muhammad, *The Condemnation of Blackness: Race, Crime, and the Making of Modern Urban America* (Cambridge, MA: Harvard University Press, 2010); Michelle Alexander, *The New Jim Crow: Mass Incarceration in the Age of Colorblindness* (New York: New Press, 2010); Elizabeth Hinton, *From the War on Poverty to the War on Crime: The Making of Mass Incarceration in America* (Cambridge, MA: Harvard University Press, 2016); Cornel West, *Democracy Matters: Winning the Fight against Imperialism* (New York: Penguin, 2004); Angela J. Davis, ed., *Policing the Black Man: Arrest, Prosecution, and Imprisonment* (New York: Pantheon, 2017); Christopher J. Lebron, *The Making of Black Lives Matter: A Brief History of an Idea* (New York: Oxford University Press, 2017); Wesley Lowery, *They Can't Kill Us All: The Story of Black Lives Matter* (London: Penguin, 2017); Barbara Ransby, *Making All Black Lives Matter: Reimagining Freedom in the Twenty-First Century* (Oakland: University of California Press, 2018); Keeanga-Yamahtta Taylor, *From #BlackLivesMatter to Black Liberation* (Chicago: Haymarket, 2016); Patrisse Khan-Cullors and Asha Bandele, *When They Call You a Terrorist: A Black Lives Matter Memoir* (New York: St. Martins, 2017); Haki R. Madhubuti, *Taking Bullets: Terrorism and Black Life in Twenty-First Century America* (Chicago: Third World Press Foundation, 2016); David Cole, *No Equal Justice: Race and Class in the American Criminal Justice System* (New York: New Press, 1999), and for the complicity of the United States government in domestic drug peddling, see Gary Webb, *Dark Alliance: The CIA, the Contras, and the Crack Cocaine Explosion* (New York: Seven Stories, 1998).

# Epilogue

WESLEY C. HOGAN AND PAUL ORTIZ

A series of self-inflicted catastrophes in the early twenty-first century demonstrated that the United States was broken for all but the wealthiest members of the society. Hurricane Katrina, the Great Recession, endless wars, mass shootings, and the COVID-19 pandemic were debacles rooted in the troubled history of the republic. Each calamity proved to be a great investment opportunity for "disaster capitalism" and the One Percent. The rich got richer more rapidly than ever. Wealth and income inequalities deepened while Pentagon and policing budgets soared. In public schools, police officers replaced nurses, social workers, and music teachers. Incarceration rates skyrocketed.

The presidential election of 2000 and the aftermath of Hurricane Katrina demonstrated that white supremacy and "the new Jim Crow" inequalities were alive and well in the United States. State voter suppression of hundreds of thousands of African Americans in Florida set the stage for more years of corporate rule, war profiteering, and policies that starved cities like New Orleans, Atlanta, Nashville, and Houston. However, what happened to the citizens of New Orleans in the wake of the hurricane was also a bipartisan political crime. The people of the Gulf Coast paid the price for President Bill Clinton's boast that "the era of big government is over," and for the Republican dream of dragging government into the bathroom and drowning it to fund tax cuts for the wealthy. It was obscene to hear media experts claim that Hurricane Katrina had forced the society to once again pay attention to race and class in America. That was all the nation had been doing for the previous three decades since the presidency of Richard Nixon. Between 1970 and 2000, public policies ranging from urban development to education were formulated more on the basis of enhancing the race and class privileges of the few rather than delivering the greatest good to the many. As more than one commentator noted in the final years of the twentieth century, the once noble dream of a War on Poverty degenerated into a war on the poor and the creation of the largest prison industrial system in human history.

The ascent of Donald J. Trump to the White House would not have surprised Larry Goodwyn in the least. Echoing the themes that underpin the essays in this volume, Larry would have ascribed the victory of Trump's reactionary electoral movement in 2016 to three factors. Above all, those who viewed themselves as standing in opposition to Trump displayed a general lack of organization and failed to ignite sustained, grassroots organizing. Equally important was the failure of Democratic political leaders to understand the power of white supremacy to mobilize aggrieved constituencies for Trump. Finally, the neoliberal and pro-corporate politics championed by both major political parties has demobilized millions of potential voters into believing that their ballots do not matter. This latter phenomenon is what Goodwyn once called the "mass resignation" of too many citizens who opt out of voting or any form of civic engagement. It was a political inertia fatally reinforced in the popular wisdom—affirmed in 2000 and in 2016—that, democracy aside, there's always corporations, the US Supreme Court, and the Electoral College to make sure that the will of ordinary people does not triumph. When Aundray Dogain, a shift manager at a Cross City restaurant raising a family on $5.15 an hour, was asked by a *New York Times* correspondent if she planned to vote in the 2000 presidential election, she threw the question back in the reporter's face: "Why vote? I don't want to waste my time. I don't even pay attention to those two [candidates,] and all my friends say the same thing. My life won't change."

Another reason to not participate in politics is the ideology of American exceptionalism, the belief that the history of the United States has been so blessed by God, so extraordinary, that we've managed to avoid the problems other nations commonly face. In contrast to authors such as Jesmyn Ward, Kurt Vonnegut, and James Baldwin who presented a literary vision of what Larry called in his classes "American endurance under tragedy," Goodwyn often lamented of the nation's historians, "Their song is one of celebration." By erasing the problems of ordinary people from the historical record, historians had created a narrative of steady progress: "Secure in a society that works, Americans are indeed spared the vicissitudes elsewhere afflicting the species."[1] From his vantage point as a scholar and an organizer in the multiracial civil rights movement in the South, Goodwyn could clearly see why this belief in a Shining City on the Hill was so false and so deadly to small-*d* democracy: it gave the bipartisan ruling class a false sense of righteousness. American exceptionalism defined as dysfunctional anyone who did not achieve middle-class status—the majority of the population in every era of our history.

This belief in a republic making steady progress on all fronts also robbed white people of their moral incentive to deal with systemic racism and economic inequality. It choked off citizen input into basic decisions that govern their lives. Indeed, Goodwyn's assessment of the modern civil rights movement was that "the moderates," meaning Martin Luther King Jr., were defeated because the nation was unable to respond positively to even the nonrevolutionary demands of Dr. King's Southern Christian Leadership Conference including fair housing, economic security, and a prioritization of social needs over waging foreign wars.

Goodwyn's insistence that those in power in the United States must drop their rose-colored historical glasses and come to grips with the country's fundamental flaws animates the essays in this book. The authors herein write about a system that doesn't just fail Black and brown people but an increasing number of white folks as well. Goodwyn's chronicle of the decline of American democracy after the fall of the Populist movement in the 1890s may be jarring to readers steeped in the US history textbook tradition of ever-expanding freedom. However, it will not surprise community organizers who grapple every day with the overlapping crises of mass incarceration, chronically low wages, environmental degradation, and permanent war.

It may be that the decisive factor in the 2016 presidential election was that moment when the Trump campaign grasped the power of an historical illusion that could not be argued against, given the conventions of American politics, and used it with laser-like efficiency against the opposition: "Making America Great Again," indeed.

It is up to all of us to fix this mess. We wrote this book to provide readers with tools, historical case studies, and examples from struggles past and present that provide pathways to building the kind of solidarity needed to mobilize people power. Many readers of this volume are already involved in activist and organizing commitments. It is our hope that you will find this book useful—and will be inspired to join or start or keep on within a movement that challenges the injustices and inequalities that continue to plague the twenty-first century. We know that there are many campaigns, tools, and movements we have not included. We hope others will continue to share their stories until we have a very large library of books, films, archives, and other permanent resources for future organizers and activists to reach for when they face these struggles in their own time. Right now, the archives and books on the movements for small-*d* democracy are but a mere fraction (less than 5 percent) of the world's archival space and book content. The vast majority of our collective memory focuses on other aspects of culture and politics. As we conclude, we'd like to return to an intimate glimpse of the personal politics of organizing. The first step in creating a social movement is to build relationships of trust.

Ralph Nader, who knew Goodwyn for at least five decades, called Goodwyn a multiplier. "His lasting contribution," Nader reflected, was that he "searched for talented students and young scholars and activists and in all kinds of ways assisted, advanced and elevated their talents, their missions and their positions." Less visible than his scholarship, it was "this networking, support and instruction provided to a whole generation of seekers for historical and contemporary truth" that would "continue to have a lasting impact." Journalists, colleagues, activists, and even perfect strangers "would send manuscripts to Larry because they knew he would not reject their request for his criticism. He was as generous with his time as he was with sharing his insights." It was rare, but it doesn't have to be—both the sharing of time and the insights themselves. Few were and are as "acutely aware of the connection between valid knowledge and long-deferred justice."[2]

Inherently this "multiplier" talent led Goodwyn to allocate time in unusual ways for a scholar. He spent days with students, sometimes for hours going over a single paragraph. Larry treated teaching and one-on-one student mentoring as a sacred calling. Many of the writers in this volume spent late Friday afternoons in Goodwyn's office poring over dissertation drafts or explaining what their main thesis argument was, only to have the session interrupted by a phone call from an editor for the *Nation* or a literary luminary such as Molly Ivins or Bill Greider. Inevitably, Larry's response to Ivins or Greider: "I'll have to call you back later, comrade. I'm in the middle of a serious discussion with a student." In an academic world based on status and name recognition, this was a truly liberating experience for many young people.

Goodwyn spent a good portion of his life's waking moments ensconced in dive bars, college pubs, sports arenas, and honky-tonks of all description—talking with community organizers, students, and the unusual colleague willing to visit the unsteepled places. In an era prioritizing ever-increasing speed and efficiency in communications, Goodwyn practiced the long game of relationship building, played at a human pace. He told you the same story fifty-two times, or maybe fifty-three, until he thought you'd understood *intuitively* what it had to teach. Not just understood intellectually. Understood in a way that it changed your habits of thought and action. Goodwyn frequently noted that democracy was an unsanctioned cultural notion. Lip service might be paid by the powerful to the idea, but none in power supported the practice. Often their actions showed they had never in fact understood the concept.

One of the few ways we human beings could possibly find to create a democratic relationship, develop a set of democratic habits, or participate in a genuine democratic political experience was to live through it with him, together. He served as a *fundi*—that Swahili term not quite encapsulated by "master craftsman." A *fundi*, as civil rights organizer Bob Moses reflected, was a person "who masters a given craft" by learning within the community, "coming up through the community," helped along by others who have mastered it. "He plies his craft and teaches it to other people in the community," and it goes on like that, without it ever being institutionalized.[3] Democratic social relations had to be built person by person. No shortcuts. Former Goodwyn student Donnel Baird highlights this point: "Chief among his lessons is the importance of people coming together to have sustained, serious, candid conversations about politics, and what can be done."

Goodwyn came of age in the multiracial civil rights movement in Texas. This experience taught him fundamental truths about human relations that allowed him to see clearly, and then he set out, fundi-style, to help others to see. He also learned from people like Thelma Kithcart, Donnel Baird, and Ernie Cortés and then passed these lessons down to later generations of organizers and students. This is a reminder of the precious importance of intergenerational movement building. The anticolonial scholar Walter Rodney referred to this intense process of getting together as "grounding." There is no substitute for holding face-to-face discussions in order to challenge the received cultures that keep us chained to the status quo.

Larry's encouragement led people to be kind and patient with themselves. As he told Faulkner Fox, "You can't stay hitched to the idea of [an] open life unless you conceive the inevitability of error." All of us make mistakes, he said. Don't let those errors deter you. He encouraged people to let go of ego, to give "yourself permission to make all the errors you know you're going to make." It meant "you can try anything." Lane Windham's undergraduate experience with Goodwyn led her to understand that "what mattered was learning that social progress is never inevitable; it grows from collective efforts, and those collective efforts rarely succeed without mindful and careful organizing." She, like so many others who interacted with Goodwyn, moved with speed and passion into a life of political organizing in large part due to his sustained influence and encouragement.

Goodwyn had a fundamentally antagonistic relationship to institutions in general and the historical profession in particular. As a journalist in the 1950s, he discovered that newspapers bamboozled by oil money and enthralled by power were not reporting the central stories of the state of Texas. As a civil rights activist, he began to recognize the depth of his own personal white supremacy. He soon realized that this flaw was not unique to him but in fact saturated every institution in the land. As a graduate student, he could not understand his professors, so he read each of the presidential addresses of the two primary professional organizations: the Organization of American Historians and the American Historical Association. His conclusion was similar to the one he reached about the top newspapers: "We are trained by the historical literature to avoid the central issues of the republic." Thus his basic message to students from the 1970s through his retirement in 2002 was direct: "March to the margins. We need your view of history to get the story straight, and get it back on track. Tell us what you're learning."

Along the way, there were disappointments. Barack Obama's historic election in 2008 did not lead to the types of reform that most Obama campaigners—including some contributors to this volume—expected. In retrospect, it may have been unrealistic to expect that any president elected in the midst of the US-imposed "global war on terror" could have moved the dial much to the progressive populist side of the political spectrum. This is not to say that President Obama did not accomplish much during his two terms in office. However, just as the US war in Vietnam drained resources away from LBJ's Great Society, the endless wars in Afghanistan and Iraq essentially took goals such as closing the Guantanamo Bay detention camp and other reforms off the table.

This is why groups like the International Indigenous Youth Council, the Movement for Black Lives, and Jewish Voice for Peace have emphasized the need to confront the histories of American settler colonialism, white supremacy, and foreign policy as a whole rather than piecemeal. In doing so, today's organizers are reviving the nonviolent critique of American society brought forward by Dr. Martin Luther King Jr., James Lawson, Ella Baker, César Chávez and many others. The editors of a recent issue of *Against the Current* remind us of the cost of American wars abroad and at home:

The considerable damage the post-9/11 military adventures have inflicted on U.S. society in physically and emotionally broken lives and families, trillions of wasted dollars, the rise of racism and cynical and vicious domestic politics, are dwarfed—by orders of magnitude—by the unbelievable civilian suffering and devastation where the wars are fought on the ground and from the air.[4]

Living and working in Texas and North Carolina his entire adult life, battling with "the insanity of his beloved South" remained a lifelong focus of Goodwyn's work. The intensity of this fight within himself allowed Goodwyn to take seriously the political shadow of the Lost Cause, even as he remained its unrelenting opponent. Like fellow oral historian Alessandro Portelli, Goodwyn was an ardent reader of William Faulkner, and he especially enjoyed quoting *Absalom, Absalom!* narrator Rosa Caufield's stunning insight into the kind of men who led the South down the road of ruin in 1861: "Oh he was brave. I have never gainsaid that. But that our cause, our very life and future hopes and past pride should have been thrown into the balance with men like that to buttress it—men with valor and strength but without pity or honor. Is it any wonder that Heaven saw fit to let us lose?"[5] In 1964 in St. Augustine, Florida, Goodwyn came face to face with the violent legacies of the Lost Cause. When civil rights movement activists gathered to march to the city's former Slave Market, members of the Ancient City Gun Club stepped off into a violent attack on the marchers while shouting a shrill Confederate battle cry. It was the first time in Goodwyn's life he had heard the "Rebel yell." St. Augustine taught Larry that racism's hold on American culture had not weakened one iota since the Civil War.

As legal scholar Peggy Cooper Davis has recently confirmed, the Lost Cause has struck down not just those who died at Gettysburg or Antietam but generations of Americans who've been prevented from accessing "equal justice under law" through a "confederate narrative" winding its way through the highest courts in the land, through present-day decisions on corporate finance, voting rights, and racial justice.[6] Goodwyn tried to understand how Civil War generals like Robert E. Lee could make such colossal errors as Gettysburg. Never shirking a confrontation with the evidence, Goodwyn brought the puzzlements forth readily in his writing, in the classroom, or over a beer—a sorrowful but essential examination, encompassing the South's beauty and sheer undiluted terror. But the South has been the birthplace of homegrown, transformative insurgencies—many of which

Goodwyn's students eventually wrote about, including the Textile Workers' General Strike of 1934, the Student Nonviolent Coordinating Committee, the Coalition of Immokalee Workers, the Farmers' Alliance, and the Dream Defenders, among others too numerous to mention. Goodwyn would have been elated at the rallying call of the undocumented Dreamer youth movement in the South: "They tried to bury us. They didn't know we were seeds."

Meeting Larry was often the beginning of something major—of a decades-long conversation, of discerning a direction, of experiential learning. As his son Wade recalls, this made time with Larry akin to being "dunked in a barrel of stories that left me stained with democracy and never the same again." This time in our world, with democracy's fabric so threadbare, we bring together stories, methods, exhortative phrases, silences, determinations as ideas for moving forward.

To the end of his life, Goodwyn remained resolute in his hope that the "South not [be] defined by racial reaction but instead by common democratic aspirations." People "need to 'see themselves' experimenting in democratic forms," he'd note. They have to find a way to move from confabulating in the kitchen to moving in the streets and working to democratize corridors of power. "Show us how they got out of the kitchen and into the public square," he'd say, again and again. "Go seize the high ground. Tell their stories."

The momentum created by the Black Lives Matter democracy movement provides us with a remarkable opportunity to achieve the radical gains that Martin Luther King Jr., Ella Baker, Pauli Murray, and others dreamed of in the 1960s. The key takeaway of *People Power* is a lesson that Larry Goodwyn learned as a younger activist helping to weave together a multicultural coalition for justice in his beloved Texas: anyone who approaches life with humility, candor, patience, and self-reflection can be an organizer. Organizing a social movement means building relationships of trust. In the United States, this means forthrightly dealing with what Larry called "unconscious white supremacy" and confronting the fact that "We think in racist ways, even when we are trying not to. It is not so much that we consciously lie to one another. We merely utter polite banalities in order to avoid speaking difficult truths."

Larry consistently warned against the debilitating tendency of vanguardism or top-down leadership styles that sabotage promising insurgencies. In our own time, campus-based activists sometimes believe that they must gear up to lead the next movement. Nothing could be further from the truth. As Max Krochmal reminds us, Goodwyn learned in Texas that mobilizing for power meant drawing on the creative leadership of everyone from "the checker players on the courthouse lawn to the maids and porters who brought food to the houses." Larry taught that change came from "below" whether that meant hard-pressed farmers building the Farmers' Alliance in the 1890s, African American coal miners leading industrial unionism in the 1930s, or Mexican and Filipino workers organizing the Grape Boycott of the 1960s. In every movement that Larry Goodwyn studied or participated in, from the Student Nonviolent Coordinating Committee to Polish Solidarity, it was working-class and poor people who provided the critical ideas and energy to build and sustain the struggle.

In a volume featuring the reflections of colleagues, comrades, and organizers discussing a beloved, cantankerous friend, it is appropriate that a former student, Donnel Baird, has the last word: "Dr. Goodwyn was running a workshop with all of us, his students. For years. And as students and participants in Dr. Goodwyn's workshop, what greater tribute could we pay to the man than to talk among ourselves and come up with a plan to take our country back."

## Notes

1. Lawrence Goodwyn, review of *Liberty and Union: The Crisis of Popular Government, 1830–1890*, by David Herbert Donald (Boston: Little, Brown, 1978), *New Republic*, November 18, 1978, 33.

2. Ralph Nader, "Multiplier," *First of the Month*, http://www.firstofthemonth.org/love-is-the-message-tributes-to-lawrence-goodwyn/.

3. Bob Moses, "Address at 75th Birthday Celebration for Ella Jo Baker, December 9, 1978, Carnegie International Center, New York, NY," transcription by Clayborne Carson, Folder 1, Box 10, Joseph Sinsheimer Papers, Rubenstein Library, Duke University, Durham, NC.

4. "All Wars: No End, No Point?," editorial, *Against the Current*, March/April 2020, 1.

5. William Faulkner, *Absalom, Absalom! The Corrected Text* (New York: Vintage, 1990), 13.

6. Peggy Cooper Davis, Aderson François, and Colin Starger, "The Persistence of the Confederate Narrative, *Tennessee Law Review* 84.301 (2017): 301–66.

# CONTRIBUTORS

Donnel Baird is the founder of BlocPower, an early-stage clean tech startup based in New York City. BlocPower develops portfolios of clean energy retrofit opportunities in underserved communities and connects those opportunities to investors seeking social, environmental, and financial returns. BlocPower creates jobs for qualified local low-income workers, produces energy savings for community institutions, reduces carbon emissions, and provides returns to investors. Baird is a graduate of Duke University and Columbia Business School, where he was a recipient of the Board of Overseers Fellowship and a recipient of investment from the Lang Fund for Entrepreneurial Initiatives. He spent four years as a political and community organizer and more than two years managing a national initiative to leverage American Reinvestment and Recovery Act energy efficiency investments in underserved communities. Baird is a native of Brooklyn, New York, and is a perpetually exasperated fan of the New York Knicks.

Charles C. Bolton, professor of history at UNC Greensboro, works on the history of the US South. His books include *Poor Whites of the Antebellum South: Tenants and Laborers in Central North Carolina and Northeast Mississippi* (1994) and *The Hardest Deal of All: The Battle over School Integration in Mississippi, 1870–1980* (2005). A former director of the Center for Oral History and Cultural Heritage at the University of Southern Mississippi, he has also received major grants from the Mississippi Humanities Council, NASA, and the US Department of Education.

William Chafe is Alice Mary Baldwin Professor Emeritus of History at Duke University and the author and editor of thirteen books. His work has focused on civil rights history, women's history, and modern political history. He helped to start the Duke Oral History Program, the Center for the Study of Civil Rights and Race Relations, the Duke-UNC Center for Research on Women, and the Center for Documentary Studies. He chaired the Duke history department in 1990–95 and was dean of the Faculty of Arts and Sciences and vice-provost for undergraduate education from July 1, 1995 to July 1, 2004. His book on the Greensboro sit-ins, *Civilities and Civil Rights: Greensboro, North Carolina and the Black Struggle for Freedom,* won the Robert F. Kennedy Book Award in 1981. Other honors include the 1993 Sidney Hillman Prize for Book Journalism for *Never Stop Running: Allard Lowenstein and the Struggle to Save American Liberalism* and the Lillian Smith Book Award in 2003 for *Remembering Jim Crow,* coedited with Robert Korstad and Raymond Gavins. Chafe served as president of the Organization of American Historians in 1999–2000 and on the executive board of the organization for more than ten years, and in 2011 he was awarded its Roy Rozenzweig Prize for Distinguished Service.

Ernesto Cortés Jr. is codirector of the Industrial Areas Foundation (IAF), which provides leadership training and civics education to poor and moderate-income people across the US and UK. Cortés has been instrumental in the building of more than thirty broad-based organizations whose hallmark is the development and training of ordinary people to do extraordinary things. During his time as executive director of the West/Southwest IAF, organizations have produced impressive results in job training. By building the capacity of constituents to create the political will to mobilize for hard monies, IAF organizations have built ten independently operating labor market intermediaries: Project Quest in San Antonio, Capital IDEA in Austin, Project ARRIBA in El Paso, Project VIDA in the Rio Grande Valley, JobPATH in Tucson, NOVA in Louisiana, Skills-Quest in Dallas, Capital IDEA–Houston, Arizona Career Pathways in Phoenix, and Project IOWA in Des Moines. Cortés also envisioned and launched the Alliance Schools strategy, a much lauded initiative to engage communities of adults in public education. The work of the West/Southwest Industrial Areas Foundation, pioneered by Cortés, has been written about extensively. Cortés has been awarded honorary degrees by Princeton University, Rutgers University, Southern Methodist University, University of Houston, and University of St. Edwards in Austin and is the recipient of the Heinz Award in Public Policy and a MacArthur "genius grant." Cortés has completed multiple fellowships at the JFK School of Government at Harvard and MIT's Department of Urban Studies and Planning (Martin Luther King Jr.). He is a graduate of Texas A&M University.

Marsha J. Tyson Darling is professor of history and interdisciplinary studies and director of the Center for African, Black & Caribbean Studies at Adelphi University. She is the editor of the multivolume work *Race, Voting, Redistricting and the Constitution: Sources and Explorations on the Fifteenth Amendment,* was series editor for the Black Studies and Critical Thinking book series at Peter Lang Academic Publishing, and has published articles on voter suppression, gender and race intersectionality, Black women's herstory, the civil rights movement, the nation's eugenics legacy, and bioethics and governance issues related to assisted reproductive technologies, especially surrogacy.

Benj DeMott has written for the *City Sun*, the *Village Voice*, and academic journals. He edits *First of the Month* (online at www.firstofthemonth.org), which he helped found in 1998.

Scott Ellsworth was Larry Goodwyn's fourth PhD student at Duke. The author of *Death in a Promised Land*, the first comprehensive history if the 1921 Tulsa race massacre, he also uncovered a clandestine integrated college basketball game that took place in North Carolina in 1944. The resultant book, *The Secret Game*, was a 2016 PEN Literary Award winner. Despite being a native Oklahoman, Scott was able to thrive in the decidedly Texas-centric Goodwyn household. He now lives in Ann Arbor, where he writes books and teaches at the University of Michigan.

Faulkner Fox is the author of *Dispatches from a Not-So-Perfect Life*, a creative nonfiction book about feminism and motherhood. She is a grassroots organizer and voting rights activist who was a plaintiff in the recent lawsuit against the state of North Carolina for partisan gerrymandering, *Common Cause v. Rucho*, which was heard by the US Supreme Court in 2019. She was a cofounder of Durham for Obama and its lead organizer from 2008 until January 2017, when Durham for Obama became Durham for Organizing Action. She is still active with that group.

Elise Goldwasser continues to disrupt the patriarchy and challenge elitism from Durham, North Carolina. Her other publications include the cotranslation of three Arabic short stories by Egyptian author Alifa Rifaat in *Opening the Gates: A Century of Arab Feminist Writing* (1990) and "Economic Security and Muslim Identity: A Study of the Immigrant Community in Durham, North Carolina" in *Muslims on the Americanization Path?* (1998). She was a Smithsonian Fellow in 1989–90, and in 2013 she performed to "Bootylicious" with Duke's student Latin Dance group Sabrosura as a guest star. The crowd went wild.

Wade Goodwyn is a National Desk correspondent with NPR covering Texas and the surrounding states. Reporting for NPR since 1991, Goodwyn covers everthing from politics to music, with stories ranging over weather calamities, religion, corruption, immigration, obituaries, business, and high-profile court cases. Texas has it all, and Goodwyn has covered it. He's reported on the implosion of Enron and the trials of Jeff Skilling and Kenneth Lay; the prosecution of polygamist Warren Jeffs; the siege of the Branch Davidians in Waco, Texas; the bombing of the federal building in Oklahoma City and the trials of Timothy McVeigh and Terry Nichols in Denver; the Olympic Games in Atlanta; and the school shootings in Paducah, Kentucky, in Jonesboro, Arkansas, and at Columbine High School in Littleton, Colorado. Among his most recent work has been the wrongful prosecution and conviction of black and Hispanic citizens in Texas and Louisiana. With American and Southwest Airlines headquartered in his backyard, coverage of the airline industry is also a constant. Before coming to NPR, Goodwyn was a political consultant in New York City. He graduated from the University of Texas with a degree in history.

William Greider (1936–2019) was an author and editor who was great friends with Larry Goodwyn. His many books include *Secrets of the Temple: How the Federal Reserve Runs the Country*; *Who Will Tell the People: The Betrayal of American Democracy*; and *One World, Ready or Not: The Manic Logic of Global Capitalism*. He was a regular contributor and editor at the *Washington Post*, *Rolling Stone*, and the *Nation*.

Jim Hightower is a populist agitator, best-selling author, public speaker, daily radio commentator, weekly newspaper columnist, and publisher of the monthly political newsletter *The Hightower Lowdown*, which has received both the Alternative Press Award and the Independent Press Award for best national newsletter. He's the author of seven books, including *Hard Tomatoes, Hard Times* and *Swim against the Current: Even a Dead Fish Can Go with the Flow*. After graduating from the University of North Texas, he went to work in Washington as legislative aide to the populist senator from Texas, Ralph Yarborough. He then cofounded the Agribusiness Accountability Project, a public interest project that focused on corporate power in the food economy, and was national coordinator of the 1976 "Fred Harris for President" campaign. Hightower then returned to his home state, where he became editor of the biweekly *Texas Observer*. He served as director of the Texas Consumer Association before running for statewide office and being elected to two terms as Texas agriculture commissioner (1983–91).

Wesley C. Hogan is director of the Center for Documentary Studies at Duke University, and research professor at the Franklin Humanities Institute and History. She writes and teaches the history of youth social movements, human rights, documentary, and oral history. She was codirector of the Institute for the Study of Race Relations at Virginia State University from 2006 to 2009. Her most recent book, *On the Freedom Side*, draws a portrait of young people organizing in the spirit of Ella Baker since 1960. She co-facilitates the SNCC Digital Gateway, a partnership between the SNCC Legacy Project and Duke whose purpose is to bring the grassroots stories of the civil rights movement to a much wider public through a web portal, a K–12 initiative, and a set of critical oral histories.

Wendy Jacobs is chair of the Durham County Board of Commissioners and has served as an elected official since 2012. She has called Durham home since she graduated from Duke University in 1983. Wendy's path to elected office is grounded in her grassroots involvement in the Durham community and experience as a former educator. She serves in leadership roles at the local, regional, state, and national level and works with others to create change so that all people can thrive in Durham. She is married to Dr. Michael Meredith, a Duke Primary Care physician. Their three children, Caleb, Eliza, and Zach, are graduates of Durham Public Schools.

Thelma Kithcart, a Durham native, received formal education in Durham Public Schools and an Associate degree from Durham Technical College. She worked at the Duke University Department of History for more than ten years, retiring in 1992. During that time she worked in the Oral History Program with Larry Goodwyn and William Chafe. She continues to live in Durham and is the mother of three adult children, Lynette Cradle and James Kithcart Jr. of Durham and Celena Turner of Fayetteville, six grandchildren, and three great-grandchildren. Thelma attends Russell Memorial CME Church in Durham, where she is a very active member, serving as church treasurer and conference secretary and singing in the Senior Choir.

Max Krochmal is associate professor of history and founding chair of the Department of Comparative Race and Ethnic Studies at Texas Christian University in Fort Worth. He is the author of *Blue Texas: The Making of a Multiracial Democratic Coalition in the Civil Rights Era*, winner of the Frederick Jackson Turner Award of the Organization of American Historians, the Tejas Non-Fiction Book Award of the National Association of Chicana and Chicano Studies, and other accolades. He also directs the Civil Rights in Black and Brown Oral History Project, which has been supported by the National Endowment for the Humanities. Krochmal serves as cochair of the Fort Worth Independent School District Racial Equity Committee and is on the steering committee of United Fort Worth, the city's immigrant rights movement. A native of Reno, Nevada, he majored in community studies at the University of California, Santa Cruz, before earning his graduate degress in history at Duke University.

Connie L. Lester is the author of *Up from the Mudsills of Hell: The Farmers' Alliance, Populism, and Progressive Agriculture in Tennessee, 1870–1915* and several articles and essays including "Lucille Thornburgh: 'I had to be right pushy,'" in *Tennessee Women: Their Histories, Their Lives*; "Populist Scholarship as a Survey of American Political and Social Change," in *Agricultural History* 82.1; and "Balancing Agriculture with Industry: Capital, Labor and the Public Good in

Mississippi's Home-Grown New Deal," in *Journal of Mississippi History* 70.3. She has been editor of the *Florida Historical Quarterly* since 2005. She is editing the Civil War diaries of Lucy Virginia French and is working on a book-length manuscript on Mississippi economic development in the twentieth century.

Adam Lioz is an attorney and policy advocate with more than twenty years of experience working to promote political equality, economic opportunity, and racial equity through public education, policy design, direct advocacy, litigation, and electoral campaigns. Adam is currently senior counsel with the public policy organization Demos. He has litigated to promote voting rights; written extensively on structural democracy issues; been quoted, published, or featured in leading media outlets; played leadership roles in grassroots electoral campaigns that have made face-to-face contact with hundreds of thousands of voters; and taught money-in-politics law at Berkeley Law.

Andrew Neather (PhD Duke, 1994) studied with Larry Goodwyn from 1987 to 1993. Since returning to his native UK in 1995, he has followed a career in political communications and journalism. He now works in strategic communications at Transport for London, the city's public transit authority. He lives in London with his wife and three children.

Paul Ortiz's pathway to academia (PhD Duke, 2000) was the labor movement, where he worked as an organizer with the United Farm Workers of Washington State's Chateau Ste. Michelle wine boycott, which resulted in a union contract for farmworkers that is still in force. He is the author of *An African American and Latinx History of the United States* and *Emancipation Betrayed: The Hidden History of Black Organizing and White Violence in Florida from Reconstruction to the Bloody Election of 1920*. He also coedited and conducted oral history interviews for *Remembering Jim Crow: African Americans Tell about Life in the Jim Crow South*. Ortiz is currently working on two books, *A Social Movement History of the United States* and, with William H. Chafe, *Behind the Veil: African Americans in the Age of Segreg*ation. After teaching in the Department of Community Studies at the University of California, Santa Cruz for seven years, he moved to the University of Florida, where he is currently a professor of history and director of the Samuel Proctor Oral History Program. Proctor Program students recently helped to commemorate the centenaries of the Elaine Massacre in Phillips County, Arkansas, and the Ocoee, Florida, Election Day Massacre. The Proctor Program facilitates oral history fieldwork on global climate change, Latinx studies, women's history, and LGBT studies among other topics.

Gunther Peck is Bass Fellow and associate professor of history and public policy at Duke University. His first book, *Reinventing Free Labor: Padrones and Immigrant Workers in the North American West, 1885–1930*, received the Taft Labor History Prize among other awards. He is currently researching and writing *Trafficking in Race: White Slavery and the Rise of a Modern Whiteness, 1660–1860*, which explores how struggles by servants, sailors, and African slaves against human trafficking shaped the political history of whiteness, abolition, and emerging labor movements on both sides of the Atlantic, and *The Shadow of White Slavery: Innocence, Rescue, and Empire in Contemporary Human Trafficking Campaigns*, a history of imperial antislavery and human trafficking from the late nineteenth century to the present. In addition to scholarly publications, Peck has written articles and opinion pieces for publications including the *Raleigh News and Observer* and *Salon*. He teaches courses in immigration policy, ethics, and environmental history.

Tim Tyson is senior research scholar at the Center for Documentary Studies at Duke University and adjunct professor of American studies at the University of North Carolina. His most recent book, *The Blood of Emmett Till*, won the 2018 Robert F. Kennedy Book Award, was long-listed for the 2017 National Book Award, and was named a Best Book of 2017 by both the *Los Angeles Times* and National Public Radio, while the *Atlanta Journal-Constitution* named it a Best Southern Book of 2017. Vann R. Newkirk of the *Atlantic* wrote that *The Blood of Emmett Till* "manages to turn history into prophecy and demands that we do the one vital thing we aren't often enough asked to do with history—learn from it." Tyson is also the author of *Blood Done Sign My Name*, finalist for the National Book Critics Circle Award and winner of the Southern Book Award for Nonfiction and the 2007 Grawemeyer Award in Religion. Tyson was executive producer of Mike Wiley's 2008 play and writer-consultant for Jeb Stuart's 2010 feature film adaptation by that title. His 1999 book *Radio Free Dixie: Robert F. Williams and the Roots of Black Power* won the James Rawley Prize for best book on race and the Frederick Jackson Turner Prize for best first book on US history from the Organization of American Historians (OAH); it was also the basis for *Negroes with Guns: Rob Williams and Black Power*, which the OAH awarded the 2006 Eric Barnou Prize for best historical film. Tyson is coeditor with David Cecelski of *Democracy Betrayed: The Wilmington Race Riot of 1898 and Its Legacy*, which won the 1998 Outstanding Book Award from the Gustavus Meyers Center for Human Rights in North America, and is author of *Ghosts of 1898: Wilmington's Race Riot and the Rise of White Supremacy*, which won a 2007 Excellence Award from the

National Association of Black Journalists. He serves on the executive board of the North Carolina NAACP, Repairers of the Breach, and the UNC Center for Civil Rights.

G. C. Waldrep worked with Larry Goodwyn in 1992–96; his dissertation, eventually published as *Southern Workers and the Search for Community: Spartanburg County, South Carolina*, won the Richard Wentworth Prize in American History. Subsequently Waldrep has published six collections of poetry, most recently *Feast Gently*, which won the 2019 William Carlos Williams Award from the Poetry Society of America. He is professor of English at Bucknell University.

Lane Windham is associate director of Georgetown University's Kalmanovitz Initiative for Labor and the Working Poor and codirector of WILL Empower (Women Innovating Labor Leadership). She is author of *Knocking on Labor's Door: Union Organizing in the 1970s and the Roots of a New Economic Divide*, winner of the 2018 David Montgomery Award. Windham spent nearly twenty years working in the union movement, including as a union organizer. She earned an MA and PhD in US history from the University of Maryland and a BA from Duke University.

Peter H. Wood, a Harvard graduate, taught early American history at Duke for thirty-three years; he now lives in Longmont, Colorado. His books include *Black Majority* and *Strange New Land*. While working for the Rockefeller Foundation in the early 1970s, he met Goodwyn and assisted in the creation of the Duke Oral History Program. Wood aided in trimming extra pages and metaphors out of Goodwyn's powerful manuscript on Populism, while Goodwyn's lifelong fascination with the Civil War helped inspire Wood to write *Near Andersonville: Winslow Homer's Civil War*. Their enduring friendship even included sharing season tickets for Duke men's basketball.

# INDEX